Born near London in 1949, Dav   author of *Rap Attack* (1984, 1991, 2000), *Ocean of Sound: Aether Talk, Ambient Sound and Imaginary Worlds* (1995) and *Exotica: Fabricated Soundscapes in A Real World* (1999). As a composer and musician, he has released seven solo albums, including *Museum of Fruit*, *Pink Noir* and *Black Chamber*. In 2000 he curated 'Sonic Boom: The Art of Sound' for the Hayward Gallery in London. He is currently a Visiting Research Fellow at the London Institute.

Praise for *Haunted Weather*

'One of Britain's most celebrated writers on music' *New Statesman*

'*Haunted Weather* is not just a deeply thoughtful and richly populated survey of modern experimental music, it's a meditation on hearing itself' *Guardian*

'A bewilderingly complete knowledge of music, (Toop) has somehow managed to make the world of experimental music not just understandable but alluring for even the most virginal listener… this book is almost perfect' *Independent on Sunday*

'With Toop's enthusiasm and accessible style, the world of the avant-garde needn't seem like a closed club: *Haunted Weather* offers the perfect port of entry for the uninitiated' *Record Collector*

'An intensely rewarding meditation on (among other things) the secret love affair between music and silence' *Independent on Sunday*, Ben Thompson's Book of the Year

'Toop writes of music fashioned from street traffic, CD skips, egg slicers, and laptops that crash too often. He shows how even the most coldly digital music – far from being a polished procession of ones and zeroes – is, at some level, organic and rotting, earthly and imperfect' *Village Voice*

'Richly referential and receptive, intellectually supple and, thankfully, dry and lucid, this is the perfect, open-ended guide to the 21st century soundworld' *Wired*

'The best title of the year, it's also a beautifully elliptical, allusive and elusive study of the impact of new technology on contemporary music' *Sunday Herald*, Bill Duncan's Summer Reading Choice

haunted weather

music, silence and memory

◆

david toop

◆

A complete catalogue record for this book can be obtained from the British Library on request

The right of David Toop to be identified as the author of this work has been asserted by him in accordance with the Copyright, Designs and Patents Act 1998

First published in 2004 by Serpent's Tail, 4 Blackstock Mews, London N4 2BT

First published in this 5-star edition in 2005

Typeset at Neuadd Bwll, Llanwrtyd Wells

Printed by the CPI Group (UK) Ltd, Croydon, CR0 4YY

10 9 8 7 6 5 4 3 2

contents

images

introduction: beginning with a slight breeze

My father was not a great reader, or writer, come to that. After he died I found a diary he had kept. Most pages were blank, though occasional entries noted family visits and other small fluctuations in atmospheric conditions. 'A slight breeze' I remember, if only for its lack of excitement. For most of his life, he seemed to own just one book. As he grew older he acquired a few books on photography, boxing and World War II, his main interests, but from the time when I was a boy I recall only a travel book called *Tschiffely's Ride*, Aimé F. Tschiffely's account of his three-year journey from Buenos Aires to Washington DC in 1925, using only two horses.

Aside from some notable exceptions, travel writing is not a genre I particularly enjoy; too much self-aggrandisement posing as observation and no doubt I am guilty of the same crime myself. Why this one book, I wondered? My father liked horses. He rode them in Territorial Army service with the City of London (Yeomanry) Battery, otherwise known as the Roughriders, but by the time he and his wartime regiment, The Royal Dragoons, were fighting their way through France, Belgium, Holland and Germany after the Normandy landing of 1944, his horse had mutated into an armoured troop carrier. Perhaps as a young man he had dreamed about riding through unknown places on a horse. This is my speculation. Too late to ask.

Immersing myself in books as a child I was puzzled by my father's apparent satisfaction with Tschiffely, at times worrying at the poignant contrast between those dreams and the reality of our life in suburbia. During the course of researching this book, I had the opportunity to travel extensively and so considered the possibility that the travel genre might work as a Trojan Horse to contain my developing thoughts, flooding into my mind in an alarmingly haphazard fashion. Not that I've ever read through Tschiffely's journey, but he and his horses appeared in my memory suddenly, as if to dissuade me from that option. My father's almost empty diary about minutiae seemed a better touchstone than masculine adventure.

The book I found myself writing began to focus on the way technology changes our relationship to the body. Sound is simultaneously material and immaterial, a good subject through which to measure the disembodiment that comes with the digital world.

Computers can encourage the creation of new forms, though some of these will seem far from new if you've followed the history of the 20th-century avant garde. Digital software will make sounds for you. You can go away and make a cup of tea, then come back to a storehouse of sounds, some unusable, some boringly familiar and some startlingly unusual. A different software program can then integrate these sounds into a composition or real-time performance. Yet another program creates a desktop environment in which sound can be transformed in real-time, right in front of an audience. What interests me is the way in which musicians react to these possibilities: how they find creative possibilities within them, either as a user or a collaborator; how they deal with the problems that arise; how they fit them into older practices and established institutions. Does their thinking change when working without the physicality of a conventional musical instrument?

Being a musician and user of digital audio software myself, some of my investigations take the form of personal memoir as I experience a wide variety of sound events, either as participant or observer, or learn through listening to other sound artists talk unguardedly about their work. My own story stretches from playing in rock bands in the 1960s and acoustic improvisation in the early 1970s, up to the laptop era of the present. Again, for personal reasons, I look for ways to reconcile these different approaches, to find historical connections and conceptual leaps rather than to condemn one or the other.

As we move through a period of intense, unsettling and very rapid change many musicians, composers and sound artists respond by exploring subtle and subliminal characteristics of the physical environment or the almost supernatural communications that can occur in musical dialogue.

When sound artists and improvisers focus on details that would once have seemed just a tiny part of a bigger whole, I believe they are entering the microscopic in order to counter a wider sense of fragmentation: too many signals making too much noise. Some time ago I began to realise that digital technology was changing the ways in which music is perceived, stored, distributed, mediated and created. This goes beyond the frequently discussed topics of the Internet, intellectual copyright, MP3s and the (perhaps too hastily) predicted collapse of the music industry. Many of those changes are too new, or too subtle, to understand fully, yet we know for certain that the pace of change is relentless.

Digital communications have pitched the idea of space into confusion, so the relationship of sound to space has become an immensely creative field of research. This may be the resonant space of rooms, soundscape recordings of urban and natural environments, performance spaces or the airless virtual space of a computer hard drive. Some of this new creative activity is concerned with invisible forces such as pressure waves and psychoacoustics; some concentrates on inaudible, barely noticed sounds or private gestures. A greater understanding of how human perception and psycho-physiology works runs in parallel with the fascinations of the sounds that surround us yet lie beyond our conscious awareness.

Computers are relatively uniform, of course, and they never allow us to forget the corporate world in which they originate. Many artists seek to evade this by using the computer as a tool for personally meaningful, small gestures and local activities that function best within a small community.

My father's observation – 'a slight breeze' – seems less banal in this context, perhaps his recognition of the profound influence of subtle meteorology on mood and the trajectory of an ordinary life. Haunted weather prevails as change becomes mystifying and overwhelming. The most vital contemporary music searches for ways to articulate new responses to the dramas of social change, technological shifts and upheavals in how to make, how to show, how to hear with clarity, how to remember, how to move around, how to maintain poise in a world gone crazy with commercial and informational delirium.

There is so much of this work for any one person to hear, let alone absorb and form into some sort of shape, but a lot of it can be exceptionally engaging, even for somebody with little specialist interest in esoteric sound art. Everybody seems to retain memories of sound, or experience some feeling about sound in their daily lives, if only because they are angry about the party next door, oppressed by jets flying overhead at all hours of the day and night or cry floods of tears whenever they hear some faintly remembered sound from childhood. In his lecture on 'Multiplicity' (*Six Memos for the Next Millennium*), Italo Calvino talks about the author Carlos Emilio Gadda and his essay on the use of prestressed concrete and hollow bricks in modern buildings. 'There follows a grotesque description,' writes Calvino, 'both of his life in a modern building and of his obsession with all the noises that assault his ears.'

Contemporary sound work addresses such memories, sensations and reactions directly, sometimes offering solutions or insights and sometimes making it all worse. Moral frameworks have emerged in which sounds are divided into good or bad and must be judged within an adversarial court of critics, academics, theorists and practitioners. Meanwhile, a torrent of CDs and MP3s floods over systems of marketing and distribution already on the point of collapse. Arguably, I suppose, there's too much of this work and its quality is treacherously variable, but on the other hand, the vitality, evolving ingenuity and determination is astonishing. Despite all that, the greater mass is like an iceberg, invisible beneath a cold sea of increasingly mediated cultural entertainment. Perhaps we should find it disturbing that such an active sector of audio life is so rigorously excluded from a wider public. Hopefully, I can give the underwater part of the iceberg some exposure.

Links, networks and so-called coincidences can be found everywhere but the recent explosion of digital technology in sound work has established a kind of year zero. The world carries on as if nothing had happened. Some artists from before zero find the new world is full of potential; others fall backwards into the old world, resigned to a creative life that has tangible boundaries. As for young artists, some of them assume that nothing before zero is relevant. They simply embrace the computer: the faster and more fragmented the data the better. Others find useful connections from ones and zeros back into the analogue version of the sonic universe, in order to explain to themselves how music came to be this way.

I don't even pretend to be comprehensive. In the past, trying to listen to everything has almost destroyed my desire to listen to anything. I am more drawn to the ways in which sound can enrich our understanding of the world, and fascinated by the ingenious forms through which people use sound to articulate, decorate and communicate that understanding. This is an ongoing process with no end in sight.

Thinking again about my father, who was obliged in desperate times to dismount from his horse and take the wheel of an armoured vehicle, I realise the powerful nostalgic pull that horses must have exerted on a man like him. Digital technology can be seductive or repellent, yet there is no avoiding its increasing presence and influence. I have mapped a sector within sound and feel happy to report that sonic equivalents of the horse still survive and thrive.

Spatial interlude

After nightfall on new year's day. *The Ballad Artistry of Milt Jackson* was playing softly in one corner of the room. A fox turned into our road, its progress measured by echoes of a shrill bark bouncing from open spaces and walls of various heights, back into the unusually silent atmosphere of the city. Judging the right moment I opened the front door. Foraging for food in the post-Christmas rubbish, the fox turned into our front gate. I called out quietly to Eileen. The fox looked up, was gone.

1 What is happening to music?

Not strictly awake, though far enough from dreamless sleep, I am lying on this bed up here in the clouds. Outside the 12th floor window of the Shinjuku New City Hotel crows chant their death songs and in my near-hypnopaedic state I float on their air streams, gliding through dust shapes of sound. Ear pressed closely to the pillow, a body infiltrated by mournful, fog-bound melody. There are two pitches, rumbling, fugitive, maybe a distant Bowhead whale lament heard from far northern seas. Lift this head from its hollow within the pillow; pass outside the room: these notes vanish as if hidden by the real.

I think of John Cage's story about his experience in a totally soundproof anechoic chamber, a place of no echoes. Drawn to silence, he expected to discover exactly that. Instead, he heard two persistent noises. The engineer in charge of the anechoic chamber at Harvard University explained: the high sound was the working of Cage's nervous system, the low sound was blood pulsing through his circulation. In other words, he was hearing his own lifeforce. Perhaps a hotel technician would diagnose the melancholy notes filtering through this pillow as the chant of my own nostalgia.

Muffled by the wall next to this bed there is water running. My neighbour taking an early morning bath, or have I drifted in jet-lag reverie to the edge of a stream in the local park? Other sounds take up fleeting residence alongside these ambiguous intruders: body processes, faint murmurs of 5.00 am traffic from the street far below; sirens; trucks reversing in a cacophony of alarms and recorded vocal hysteria; air conditioning; the drone of that conveniently placed beer dispensing machine that squats across the corridor between the lift and my door. Some of these sounds are so peripheral they

Rolf Julius
Speaker in a tall tree

shy into nothingness, like smoke sucked into crevices of thin air, the residual traces of sound artists dreaming.

speaking glass

This was January 2000, the beginning of an arc. I was in Tokyo with my friend and colleague, Max Eastley. As it happens, Max plays an invented instrument he calls The Arc, as well as building sound sculptures that are as engagingly beautiful as they are technologically simple. We had been invited to perform a live concert and create an installation together for Sound Art – Sound As Media, an exhibition curated for the InterCommunication Center, or ICC, by Minoru Hatanaka. 'The collapse of tonal music this century has opened the way for a musical revolution,' wrote Hatanaka in the explanation of his exhibition, 'with the expansion of sound-producing materials and technological progress leading all manner of sounds to be treated as music. Forms of expression are now emerging which simply do not fit within the conventional framework of "music," and not only in terms of experimental and computer music, but even in the area of popular music. What is happening to music?'

A showcase project run by the Japanese telephone company, NTT, to commemorate the 100th anniversary of telephone service, the ICC is a hi-tech palace of marvels located on the fourth floor of Tokyo Opera City

Tower. It has been described by the art critic Toshiharu Itoh as 'a cultural facility of a sort that had never existed before, a place that would explore not only the value of future artistic culture but that also examined the issues of communication and the mind in a technological society'. In the permanent exhibition it's possible to create and evolve your own virtual organisms, be immersed in virtual reality controlled by a wooden puppet and 'converse' with virtual characters. 'Currently we could point to a whole cross-section of works intersecting with the field of media art,' Hatanaka wrote in his introduction to the exhibition catalogue. 'Indeed it would be difficult to find examples of media art which do not incorporate acoustic elements. This is certainly not unrelated to the fact that not only music, but media art in general progresses and matures in step with advances in technology. Just as our daily lives are saturated with electronic sounds, the element of sound is omnipresent in media art.'

No need to look very far to find the truth of that, though in Japan, an unusually close relationship between infrastructure media and weird sonic experiment was showing signs of strain. As recession bit deeper and deeper into Japan's institutions and their vision of what might be possible in the future, corporations began to shed their commitment to unconstrained innovation. TOA's Xebec Hall in Kobe, which I wrote about in *Ocean Of Sound*, had suspended its programme and NTT was about to restructure its InterCommunication Center. The belief that technological development, commerce and artistic experiment can march hand in hand, whistling a cheerful improvised tune, is fragile.

During a second trip to Tokyo that year, I visited ICC again for the opening of an exhibition called 'Tangible Bits: Towards Seamless Interfaces between People, Bits and Atoms'. Demonstrating the ongoing work of Professor Hiroshi Ishii and his Tangible Media Group at the Media Lab at MIT, the exhibition explored interface design. PingPongPlus was table tennis with a difference: a ping-pong table covered with digital water. Bounce the ball across the table and digital fish scatter in all directions. I risked a quick game. With or without digital fish, my returning still lets down my serve. The Curlybot is like a cross between a computer mouse and a contestant in *Robot Wars*, a cute little plastic dome that looks as if it might catapult toxic substances into your eye if you get too close. Curlybots exist to be pushed around. They remember the path they were pushed along, no matter how convoluted, and then play it back on their own initiative. Elsewhere in the room, more trade show than art exhibition, one of the inventors demonstrated his Music Bottles. Lifting the lid from one bottle I heard a jazz piano player, taking off the second lid added a double bass, removing the third completed the classic jazz trio with a drummer.

Encountered at the development stage, such gizmos can be just one twitch away from laughable. By the time I started listening to jazz in the 1960s, a revolution was in progress. Free jazz would consign anything but the very best post-bop piano trios to drinking lounges and supper clubs. Why in the year 2000 would I want to be listening to a vastly inferior version of the Ahmad Jamal Trio escaping out of three empty scent bottles? But the explanation of how this idea originated was rather poetic. Hiroshi Ishii imagined a weather report bottle for his mother, a bottle of soy sauce that would uncork a chorus of songbirds if the weather promised to be fine, the sound of rain if showers were imminent. Snow on the way, they didn't say. 'What fun it would be for his mother, who had never touched a mouse or seen a homepage on the Internet,' wrote Itsuo Sakane, Director of the International Academy of Media Arts and Science, 'to have the articles in her kitchen function as interfaces. This way of thinking is perhaps rooted in a very Asian and Japanese view of life, an ancient animistic view of nature that prizes communion with our natural surroundings.' Further possibilities for this invention were proposed: 'perfume bottles filled with poetry or wine bottles that decant stories. More practical applications might include a medicine chest full of bottles that tell the user how and when to take them and let the hospital know when they do.'

Smart glassware may or may not have a place in the future but for me, the immediate implication of this technology was musical. I don't imagine glass bottle concerts becoming any more popular than Benjamin Franklin's glass harmonica, used for one-off works by Mozart and Björk but otherwise a minor curiosity from the museum of antique audio technology. The many forms through which digital technology can distance music making from the human body broach more significant issues. I thought about Toshiharu Itoh's statement – 'a place that would explore not only the value of future artistic culture but that also examined the issues of communication and the mind in a technological society' – and wondered what was happening to the rest of the body. In the overheated climate of the *fin de siècle* cyber years, a lot of wild claims were made about the inevitability of downloaded consciousness in the post-human era, most of them written by people who spent too long gazing at their computer screens. Is human flesh already atrophied? The obsession with body image, sex, health and diet in those societies prosperous enough to fret about such things suggests not. Musical recordings triggered by disturbing a magnetic field; is that a true manifestation of animistic communion with nature or just its pale shadow? Design and lifestyle magazines are full of Zen and nature, all of which seems a superficial reaction to the loss of something profound. How to describe it, this loss? To feel in the moment, clear, without distraction, able to allow spontaneous, unmediated experience, to shed media connectivity, emotional distance and the fragmentations of this life of multiple, complex levels, tempi, shades, duties and obsessions, if only for a fleeting moment.

headphonics   anechoics

There is a tiny anechoic chamber, soundproof and acoustically dead, built within ICC. For a time, an installation entitled World, Membrane and the Dismembered Body was one of the permanent exhibits. Created by Seiko Mikami, an artist who uses computer technology to explore information environments occupied by the human body, the piece amplified the sounds of a person's internal organs as he or she sat in the chamber, then transformed these sounds into a continuously transforming polygonal mesh. 'The ear/acoustic sense, a fragment of the exhibition visitor's body,' writes Seiko Mikami in the *ICC Concept Book*, 'serves as a circuit for unfixed data – such as the heart tone, a psychological affect – that is employed according to the second-to-second changes in the visitor's psychological condition. Thus, a fundamental gap is born between the body's response, when the heart is made to palpitate and undergo change in the anechoic room, and its result as expressed in the movement of sounds emitted from the body. When the body's heartbeat is thrown off course by an intervention from the outside, the desire arises to try to control the sounds that the body emits. A gap occurs between this event and the resulting desire; thus, the visitor is overcome by the feeling that a part of his/her corporeality is under erasure.' The final experience, Mikami concludes, is a feeling of being turned into a fragmented body.

A few days after the Shinjuku New City Hotel reverie I am sitting in this anechoic chamber. A panic button is close to hand, an unusual, mildly threatening precaution for a sound art installation. Exhibition curator Minoru Hatanaka closes the thick door, leaving me alone in darkness so complete that I can barely be sure I still exist. Feeling not unlike the narrator of Edgar Allan Poe's *The Premature Burial*, dreaming of 'the blackness of the absolute Night', I wait for the start of Ryoji Ikeda's *Matrix (for an anechoic room)*.

I first met Ikeda in London, probably in 1994. At the time, he was pointing a Camcorder at people like me, asking us to hold forth for a few moments on silence. His preoccupation with silence had been established in 1993 by a compilation album called *Silence*, released during his tenure as audio visual producer at Spiral, the Wacoal Art Center, in Tokyo. The contributions to this eclectic album were wide ranging: jazz pianist Paul Bley; Can member Holger Czukay; Ko Ishikawa and Tamami Tono, both performing on the Japanese bamboo mouth organ, the *sho*; Simon Fisher Turner and Derek Jarman; sound artist David Cunningham; Masumi Nagasawa playing John Cage's *In A Landscape*. With additional music by Ikeda and Yoshio Ojima, there is also a typically faltering reading by the late John Lilly from his book, *The Centre of the Cyclone – An Autobiography of Inner Space*, a document of the effects of taking hallucinogens in an isolation tank.

Precise, reserved and utterly focussed, Ryoji Ikeda seems an unlikely follower of Lilly's radical experiments in consciousness, what the researcher into dolphin language, neurology and interspecies communication described as metaprogramming of the biocomputer. For Lilly, persistent behavioural patterns were tape-loops or faulty recordings, habits that could be altered through rigorous explorations of the self. Perhaps there are connections between Ikeda's music and the techniques Lilly had discovered during his explorations. 'Of course, I respect John C. Lilly and what he has done,' Ryoji writes in an e-mail, 'but also I'm a bit ambivalent towards his late thoughts ... it is sort of the same case as Stockhausen. His followers also make his excellent researches blind.'

Born in Tokyo in 1966, Ikeda is fascinated by the phenomenology of sound and time, the way in which minimal sound sources such as sine waves can precipitate dramatic physiological effects and mysterious perceptions for the listener. 'Yes, perhaps physiological aspects of human may be a part of them,' he writes. 'For me, the most important thing is their "relationship" to each other. I cannot focus and pick up only one element of them.' *Matrix* is the purest illustration of these interests. 'Listener' is too meagre a word to describe the perceptual invasion of his work. My own response to being temporarily trapped in this foetal state is intense. Thick snakes crawl up my spine, circle around the inside, then outside of my cranium, constrict my abdomen. Slightly nauseated, I think of Masatoshi Naitoh's shocking photographs of Komasa Ichiza, a group of old-fashioned travelling players once based in the Asakusa district of Tokyo. Oppai san, a member of Komasa Ichiza, could thread live snakes into her mouth and then out through her nostrils. To feel the fluid physicality of sound in this way is an ambivalent pleasure, erotic in part, but also close to the sensation of submitting to a virus, hovering on the brink of fear at times, simply through being uncertain about how far the experiment will go. Surrender to it and time slows to a crawl, the air turns sticky and thick, thoughts refuse to cohere. Like an optical art for the ears, the patterns mutate with movements of the body. The matrix is rebuilt with every new audition.

Ikeda's single-minded investigation into acoustic phenomena began tentatively in 1990. 'Preamble', the introductory track on the *Silence* compilation, was his first release. In 1994 he began working with Dumb Type, a performance group founded in 1984 from graduates of Kyoto City University of Arts. Since then his refinement of materials and method has only been interrupted by the media overload – news broadcasts, astronauts and cinema samples – of *1000 Fragments*, released in 1995. The stripping away of these referential elements raises the question of why they were there in the first place. Like the work of the Finnish duo, Pan Sonic, and the young German artist, Carsten Nicolai, Ikeda's recordings have an oblique but marked relationship to techno. They may be constructed from minimalist sine tones, white noise, pure pulsation and the tiniest shavings of pure sonic materials, but they still belong in some distant way to the history of disco.

This relationship has an irony to it. Disco's celebration of the body is hedonistic, flagrantly sexual, aerobic: 'free your ass and the mind will follow', as funk lord George Clinton theorised it. The work of Ikeda and his contemporaries also attacks the mind–body problem by asserting the materiality of sound while questioning the nature of perception. If we experience sound as a physical sensation via internal organs, skin responses and muscle tremors then the common perception of sound as an immaterial substance, absorbed through the ears but perceived mainly through mental processing, becomes uncertain. Heard at its intended volume, Ikeda's music is a total experience, a white-out of pure data. As a preface to his ICC release of a retrospective DVD, *formula*, he quotes architect Mies van der Rohe – 'Less is more' – and pianist David Tudor – 'More is more'. From minimalism comes excess. His work could be heard as a branch of architecture, the school of invisibility. *formula* is a clarification: photographs of environments/white rooms with no discernible boundaries or internal lines, a red metal container, the ICC anechoic chamber/diagrams of concert halls/enclosures of air within which sonic textural mapping has been perceived. What's missing, from a conventional point of view, is any sign of human activation.

Matrix (for an anechoic room) is an installation that relies almost entirely on electronic technology, yet that technology is invisible within the piece. A year after experiencing Ikeda's installation in Tokyo I saw him perform in a London concert hall. The stage was completely empty, dressed to look as neutral as possible, and Ikeda sat in dark anonymity at the mixing desk, half way up the auditorium, equipped with a laptop computer and Zip drive. The only visual element of the show (is show the best word?) was a film created by Ikeda with Shiro Takatani and Hiromasa Tomari of Dumb Type, closely synchronised to sound. Despite the absence of any performers to look at, a sell-out audience sat spellbound by the visceral effect of sound.

As the apparatus of music becomes less apparent, particularly in the digital domain, so sound becomes more completely itself, the purest manifestation of a disembodied, time based art. Freed from the distraction of ranked violinists dressed in black and white sawing at their instruments, guitarists leaping around on a stage, entire typing pools of keyboard players, choreographed dancers, drum risers, video walls and pyrotechnics, the intangible core of music, the part that makes some people close their eyes when they listen, is allowed its full power. Aside from the enticing reasons for combining music with other media – the dream of creating an overwhelming synaesthesia from mixed art forms or simply the need for some eye candy to distract from the tedium of most live music – this gain comes with some profound losses. Whether based on false assumptions or deep-seated needs, the sight of musicians playing in real-time, engaged in actions that have a discernible link to the sounds they are producing, makes an audience feel a warm glow of communication. The fact that this warm glow might freeze before the end of a concert doesn't detract from the persistence of that basic need.

noise as silence

Days after *Matrix* and my hotel reverie, still flagging from the effects of jet lag, I was persuaded to visit Gendai Heights Gallery for an event called Noise As Silence. A small art gallery, record shop, performance space and bar in the dark back street suburbs of Tokyo's Shimokitazawa district, Heights Gallery was packed by the time we arrived on a Saturday night. The performance had already started (performance is no better than show, but most of these words just don't work properly anymore). Just inside the door was Sumihisa Arima, manipulating sound through MAX software on a laptop computer. Almost hidden by the bar, at the far corner, was Akira Kosuga, controlling a loop sampler and electronic effects. Seated by the wall, to the far left of the room, was Christophe Charles on laptop, also using MAX software, and in the centre, in the spot we would normally associate with the stage area, were Shunichiro Okada, Carl Michael von Hausswolff and Carsten Nicolai. These three were crammed together in a line behind a small table, like the three monkeys who see, hear and speak no evil. In the middle, Michael von Hausswolff tweaked a mixing desk, panning an 11,000-Hertz tone around the room. On either side of him, Okada and Nicolai stroked the trackpads on their laptops.

One of the few outward indicators of difference with this technology is the presence or absence of an Apple logo on the raised lid. Musician Steve Beresford describes a performance given by three improvisers in a London club: the group sat at a table on stage, though instead of flipping up the displays of expensive laptops, they opened pizza boxes, each with half an apple glued to its lid. Acutely conscious of displaying ostentatious branding in No Logo zones, some Mac users cover the glowing Apple on their G3s and G4s with black tape or cute stickers. Otherwise, the only way to tell what kind of music programs are in use is to learn to aurally recognise the clichés of the software. But in a group improvisation involving six participants, all using electronic equipment, the importance of difference, the individual voice, is a moot point.

A traditional rock band – the Rolling Stones, say – represents a fairly simple hierarchical model: vocalist Mick Jagger sharing the top of the heap with the Tommy Hilfiger logos, the rest of the band strung out below, followed by the hired hands – bass and keyboards – then an army of production functionaries and anonymous crew members packed down into the base of a vast pyramid. Even the way the band sets up on stage follows this model: singer at the front, drummer at the back, road crew adopting that ridiculous half-crouching run that signifies invisibility when something goes wrong with a microphone or cable. There are plausible reasons for this model. Nobody wants to see the hot dog stands, merchandising franchises, accountants, riggers, ticket sellers, car park attendants and security muscle up on stage with the band, but the symbolism remains telling.

At Gendai Heights Gallery, the physical organisation, along with the musical structure, was more like a web of distributed consciousness than a pyramid. For the audience, squashed up together with the players in amongst them and unable to identify sounds by easy visual references to saxophones or piano, the source of any given sound was ambiguous. For most people, I would guess it was unimportant. The way to enjoy this event, to build structure and meaning, was to find a location somewhere within the web, then feel the threads grow and mutate in all dimensions. This was true for the players, too. I hesitate to call them musicians because not all of them think of themselves as belonging within that category. At points of high complexity, when musicians are utterly absorbed in what they are doing, even improvisations using instruments such as double bass, trumpet and guitar can become confusing to the participants themselves. Who's doing what? Where's that coming from? As in cooking, combinations of flavour transcend simple addition. When the sound sources are electronic, using racks of analogue effects, or exclusively digital, generated from software, then the sounds will tend to bury themselves and their origins in the mix.

moving through haunted weather

Having joined the audience at Heights Gallery, initially reluctant to be there at all, I surrendered to the mix, accepting its seductive siren song, immersing myself in the oceanic. For more than forty minutes my senses felt bathed in transmissions from a distant planet. Like the slow spin of a short wave radio dial, the music slid softly through voice fog, tongues unknown, electrical radiance, hollow pulses, freak atmospheres, a tapping ghost, occult broadcasting, flickers at the edge of human audio, the munch and spittle of software scoffing on chaff. When I listen now to the CD-R document of that night a phrase from James Hamilton-Paterson's novel, *Ghosts of Manila*, creeps into my head: '... moving through haunted weather.'

Something in the sensitivity and textural variety of this exchange reminded me of improvisations by the Spontaneous Music Ensemble, a group of varying membership with the late John Stevens a constant inspirational presence at its centre. But that was thirty years ago, mostly acoustic, created on technologies of wood, metal, skin, plastic, wire, flesh and little pads of cloth. John believed that a musical instrument should be a direct extension of the human body, reaching out into physical space: breath and muscle, the dance of elbows and ankles, fingers, ears and instinct all working together in fluid motion, filling the air of a room. In 1971, when I took part in his improvisation workshops with percussionist Paul Burwell, John made us think hard about what it meant to play guitar through an amplifier or shake a wooden rattle. Both ways of playing involved devices or consequences that were one step (or a guitar lead) removed from human physicality. The seeds in a rattle collide with unpredictable volition once shaken; like all music, the physics business as much as the music business, but proportionally high in randomness. Strictly to myself, I thought so what? Giving up electric guitar in 1971 felt like fleeing the city to live in a teepee in Wales: totally unacceptable. Over time I came to realise that this apparent purism was one of John's methods for teaching us novices how to grasp and intensify the experience of being in the moment. Now I wonder, had he not succumbed to heart failure in 1994, how he would have reacted to this kind of improvisation, a new generation of players working according to his blueprint yet conjuring sounds out of virtual space with only the slightest tremor of a fingertip.

Just as I assumed the music was drawing to a close at Heights Gallery, the whole picture shifted into a different frame. So far, all of the players could be mistaken for members of the audience, their concentration on technology no different from the screen gazing you see on a train or in a café: somebody texting a secret lover; adding cereal, rice and milk to the Palm Pilot shopping list; furtively perusing porno JPEGs on a laptop. They could even be me, writing this book. The melodrama of being a musician, that Slim Shady, royalty on drugs, full makeup and chainsaw in broad daylight thing, was entirely absent.

The appearance of Tetsuo Furudate, plugging in his electric violin in front of the three monkeys, transformed this art-as-life scenario into something truly odd. A past collaborator with such notorious luminaries of the Japanese underground noise scene as Keiji Haino and Masami Akita, otherwise known as Merzbow, Furudate lives up to the image of a Tokyo boho with his floppy hair, long black coat and decadent demeanour. I imagine him drinking sake in the company of *demi-monde* Edwardians such as Arthur Machen and Austin Osman Spare. Furudate's first notes emerged from the swamp dripping with reverb, a reminder of another world, a different era. As H. P. Lovecraft might have written, 'I heard afar on the moor the faint baying of some gigantic hound.'

Feedback trembled at the edges of control, as Yurihito Watanabe tested a microphone through the mixing desk. Watanabe is a small man with long straight hair who might have been a member of Monsieur Debussy's salon, had he lived a century earlier. His voice turned out to be a plummy, operatic counter tenor, albeit untrained, a bird of vivid plumage that rose out of this forest floor of electronic abstraction, then hovered high above it, conscious that such a conspicuous display might quickly become a solo flight but determined to make a show. If those were his misgivings, they proved to be close to the truth. Most of the participants in the first phase shut down rather quickly. This withdrawal meant that those who stayed with the new direction were disengaged from an intricate web. Their location in physical and musical space grew clearer. The alarming contrast between distributed consciousness and the distinctive musical signatures of Furudate and Watanabe was more marked for being less dense, less interpenetrated than it might have been with all participants fully involved. By the end, the only survivors were violin, sporadic voice and what sounded like the snuffling of a giant cyber-dog. Sometimes sounds appear to be hemmed in by a vast, ambivalent silence, an eraser that threatens to rub out anything in its grip. This was one of those moments.

The performance ended after seventy minutes, perhaps with the faint scent of a mismatch left hanging in the air. Without any dramatic transition, Heights Gallery became a social space, the players standing up from their electronic devices to mingle cheerfully with people who had been audience members just a few minutes before. Later, some of us went to a restaurant. I talked with Furudate, though I don't remember asking him his feelings about the music. That came later, as I began to appreciate the strength of my own reactions.

The more I thought about it, the more I realised I had experienced a public enactment of a confrontation that had troubled me for years. Six months later I was lecturing in Saalfelden, a pretty village close to the Austrian Alps. To reach Saalfelden, first you fly to Salzburg, which means that the ghost of Mozart blips loud and strong on the tourist radar. Every summer, Saalfelden hosts a jazz and improvisation festival. I lectured on the subject I'm circumnavigating right now: the impact of digital technology on our humanistic conceptions of music and performance. After I'd finished, the Viennese DJ Patrick Pulsinger approached me. He was enthusiastic about what I'd said in the lecture and as we chatted he handed me a white label 12 inch EP called 'Easy To Assemble – Hard To Take Apart'.

Later that night I listened to a couple of the live concerts before going to bed. Singer Shelley Hirsch was playing in a duo with DJ Olive. Over dinner, Shelley didn't look in the best condition to play. She was wracked with period pains and clearly should have been somewhere comfortable with a hot water bottle and a handful of painkillers. As it turned out, both of these New Yorkers were magnificent. Olive cued up a succession of quietly complementary records on two decks; Shelley did her free-associative thing: babbling, singing in a bewildering confusion of styles, whispering asides, acting out little dramas, using two microphones to shift spatial illusions and personae, generally bouncing off any available stimulus that struck her. She even threw a little of our dinner conversation into the pot. It was a demonstration of how to be utterly, demonstrably human yet interact beautifully with a technology that exemplifies art in the age of mechanical reproduction.

Back in London I listened to 'Easy To Assemble – Hard To Take Apart'. The first thing that struck me was the list of musicians, a jazz septet that included trombonist Radu Malfatti. Radu lived in London in the early 1970s, heavily involved in the free jazz and improvisation scenes of that time. Lately he has developed a different reputation, notoriety even, as a proponent of extreme minimalism. Some of his recent albums are so sparse that you assume the laser in your CD player is kaput. For a lot of people, this is going to sound like another instalment in the Carl Andre 'Tate bricks' saga, but Malfatti is reacting against verbosity in contemporary composition. As for improvisation, he argues that success on the live circuit requires an active, energetic style of playing that leads to cliché. More interested in challenging cultural expectations and developing forms that heighten awareness rather than spread uniformity, he has subtracted activity from his music to the point where almost nothing is left.

At the same time, he's a capable post-bop jazz player and that's how Pulsinger used him, along with pianist Josef Novotny and the others. The idea was to rework their acoustic music electronically, feeding their acoustic sound through Pulsinger's computer, where it could be shaped and transformed with audio software. The output mixes both acoustic and electronic signals, giving the listener a sense of encounter between two different worlds, one of physical room spaces, real-time and human interactions, the other of virtual space and digital processes. I e-mailed Patrick and he told me about his real ambition, which was to present this concept in concert. Ideally, the jazz ensemble would be on stage in a soundproof glass box. They would play but their sound wouldn't travel beyond the confines of the enclosure. Pulsinger would be outside the box with his laptop, transforming the sounds in real-time. He wanted to do it, he said, but there were technical problems.

Cruel to ask (so I didn't), but I assume some of those problems were not unrelated to the issue of soundproofing. To make the glasshouse completely soundproof I imagine you'd have to start by making it airtight. A small airtight glass enclosure full of musicians all moving and blowing would soon get pretty stuffy. Condensation would mist the walls and ceiling until the structure took on the outward appearance of the Palm House at Kew Gardens. After a time the players would get sleepy, maybe collapse one by one over their instruments. If the concert was long enough they might even suffocate, their souls wafting away into the digital domain like those paintings of The Rapture enjoyed by born again Christians during the Ronald Reagan era. In normal circumstances this would signal the end of the evening but Patrick would still be there, plenty of sounds stored in his hard drive, more than enough to shape and transform until the police arrived.

> hard
>
>> to
>> assemble
>>
>>> perhaps
>>>
>>>> but
>>>>
>>>>> easy
>>>>>
>>>>>> to
>>>>>>
>>>>>>> take
>>>>>>>
>>>>>>>> apart

ants   hub   code

September 2000: a month after Saalfelden; the city was Berlin. I had been booked to perform in an event called Quasi Amazonia, the slightly subversive adjunct to a more official German celebration of traditional music from the Amazon region. Appearing on the same bill as Silvia Ocougne and Chico Mello, who played John Cage compositions in bossa nova style, I gave the debut performance of *A Journey Sideways*, a project that addressed my experiences of recording Yanomami shamans in Amazonas. Our show was held in the smaller theatre at the Haus der Kulturen der Welt, the hall that Berliners call The Pregnant Oyster. The night I arrived in Berlin the main festival programme featured Afro-Brazilian trance music from Amapá in Brazil. The large auditorium at the house of world culture certainly represents an aspect of global culture: the architectural culture that purports to democratise concert-going by redesigning the hall in which it takes place. Seats are raked on a barely perceptible incline that sweeps in a gentle wave around the stage. The platform is very low, deep and wide, the beach at the centre of the bay, and within touching distance of those audience members sitting in the front row. In this kind of hall you're supposed to feel equal to your neighbours, relaxed, informal and just a second away from becoming close personal friends with the musicians on stage.

There is a long and tortuous history of European concert promoters presenting music from regions that do not share the values embodied in concert venues designed for classical orchestras. Modern bands using electric instruments, virtuoso soloists and formalised music traditions such as Indonesian Gamelan, Hindustani Ragas and Japanese Gagaku can work tolerably well. Even if the structure and meaning of the music is only superficially understood, the power of the performance and skill of the performers is easily appreciated. The effect of transposed ceremonies that belong in secret night gatherings, seated on desert sand, or in a longhouse hidden deep in a Pacific rainforest, ranges from surreal to excruciating. Once upon a time I took my seat at this type of event full of great expectations. Now I slump down in a resigned air of cynicism and dread. Given the choice of going back alone to my hotel by the only remaining stretch of the Berlin Wall, or hearing some Brazilian trance music, I made a mistake. Anybody involved in the music industry for more than thirty years suffers excess awareness. This affliction is a type of repetitive strain injury that goes with the occupation. So as the musicians filed out on stage, drumming and dancing, my eye was drawn to the identical ironed creases in their identical shiny smocks. I thought of suitcases loading onto jumbo jets, travel irons and clothes hangers, the hopeful showbiz acumen that led one member of a distant community, or perhaps a tour agent, to suggest matching band uniforms, just like James Brown and the Famous Flames or The Beatles.

The drumming and singing began, their clarity unimpeded by the dynamic ambience of a communal living space: no babies crying, dogs barking, no night insects or generators throbbing. As with comparable situations in the past – hearing the Ketjak monkey dance in a performance for bored package tourists in Bali, or Australian Aboriginal ceremonies at London's Institute of Contemporary Arts – I can't stop thinking that this shouldn't be music solely for spectators. Exoticism and voyeurism are compounded by alienation. In all its manifestations, this problem is an adversary attacked repeatedly by every conceivable strategy during the 20th century: a few performers address ranks of passive observers in the atmosphere of a mausoleum. 'The modern concert hall is built on the assumption that a musical performance is a system of one-way communication,' wrote musicologist and educator Christopher Small in *Musicking*, 'from composer to listener through the medium of the performers. That being so, it is natural that the auditorium should be designed in such a way as to project to the listeners as strongly and as clearly as possible the sounds that the performers are making.'

As for the rhythmic patterns and repetitious vocals, they are supposed to facilitate trance states, not fashion critiques. Neither should this music be a purely performative spectacle, a 'thing' to observe. Just sitting in this everytown hall, listening in a disengaged way, dispassionately watching events unfold, my mind began to run amok. I thought about endings, how problematic they are for musicians unaccustomed to the formality of defined beginnings, appropriate duration and co-ordinated conclusions. A senior member of the group dealt with the endings problem by tapping one of the drummers on his shoulder. The second the signal came, everybody stopped abruptly. After a short pause, they began the next piece. Towards the end of the concert, one of the younger musicians invited audience members from the front rows to join them on stage. Certain incidents in this category of horror stick in my mind like pieces of unwanted chewing gum: the woman called up on stage to be a Juliet to Barry Manilow's Romeo, then presented with a video tape of her impossible dream come true; the woman inveigled into sexy dancing by the SOS Band, her ample backside crotch-bumped in front of a packed concert hall; the woman (you see a pattern here) seduced into the spotlight by Eighties soul hunk Alexander O'Neal, then serenaded and virtually dry humped on his big brass bed.

In Berlin, a woman took one brave step towards Amapá, delighted to enact the role of the sexy northern European. She was followed by a mother, cautiously swaying, her baby cradled in one arm. Finally a few men bold enough to confront their own inhibitions jumped up on the platform to dance. I slapped myself on the wrist for my malicious train of thought. The scene was rather sweet. The source of these so-called problems was traceable to my own jaundiced and contradictory views. Participation of some sort, no matter how awkward, is better than none at all; that's so long as it's not me up there. Better for people to express a physical response to the music than just sit like a bunch of Euro-stiffs at a Brahms conference. Actually, what I really thought after flirting with these positive messages was more a tumble of remorse than a limp apologia. How pallid this experience had been from the outset, how brutal the wrench that pulled the music out of its social and spiritual context and away from its climactic purpose. To see somebody fall into trance can be disturbing, shocking, like watching a time slip. Where was that disturbance, or the vigour latent in the music? Held in check, of course, by the bureaucracy, the design, the managerial tedium of contemporary concert-going, by the uneasy confluence of anthropology and entertainment, by the dissonance inherent in the event, by the bogus neutrality of the environment. Should we blame the Brazilian musicians for wanting to expand their horizons and make a bit of money to take home, the festival organisers for focussing attention on a rich cultural region, the audience for indulging their pleasure in hearing the remains of an unusual musical tradition or the uniformity entrenched within such performance environments?

Like Patrick Pulsinger's unrealised ambition to encase acoustic musicians in a soundproof glass box, or the confrontation of digital and corporeal at Heights Gallery in Tokyo, this Berlin concert presented me with a symbolic encapsulation of some of the challenges now affecting live music. What remained unresolved was the reason for those challenges and the way in which live music might adapt to accommodate them. Based on my experiences as a fan, as a concert reviewer and as a performing musician, I had begun to feel that live music was anachronistic. Concerts continue to flourish, of course, but too many of them are content to be signposts to the past: musicians twenty or more years past their best, bands re-formed to feed the illusory nostalgia of an audience too young to be aware of them first time around, the stubborn endurance of the pre-20th century classical repertoire, copy bands selling fakes of U2, Abba or The Doors in the absence of the originals, 'classic' jazz and rock groups recreating past eras with young substitutes depping for the dead or otherwise indisposed stars, new bands copying old bands or playing music so perfected and dominated by control systems that the audience might as well be watching DVD. As the adverts used to ask (somewhat optimistically, since this was analogue cassette tape under discussion), is it live or is it Memorex?

the listening room

If you pass through the hub airport of Frankfurt on your way to Cologne, Linz or some other destination, you may find yourself walking along a long tunnel. There is a sound in this tunnel, a synthetic rushing wind, that seems to rush you on your journey. I assume this is a commissioned sound installation, though many contemporary spaces possess their own peculiar acoustic characteristics.

In 1997 I took part in an event organised by the Cologne DJ Frank Schulte. A year before, I had seen him working in Switzerland with the expatriate, chess playing American David Shea, both of them building up complex soundscapes together with recordings and turntables. Shea had made a number of albums that collaged and sampled music history, primarily using record decks. In the courtyard of the Bern squat where we were both performing, he told me about the time that easy listening composer Ray Conniff phoned him at home, apoplectic with rage, demanding to know how Shea could sample his music and consider himself an artist, not a pirate. Imagine lifting the phone and hearing the words: 'This is Ray Conniff speaking ...'

Interested in improvisation, old school and new, Schulte assembled a number of musicians who might create a hybrid of some interest within the post-ambient club context. He called this concept The Listening Room. Among the other acts that weekend were Ryoji Ikeda and Burnt Friedmann, who played solos, and ex-Can drummer Jaki Liebezeit's Club Off Chaos. Our group of five – Frank, myself, Robin 'Scanner' Rimbaud, American percussionist and raconteur David Moss and New Zealand reeds player Hayden Chisholm – attempted to find common ground, distributed spatially around a room full of young Germans whose reference points began, I would guess, with post-Detroit techno and club culture.

Frank's idea was to shift the action from solos to small groups, allocating each segment a time scale: duo Rimbaud/Moss, about 5 min./+ reading by David Toop + sounds of Moss and Rimbaud, about 5 min./fade-in of Hayden Chisholm – duo with Schulte, about 5 min....short comment by Toop, about 1 min, all changes being cued by one of the players in action. That was the gist of Frank's score, with a start time of 22.00 and the projected finish at 01.01. During the soundcheck my short comment was 'fuck this'. David Moss and I had been improvising for decades. Scanner, Hayden Chisholm and Schulte himself were all accomplished improvisers. Nobody needed to work to the timings of a cook book. Given the fact that we were so dramatically separated in space, we had never played together and, in a number of cases, never met, and given the fact that the audience didn't really have a way of entering into this kind of fragmented, genre-shifting form, the gig seemed to go pretty well.

The following morning, I joined an animated discussion with Andres Bosshard and David Moss. Bosshard is a soundscape recordist from Zurich who travels the world with his own mobile recording and playback vehicle. In Cologne he had driven this van into the Stadtgarten parkland surrounding the venue, fixed loudspeakers in the trees and played a lengthy, shifting montage of his recordings. At breakfast, Moss was delivering a soliloquy about The Listening Room event and all its consequences, implications and repercussions. The permeable, liminal, come-and-go environment of bricoleurs, stateless persons, chancers and bladerunners that had grown from the ambient chill out rooms of the early 1990s was destroying focus, he complained. People who came to these things didn't know how to listen any more, couldn't concentrate, had no language for evaluating the specific, only the capacity to wander through post-modernity in a state of vacancy. I countered by saying that this situation had opened up many new possibilities for musicians from different generations, backgrounds, styles and levels of ability. A significant audience had evolved, comfortable with odd mixes of genre, eager to learn and far more civilised than the hostile bastards who might have thrown missiles and yelled abuse during previous decades. So what, he said (and I paraphrase). At least they were passionate, whether for or against. Nobody's listening closely, or truly engaged. It's all background for some sort of lifestyle behaviour.

His discomfort stuck in my mind. Four years later I asked him for his views on performance, how audiences were changing, how technology was changing the way gigs are set up, the way musicians play and the way an audience listens (or doesn't listen). In response, he e-mailed me this story: 'Spring, 2001: I was performing in an alternative theatre/performance space in a suburb of Florence on a Saturday night. After my 10 pm show, there was a midnight dance/disco for the "younger" crowd. As I finished my show for a largely "art-type" audience, and began to pack up my drums, electronics and other eccentric objects on the stage, I saw a young man, about 17–18 years old, at the front of the stage watching me intently. After a few minutes, I asked, "Can I help you?", and he asked me, "How do you do it?"

'I thought he was asking about my electronics, 80s style "live" sampling or the simple drum triggering of pre-recorded cassettes. As I started to talk about that he broke in: "No, no, I mean how do you play it?" And then I thought he meant how do I perform as an improviser and so I started another explanation. But he broke in again and said, "No, no, that's not what I mean. I want to know how you play on stage and make all that sound yourself."

'And then I realized the incredible truth: "Are you asking how I can play 'live'?" I said. "Yeah," he answered. "I've only seen playback and laptop and DJs and MTV, never saw 'live' musicians on stage and you're not even a band. I just came here early for the disco and saw the last part of your concert. Why do you do this?" Well, I would gladly have stayed there and discussed my personal obsession with "live performance", but they wanted me off the stage and I had to keep on packing up.'

With the notable exception of free improvisation and its derivatives, the new music or sound art that I find exciting is rarely conceptualised as a performance medium, in the conventional sense at least. Techno, hip-hop, electronica and all the other studio-based music forms of the early 21st century make efforts to engage in familiar performance routines, yet the results range from reasonably satisfactory compromise to pointless travesty. Ultimately, these musics are made in close partnership with machines. A century of recording has changed our expectations of the way in which music is created, how it should sound, where and when we hear it and in what format. Add to that twenty years of music video and the necessity of a human presence becomes optional. Promethean fictions based on the dangers of animating machines or humanoid creations such as robots and replicants – Ernst Hoffmann's *Automata*, Mary Shelley's *Frankenstein* or the evil robot created by Rotwang in Fritz Lang's film, *Metropolis* – have been absorbed into midnight movie kitsch. Their anxieties linger, apocalyptic technophobia now scaled back to the personal, the tribulations of capital: will I become an economic reject if I don't learn Windows? How can old-media companies encrypt their cultural property to prevent digital theft? Will I need to buy a new computer with vast gigabytes of capacity if I fill up the hard disk with digital pictures of my cat? But warnings that the robots will take over from us humans were displaced around the same time that Arnold Schwarzenegger turned friendly and sushi came served on a conveyer belt.

For music theorist and 'concept engineer' Kodwo Eshun, such concerns are barely relevant. 'Underground Resistance is not a group but the symbiosis of the soundmachine with producer Mike Banks,' he writes in his book, *More Brilliant Than the Sun: Adventures in Sonic Fiction*. 'The producer is caught up in machinemutation, played by the machinery he plays.' The roots of this 'symbiosis of the sound machine' fork in any one of three different directions. One reaches back to the beginnings of disco and funk in the 1960s, one returns to the first experiments in electronic music, the third goes back to 1890, to the beginnings of commercially available recorded sound. In the case of the Detroit recording act (brand, they might be called in 2001), Underground Resistance, all three.

intensity

> 'He led her to the hive, where the bees were making a horrifying drone. In went his left hand. And out it came unharmed, even with seven or eight bees on it, some fanning their wings, some moving their legs, others crawling between his fingers.'
>
> Izumi Kyoka, *The Holy Man of Mount Koya*

of

That Saturday night at Gendai Heights Gallery continued to bug me. I e-mailed Tetsuo Furudate, who sent me a CD-R recording and some photographs of the gig, along with the e-mail address of Yurihito Watanabe, the singer who appeared towards the end of the performance. Watanabe speaks very little English. His friend, the artist Mariko Sugano, translated the replies he sent in response to my questions. From his point of view, the evening had presented unique difficulties. 'No one of us knew in advance what happened that night,' he wrote in his first letter. The performers using laptop computers, samplers and mixing desks created a sound so complete that there seemed no opening through which he could gain entry.

vibration

Openings, gaps, ambiguity and hiatus are very important elements in improvised music. They are portals that allow unpredictability, lateral movement and variety. They resist closure and domination. Certain types of improvisation fuelled by drugs like cocaine and amphetamines, or founded on an unspoken code of exaggerated masculinity, may develop within their own logic yet allow no clear openings at all. One example might include the mid-70s electric music of Miles Davis. In these situations, musicians who feel as if they are outside the perimeter need an enormous effort of will to enter the fray. The performers at Heights Gallery were hardly raging on speed or testosterone; nevertheless, an apparent impermeability emerged out of the compatibility and inexhaustible energy of their sound generating tools. The resultant web – intricate, immersive, lacking any discernible narrative – would have been easy enough to enter with similar tools but virtually impenetrable for a musician dependent on a highly individualised vocabulary and an immediately recognisable instrument. In this context, a voice (perhaps the ultimate signifier of human nature) is highly problematic.

'Although such a fullness of sound was interesting,' Watanabe wrote, 'I couldn't easily find a chance to sing passively there. I couldn't gauge the physical rhythm of the laptop contingent and then I was imagining a certain event inside me. It looked like the image of a criminal awaiting death by hanging, on the gallows, a rope around his neck. It seemed I couldn't wait any longer so I kicked away the foothold by myself. Actually my voice was similar to the cramp of the hung body. Of course, this was an imaginary event which happened inside me, not an objective understanding of the bigger event on the stage. However, I realise that a kind of suffering can play a suitable part in an event.'

These images of death row, suicide, the paroxysms of strangling, seem rather melodramatic when applied to a performance of spontaneous music in a small Tokyo club. In fact, they give voice to the strong feelings that arise quite frequently from informally structured sessions of this kind. Watanabe's personal aesthetic simply adds an interesting coloration to commonly expressed reactions. Trained for two years in the singing, dancing and theory of Noh theatre, Watanabe's influences are broad. He cites a long list that includes Hildegard von Bingen, Machaut, Thomas Tallis, Gesualdo, Mahler, Giacinto Scelsi, Edgar Allan Poe, Stéphane Mallarmé, Antonin Artaud, Japanese poets Teika Fujiwara and Kohnosuke Hinatsu, visionary novelist Kyoka Izumi, Samuel Beckett and the philosophers Deleuze and Guattari. 'What I have learned from these artists,' he wrote, 'is the intensity of vibration that may change the limitations of space and body. I sometimes feel that the outline of my body, vibrating and breaking into fragments, chases after many sounds and silence that are scattered about space.'

He continued by talking about the way in which the voice maps the limitations and extent of the human body, connecting and separating inside from outside, self and other. Passages from Steven Connor's rich study of the disembodied voice, *Dumbstruck: A Cultural History of Ventriloquism*, help to illuminate this subject, particularly the way in which the voice articulates the body and its orientation in space. 'So here is the essential paradox of the voice,' Connor writes. 'My voice defines me because it draws me into coincidence with myself, accomplishes me in a way which goes beyond mere belonging, association, or instrumental use. And yet my voice is also most essentially itself and my own in the ways in which it parts or passes from me. Nothing about me defines me so intimately as my voice, precisely because there is no other feature of my self whose nature it is thus to move from me to the world, and to move me into the world.'

With his 1950 film *Rashomon*, Akira Kurosawa examined the elusive nature of reality, the subjectivity of interpretation that can make a single event into an endlessly proliferating source of meanings. The film was based on two short stories by novelist Ryunosuke Akutagawa. In Kurosawa's version, a woman is raped, her husband is murdered. A bandit is arrested and tried for the crime. A woodcutter who witnessed the event gives testimony at the police court, along with the two living protagonists, the dead man (speaking through a female medium) and others. Naturally, their stories all differ and at the conclusion, there is no conclusion. 'In more ways than one,' wrote Donald Richie in his study of Kurosawa's films, '*Rashomon* is like a vast distorting mirror or, better, a collection of prisms that reflect and refract reality ... Here then, more than any other single film, is found Kurosawa's central theme: the world is illusion, you yourself make reality, but this reality undoes you if you submit to being limited by what you have made.'

In confrontations with unfamiliar experiences, such as a music performance in which the unfolding of events runs contrary to any previous norm, all of the models that help us make evaluations are smashed. Rejection may follow, or the emergence of a model that encompasses these new discoveries. Analysis of such a performance is not so different to the dissection of a friendship, a marriage, a teaching relationship: an apparent unity can be built from wildly divergent perceptions of the event's internal dynamics and goals, its eventual success or failure, even the factual details of its unfolding.

By e-mail I asked Carl Michael von Hausswolff and Carsten Nicolai for their thoughts. 'Sometimes I didn't know who was doing what and the whole became a real whole,' wrote Hausswolff. 'I tried to keep my sounds as basic as possible – droney – backgroundish. Mostly just an 11,000-Hz tone panning in the place. Then when the opera started I was stunned by fascination and surprise. It was fantastic. I don't remember how it ended ... I suppose it just faded away.

'I really love these occasions. A few years earlier when I, Graham Lewis (of Wire fame) and Jean Louis Huhta (DJ and musician from Stockholm) formed the band OCSID, we all agreed upon not rehearsing, full respect for each other and a total giving and taking. We played our sounds, others, machines, oscillators, computers, toys, CDs, LPs, cassettes, samplers – sampling each others sounds, developing the stream of sounds into a dense and complex world, then slowing it down, taking it easy, relaxing, then intensifying it again – mostly in bars, where the normal sonic ambience is pretty loud. I think it has a similarity to free jazz, the difference being the instrumentation and the fact that there's no key tone.'

As for Carsten Nicolai, he agreed that the concert had fallen into two distinct halves. 'For me, the start was very sensitive and more based on the structures and non-musical sounds,' he wrote. 'I think part two started as Watanabe plugged in the mike to the PA system and produced a kind of hum and feedback. I found this was still OK. In the moment as he started testing the mike with his voice over the ongoing sounds I lost track and stopped playing. There was a very different kind of sense. For me this was too over-pronounced, in many layers. In this time I was much more working on a kind of self-organisation of sound, in sounds that we would not define as music, or noise, but sound we live in, like my hard drive in the moment I write you this mail. In this level of perception you can imagine ...'

games   empathy   microbehaviour

Two years after Gendai Heights Gallery I sat with Yurihito Watanabe and Mariko Sugano in my dining room in London, face to face rather than in cyberspace. 'In improvisation, they always use signals,' said Mariko, translating for Watanabe, 'but at Heights Gallery, everybody had their own style. It was like being in the subway, everybody living their own life.' This

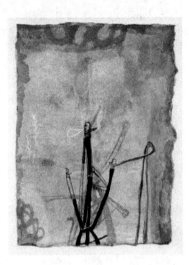

Mariko Sugano
mutus liber

image made me think of ants, as subways in the rush hour often do. Ants are interesting creatures since they perfectly illustrate the emergent intelligence, or swarm logic, of self-organising systems in action. 'Popular culture trades in Stalinist ant stereotypes – witness the authoritarian colony regime in the animated film *Antz*,' writes Steven Johnson in *Emergence: The Connected Lives of Ants, Brains, Cities and Software*, 'but in fact, colonies are the exact opposite of command economies. While they are capable of remarkably coordinated feats of task allocation, there are no five-year plans in the ant kingdom. The colonies that Gordon studies display some of nature's most mesmerising decentralised behaviour: intelligence and personality and learning that emerges from the bottom up.'

The Gordon he refers to is Deborah Gordon, a researcher in behavioural ecology, and the colonies she studies are the harvester ants of the American Southwest. Although ants and people are demonstrably different in many ways, not least in their choice of morning newspaper, Gordon's quest to find the 'connection between the microbehaviour of individual ants and the overall behaviour of the colonies themselves' (in Johnson's words) may help to illuminate some of the mysteries of collective improvisations. Johnson is careful to distinguish between outright anarchy and emergence. Explaining

StarLogo, a computer program devised by Mitch Resnick to simulate self-organising systems such as slime mould, he makes the following point: 'Systems like StarLogo are not utter anarchies: they obey rules that we define in advance, but those rules only govern the micromotives. The macrobehaviour is another matter. You don't control that directly. All you can do is set up the conditions that you think will make that behaviour possible. Then you press play and see what happens.'

To the uninitiated observer, free improvisation has no apparent rules or conditions. Does this mean it's the musical equivalent of anarchy? Some musicians who use improvisation as an option, a method that can work alongside other strategies for organisation, impose conditions at the outset of a session. These may include visual signals, the rules that Yurihito Watanabe uses to distinguish a music improvisation from rush hour in the subway, or they may be developed into sets of instructions and directions for musicians, such as those used by John Zorn for game pieces such as *Cobra*, or by Lawrence 'Butch' Morris for his 'Conductions', or conducted orchestral improvisations. 'Butch Morris gives clear signs which have to be learnt like a language by the musicians who have never worked with him before,' wrote Fredi Bosshard in the liner notes for *Conduction #70 TIT for TAT*, released on the For4Ears label. 'There are various signs. They can demand a repetition of fragments of music that have just been played or recall some that were played some time ago. A composition is being created out of the moment. It demands of the musicians a great ability to memorise, almost to the capacity of a sampler, and yet it still leaves room for individual expression and variations.'

In the most straightforward case, such rules can be used as a safety net. For musicians who feel no need for caution, like Zorn or Morris, they are more likely to have evolved as a response to the emergence of habitual patterns. Very large groupings can settle into sonic uniformity, a featureless mass that offers far less variety than the potential sum of its parts. Timid can be overshadowed by brash. How can this be redirected into structural diversity, or coaxed into balanced oppositions without resorting to the hierarchical model of composition? Is it possible to develop a group mind that thinks compositionally?

Listening to the consummate skill of New York composer and saxophonist John Zorn suggests an overwhelming love of sound. Yet Zorn has claimed that music is not about sound, not even about time, but at a fundamental level an instantaneous communication of thought. Much of his music is an audible realisation of actions set in motion. One of his recent releases, *Songs From the Hermetic Theater*, in particular the track called 'Beuysblock', returns him (via the inspiration of artist Joseph Beuys) to preoccupations of the mid-1970s, when loft performances of his *Theater of Musical Optics*, 'shifted the focus from the performer's manipulations to the objects themselves ... the objects became for me like solid sounds, different shapes, textures, colours, histories, to be ordered in musical fashion.'

This is relevant to Zorn's relationship to genre and image. His instructions to blues guitarist Albert Collins for the recording of 'Two-Lane Highway' in 1987 were given as images: 'now you're in the desert, now you're in a car, now you're walking into a chilli joint.' The smell, the air, the heartbeat of these situations is comparable to the associations of genre music. Despite a constant pressure to reduce these things to marketing aids, it could be said that genres exist to satisfy particularised needs, just as categories of pornography appeal to certain species of desire. Zorn's *Treatment for a Film in Fifteen Scenes* is a naked list: scenes 80 through 84, for example, are 'Light bulb being painted black; Stirring a Martini with olive/toothpick; Blotter on signature; Three friends arm in arm; Sand poured on paper.' Only one of these scenes has any obvious sonic component (perhaps two, should you stir your Martini with enough vigour), yet all are highly suggestive of audible event blocks within the context of a music that has neither sound nor time.

This is the clearest exposition of Zorn's interest in structures based on linear assemblages of blocks. There are precedents for this way of working – the composing of Edgard Varèse, Karlheinz Stockhausen, Frank Zappa and Carl Stalling, along with certain strands of 1970s European improvising – but through the evolution of game pieces such as *Cobra*, *Archery* and *Pool*, an intense appreciation of film editing and a generous, highly informed knowledge of so-called genres in all media, Zorn brings unique gifts to this method. Quoting Gershom Scholem on the sleeves of his *Masada* albums, Zorn asserts his own position in relation to historical material and memory: 'There is such a thing as a treasure hunt within tradition which creates a living relationship to tradition.' The tradition referred to here is Jewish but by establishing connections through the *Masada* project with the African-American experience (notably the innovations pioneered by Ornette Coleman), and to many other 'traditions' elsewhere within the body of his work (cartoons, film soundtracks, exotica, speed metal, and so on), Zorn flies above the pastiche of which he is sometimes accused to an omniscient vision state.

To listen to two albums back to back – *Cynical Hysterie Hour*, recorded for Kiriko Kubo's cartoons in 1989, and *Cobra: Tokyo Operation '94*, a version of Zorn's game piece performed by Japanese musicians – is to plunge into a vortex in which simultaneous memory and precognition of all stimuli within the pleasure dome is permanently switched to stun power. The music fulfils his criteria of an immediate communication of thought, an insight into the idea-streaming of a person wholly alive to the chaotic marvels and horrors of 20th- and 21st-century culture.

One of Zorn's contributions to contemporary music is his search for new compositional means to organise this illuminated consciousness, both in himself and his collaborators. The game pieces were a stage in this process. Heavily influenced by sports rules and martial strategy (*Ganryu Island*, the title of an early Zorn duet album with shamisen player Michihiro Sato, was the site of swordsman Miyamoto Musashi's legendary duel with Kojiro Sasaki), they began as methods for raising the potential of group improvisation to a vehicle for extreme diversity: silence, panic, tenderness, rebellion, overload, bathos, fury, tension, immolation, broken glass, Fred MacMurray's raincoat, the staring eye of a voodoo doll seen through bamboo in black and white, pink panties glimpsed in Shinjuku, the opium monologues of Foghorn Leghorn, Turu Satana crushing a man with her car, the astronaut echo of a Fender Jaguar, twenty seconds of rockabilly stolen from the single high point in the short exploding lives of four white devils from Arkansas. Within the game format, specialist skills and divergent personalities could be juxtaposed fruitfully, allowing wide latitude for individual expression yet at the same time retaining control of densities and other elements envisaged by the composer.

With or without overt rules, improvisation comes in many different guises. Certain groups stand out as landmarks in the evolution of this group mind. The 1965–68 Miles Davis Quintet – Tony Williams, Herbie Hancock, Ron Carter and Wayne Shorter – that recorded albums such as *E.S.P.*, *Miles Smiles* and *Filles De Kilimanjaro* played an abstracted music of murmurs and hesitations, feints and diversions, flitting around a barely stated pulse like moths drawn to a flickering light. The absence of strong central themes, emphatic chord sequences, parallel movement or driving rhythms highlights the remarkable currents of empathy, almost an extrasensory perception, that flowed between these musicians. Their interplay was more like a conversation of chess players, pearl divers, calligraphers and wushu masters than the formalised debates of late 1950s hard bop. This was not free jazz, the movement that had abandoned most of the structuring principles of jazz, but underlying structures were masked so artfully or addressed so obliquely that only the barest skeleton remained.

Seasoned improvisers – musicians who are familiar and comfortable with an ad-hoc way of working – tend to operate with unspoken, even unconscious sets of conditions that differ according to the players and the overall environment. At its most basic the formula is: rule=no rules. They are used to variations in quality but at their sophisticated level, disasters are unusual. Musicians who prefer to work from clearly defined structures but who involve themselves periodically in unstructured performances often express extreme reservations about the chaos that can ensue.

Nearly two years after the event, I e-mailed Tetsuo Furudate to ask for more details of his feelings about the Heights Gallery gig. 'At the time,' he replied, 'I was especially interested in putting together a concert based on group improvisation by several experimental musicians. However, this was something that would not work with a bunch of young musicians, and all my musician colleagues also shared my feelings about this kind of event. We'd all had such bad experiences in this area. Nevertheless, with a group of musicians for whom the priority is the music itself within the time–space, it could lead to different combinations of sounds, various musical happenings and a musically interesting swell of sounds. I knew this, from my experience in this field, with occasional successful results.'

In other words, working with inexperienced players risks public humiliation; you might find yourself sharing a stage with a bunch of newbies too fresh-faced to have penetrated the mystery of the hidden rules. Even the theorists and reporters of swarm logic assume that improvisation has no rules. 'In traditional games like Monopoly or go or chess, the fun of the game – the play – is what happens when you explore the space of possibilities defined by the rules,' writes Steven Johnson in *Emergence*. 'Without rules, you have something closer to pure improv theatre, where anything can happen at any time.' Anybody with practical knowledge of 'pure improv' knows this is only partially true. Expect the unexpected, of course, but some things never happen unless conditions are set in place to encourage or sanction them.

hub

So what are these rules and how do they evolve if they are rarely discussed and never written down? What about refusals to play according to rules that only exist at a substratum of awareness? When are such refusals anti-social gestures or blunt social incompetence and when are they symptoms of a desire to shift tacit boundaries?

In July 1999 I had been involved in an ambitious, if relatively unsuccessful experiment that highlighted some of these issues. Hub was a loose grouping of musicians convened by Jon Tye, London-based proprietor of the Lo Recordings label and *éminence grise* behind post-techno studio creations such as MLO and Twisted Science. An inveterate fixer, Jon realised sooner than most that a convergence was taking place at the margins of music. In the language of consumer technology, he was an early adopter. What he had perceived was a drift towards improvisation among younger musicians experimenting with electronics. Perhaps this was inevitable. Sound had become more important than structure. In the wake of all the post-techno, post-hip-hop isms – electronica, DJ mixing, digital sampling, turntablism, trip hop, illbient, gabba, drum'n'bass, darkcore, digital dub, glitch music, digital hardcore, the sharper end of ambient, microhouse and the new wave of sound art – live electronic music was in the process of rehabilitation. Musicians born after the break-up of The Beatles, the death of John Coltrane, the publication of John Cage's *Silence*, the invention of the Moog Synthesiser, after whatever marker seems adequate to register a certain sea change in sound culture, were suddenly keen to collaborate with improvisers whose experience was visible in their facial lines. Consigned to the freezing darkness in the 1980s, improvisation crept back towards the companionship of the fire.

Jon Tye was searching for ways to throw studio hybrids into the clubs, in front of a virgin audience. Hub aspired to its name: a central point connecting radial spokes. The spokes could be interchangeable but the centre point always featured one of the main protagonists. Jon had been working with Luke Vibert, a DJ and recording artist otherwise known as Wagon Christ or Plug, and Tom Jenkinson, a bass player who had staked out the furthest reaches of hyperactive drum'n'bass programming under the name of Squarepusher. The night I was invited to become a spoke radiating out from the central hub of Tye, Vibert and Jenkinson, the other players included improvising drummer Eddie Prévost, revered as a founder member of improvising group AMM, electronic trumpet player Richard Thomas and saxophonist Tom Chant, a collaborator in various line-ups including Eddie Prévost's trio, The Sycophants and The Cinematic Orchestra. Although it sounds like jazz and calls itself an orchestra, the most active member of The Cinematic Orchestra is a digital sampler. A talent for navigating both acoustic improvising and studio loops and samples typifies Chant's generation, though the transition from studio to stage is more hazardous.

We played at The Spitz, in London's Spitalfields Market. The club was full to capacity, most people drawn by Vibert and Jenkinson, so the noise level generated by conversation and drinking was considerable. The stage was similarly overcrowded, being covered with electronic equipment, Squarepusher's drum kit and bass amp, my steel guitar and effects, Eddie Prévost's gargantuan barrel drum, Luke Vibert's record decks and eight musicians. I found myself perched on the edge of the platform, within close range of the audience front row's most intimate displeasure. We had agreed a simple rule beforehand: each player would go on stage one by one so the music would build through an additive process. We also agreed to leave plenty of space for each other until a specified time during the first set. But simple rules are useless when the underlying conditions of successful improvisation are not in place. Within ten minutes of the beginning, everybody was struggling to establish their own contribution, fighting to maintain a presence, ultimately abandoning any hope of being able to listen in any detail to the total sound field. Reviewing the concert in *The Wire*, Rob Young noted the necessary resurgence of what he called 'loose-fit improvisation companies' (a reference to Derek Bailey's Company, a long-running experiment in improbable improvisation groupings). 'At best, it makes for gripping collective music making,' wrote Young. 'At worst, it can lead to an amorphous mess where no one has the courage to take a lead, so everyone ends up poised on the edge of explosion without consummating the relationship.'

Luke Vibert's DJ set seemed to flow naturally into the second set, though his strategy of playing drum'n'bass beats throughout ensured that any empathy developed during the first hour was lost in the shift to an entirely different focal point. A trumpet player in the audience worked desperately hard to sit in, finally getting a nod of capitulation from Richard Thomas. Forcing his way into a gap on the platform, he then played the way these people always do – inputs on zero, outputs on eleven. Eventually, Eddie and

I capitulated to the inevitable. With no possible escape route from the stage, we both made a psychological retreat from the chaos, hoping the end would come soon. Conveniently placed at the back, where drummers inevitably lurk, Eddie quietly packed up his kit. Deprived of that option, I sat in silence, counting sheep. After the music had stumbled to its conclusion, friends mumbled faint praise or apologies and drifted away; most press reviews were scathing, if lamentably ignorant; a feeling of embarrassment prevailed among the participants. This was one to tick off to experience.

Later that year I lectured at the Birmingham Conservatoire. Two of the students had travelled down to London for Hub. They both agreed: one of the best live gigs they had ever heard; a way forward for music. I was surprised, though only mildly. In a media environment obsessed with lists, top tens, 100 best and definitive moments of nostalgia, subjectivity still prevails. Over two years later, writing this account and curious to measure my memory against the audio document, I listened to a minidisc recording of the first set. Rob Young's metaphor of sex and seduction seemed highly appropriate. The music sounded episodic and excessively voluble, a disconnected series of paroxysms and interventions too nervous to allow for deep communication. On the other hand, this retrospective listening experience was more engaging than the real-time playing experience. How often is this the case, and how often is the opposite true? I asked Tom Chant for his opinion. The answer he returned opened another door for me. 'As a (I think I've heard it called) "user interface",' he wrote, 'traditional musical instruments seem for speed of response very good but for range of sound, say volume or pitch, quite limited compared to some electronic devices. When improvising with electronics I've found I have to follow the electronics as they haven't the speed of response to follow me.' In other words, as technology evolves, you win some, you lose some.

During a telephone conversation that took place in the middle of these thoughts, guitarist Derek Bailey pointed out to me that failures are more conducive to analysis than successes. Nobody goes to Relate to pick over the positive aspects of their relationship. In *Agapé Agape*, William Gaddis quotes Tolstoy: 'Reading bad books helps me to detect my own faults more than good ones. Good books reduce me to despair.' To further complicate the issue, music can improve over time. This is particularly true when incompatibility of performance style, longueurs and the social friction of public performance become a distant memory. Recordings are notorious for their habit of failing to mirror the pleasures (the horrors) of performance – what musicians of a dry disposition used to call the roar of the greasepaint, the smell of the crowd. Really, they are two entirely discrete modes of audition –

      which is where the difficulties once began

   which is where the difficulties now begin

            which is where the difficulties have begun

2 Space and memory

'Isn't it strange how history has been replaced by technology?'

from Jean-Luc Godard's *Éloge de l'Amour*

December 2002: Angela Flowers Gallery, Cork Street, London. Wandering into the gallery with no particular purpose in mind, just pressing the pause button for a moment on an amiable day of Christmas shopping, I'm surprised to see a painting by Trevor Sutton. We were students together at Hornsey College of Art, in the student sit-in year of 1967–68. Trevor appeared in one of my Super 8 loop films of semi-naked people engaged in pointless tasks. Other than that, and a shared interest in the cool abstractions of Robyn Denny, our work had little in common, but this painting here – uneven strokes of horizontal texture on a small, three inch deep, circular panel – is one in a series entitled *Sound Of No Sound*.

ma   shapeless

This is a paradox. Listening can direct you to silence. Noise pollution is an obvious example, an involuntary aversion therapy that drives people to the edge of madness, but enjoying noise, sound, music – whatever we want to call this phenomenon in all its forms – is a habit that can progress from excess into absence. Cage taught us, there is no silence, the body is working perpetually, beating, vibrating, and emitting energy even in repose or sleep. Concentrated listening (or deep listening, as composer Pauline Oliveros describes it) is a process of refinement. One drop of sound may be enough.

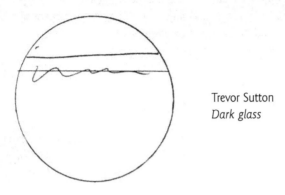

Trevor Sutton
Dark glass

Sound exists in relative silence, easily imposing itself as an unwanted interruption. This interruption is an entertainment, of course, and a refusal to be entertained seems quite natural in a world that has been transformed into nothing more than entertainment. What existed before and after the interruption may have a greater potency. One section of Ooka Makoto's *What Is Poetry*, written in 1985, begins as a questionnaire: 'Among many richly useful Japanese words is the word "ma" which signifies "interval" in time and space. What does "ma" mean in your work?' Ooka gives eight responses. Among them, he writes:

> '(if you would see the stars clearly,
> look hard at the surrounding darkness)'

and:

> 'If you think of "ma"
> as something between one thing and another,
> you're wrong.'

I would suspect this 'wrong' conclusion is not uncommon: silence perceived as blocks of 'anti-thing'; sounds heard as blocks of 'thing'. As foundation students at Hornsey College of Art, working to a programme based on the teaching methods of designer and educator Harry Thubron, we would have to draw radiators, giving particular emphasis to the spaces between the pipes. Did these air drawings develop my sense of *ma* or simply entrench the falsehood of anti-thing between one thing and another?

Ooka also describes *ma* as shapeless:

> 'Because it is shapeless,
> it becomes the source of all shapes, which is a *force*.'

Perhaps this is one of the most important lessons to learn in improvisation. Sounds grow out of silence, but not as significant events enlivening nothingness.

Sounds are woven with memory.

For this reason, they may need to be undone as memories become an anchor, dragging in the mud of accumulated personal history and nostalgia.

Silence is woven with memory.

Rituals acknowledge the power of silence, just as they exploit the otherworldly aura of sound. Though silence is supposedly an absence, the withdrawal of noise (in all its senses) is replaced by a louder phenomenon, a focussing of attention, an atmosphere, which we mistakenly describe as silence. Jonty Semper's *Kentaphion* is a double CD that collects together 81 archive recordings of 2-minute silences, observed either on Armistice Day or Remembrance Sunday at The Cenotaph in Whitehall, London. The recordings date from 1929, since for various reasons – Home Office obstruction, for one – that was the first year in which outside broadcast of the event had been allowed. Inevitably, the grain of recordings – their fluctuating hum and frizzing, fretful highs – adds individual character to each of these 'silences'. Essentially, the format is the same throughout: echoing gun salutes, the chiming of Big Ben, a silence, then guns again. Ma – something between one thing and another? But listen closely, on headphones. In 1986, two pigeons flapped their wings. In 1988 a baby was crying, a child coughed, voices were raised and tape deterioration overlaid a patina of decay that suggests 19th rather than late 20th century. In 2000, seagulls flew overhead and a strange absence of lower frequencies emphasised the vibrato in Big Ben's tolling strokes, more Kyoto Buddhist temple bell than internationally famous London soundmark. The final gun salute is richly captured, though abruptly truncated since Semper is presenting the silences here, rather than the entire ritual. This is the full stop at the end of this collection. Future recordings will no doubt enable us to follow changing fashions in mobile phone ring tones.

In his liner notes to this release, historian Dr Adrian Gregory describes the peculiarity of broadcasting silence, peculiar not only because radio administration enforces a neurotic commitment to incessant aural activity but because the experience of listening to this silence on radio, in the home, was perceived as collective rather than private. He quotes the *Radio Times* from 1935: 'Here is one of the great paradoxes, that no broadcast is more impressive than the silence following the last dashing strokes of Big Ben. The impressiveness is intensified by the fact that the silence is not a dead silence, for Big Ben strikes the hour, and then the bickering of sparrows, the crisp rustle of falling leaves, the creasing of pigeon wings as they take flight, uneasy at the strange hush, contrast with the traffic din of London some minutes before ... our job is to reduce all local noises to the right proportions, so that the silence may be heard for what it really is, a solvent which destroys personality and gives us leave to be great and universal.'

The author of *The Silence of Memory*, a study of Armistice Day commemorations, Gregory discovers a contemporary account of the first 2-minute silence, held in 1919, in which the scene in London was compared to a mechanical toy coming to a halt. Silence is equated with stillness, often, and tranquillity, which is close to tranquillisation, of course, through which either the body is rendered inert or the mind and emotions are wrapped in immobilising chemical felt in order to quell a tendency towards chaos. On 11 November 2002, I was standing in a check-in queue at Heathrow's Terminal Three, on my way to Canada, when an announcement was broadcast, requesting 'cooperation' in the observation of a 2-minute silence. Few scenes in modern life are more redolent of a mechanical toy in action than a major airport during peak hours. The sensation of highly controlled, perpetual and repetitious movement is overwhelming. An atmosphere of fairytale entrancement suppresses the underlying panic that afflicts all sensible travellers (one reason why I like artist Mariko Mori's projected work, *Miko No Inori*, or *Shaman Girl's Prayer*, with its plaintive incantation performed by Mori as plastic spiritual cyberbabe in the ultradesign of Osaka's Kansei airport). For those processing through this environment, a silence to honour the dead is reluctantly conceded (death may be imminent, after all), easily observed by those like me who still wait in a queue but almost impossible for the airline staff and travellers who have reached their moment of ecstatic confrontation at a desk. Almost imperceptibly, hush oozed downwards through Heathrow, a gentle slide that softened the outlines of jagged chatter, audio alerts, luggage belts and disembodied unwanted information speak. The mechanical toy took perhaps 118 seconds to crawl to a complete stop, then another 2 seconds to relocate its life force.

apparent silence   a life of their own

Silence and quiet are not the same condition. Quiet can be quieter than a silence, even though silence has pretensions towards the absolute. Silence is more of a social or technical condition (they made love in silence, he fell silent, she worked in silence, digital silence is quieter than analogue silence, are you determined to remain silent, silence!, the breakfast room was horribly silent).

In *Audio-Vision: Sound on Screen*, composer and theorist Michel Chion writes about the 'absent noise' type of silence in relation to film sound: 'In a well-known aphorism Bresson reminded us that the sound film made silence possible. This statement illuminates a paradox: it was necessary to have sounds and voices so that the *interruption* of them could probe more deeply into this thing called silence. (In the silent cinema, everything just suggested sounds.)

'However, this zero-degree (or is it?) element of the soundtrack that is silence is certainly not so simple to achieve, even on the technical level. You can't just interrupt the auditory flow and stick in a few inches of blank leader. The spectator would have the impression of a technical break (which of course Godard used to full effect notably in *Band of Outsiders*). Every place has its own unique silence, and it is for this reason that for sound recording on exterior locations, in a studio, or in an auditorium, care is taken to record several seconds of the "silence" specific to that place.'

Chion also talks about the way in which cinema directors and sound designers will use sound, then silence, to highlight drama. He gives an example: Ridley Scott's close-up of the ship's cat in *Alien*. Every small sound in *Alien* resonates in emptiness and foreboding. As Harry Dean Stanton searches for Jones the cat in the bowels of the Nostromo, we hear the shifting hum of the craft at work, Stanton's 'miaow', his 'here kitty kitty', a faint answering miaow in the distance, footsteps, an explosive burst of water and cat as Jones jumps away from him, a sliver of scaled skin shed by the Alien dropping on the floor, water drips and the musical tinkle of hanging chains, water dripping heavily on Stanton's cap brim, the growls of Jones as it sees the Alien, Stanton's death cry, a gentle music of chains that lingers and fades as the shot cuts to Yaphet Kotto in a quieter room, his intake of breath. 'So silence is never a neutral emptiness,' Chion writes. 'It is the negative of sound we've heard beforehand or imagined; it is the product of a contrast.'

After the house has emptied, the clockwork radio has wound down, the CD player is switched off, the postman has delivered, the cat has gone back to sleep, I love the quiet at breakfast, just listening to the murmur of central heating, the fugitive sound of breath, spoon, poured liquid, body processes, a passing car, rain on the window, faint voices in the distance, a passenger jet overhead. At the Molecular Gastronomy Research Centre in Bristol, research is being conducted into the sounds of food, how the sound of a particular food can influence its taste. Dr John Prinz has studied the way in which the sound of mastication enhances the perception of texture. Chewing sounds such as a crunch provoke immediate delicate adjustments of tooth and jaw action. Chef Heston Blumenthal was given a demonstration by Dr Prinz: 'He gave me a set of headphones and a piece of chewing gum, and then asked me to chew so that my jaw closed in time with the recorded crunching noise coming through the headphones. Something really bizarre happened: the noise triggered a signal in my brain, which in turn stopped my jaw from closing, almost as if I had lost the full use of my jaw. Subconsciously trying to counter this effect, I ended up bashing my teeth together while chewing the gum.'

In all of these situations, we listen with remarkable intuitive sophistication to the defining of contrasting spaces: the interior of a mouth, immediate social space, the room, the surrounding building, near exterior and distant exterior, the nature of a space. During a period of grieving I kept a diary. One July night in 1997 I wrote the following: 'Monday evening, a warm night, a vivid blue sky at 10.00 pm. The perfume of jasmine from the garden is filling the room. I light a candle, open a beer, enjoy the peace. Tonight I wrote a poem for Juliette [my daughter] about her tummy ache, the one that steals up on her before she goes to sleep, the malicious one that reminds her that she's supposed to be a sad girl. I want to help her find ways to send it back to its source.

'A line from The Poetics of Reverie by Gaston Bachelard: "A forgotten author has written: 'for odours, like musical sounds, are rare sublimators of the essence of memory.'" I will remember sitting here at the table, smelling jasmine on the air and hearing the tiny quick ticking of bubbles rising in my beer glass, amplified up to the threshold of audibility by the wooden tabletop.'

In *Soundscape Newsletter*, composer and pianist Tadahiko Imada wrote about the early Showa period (1925–1989) custom of gathering to hear the sound of a lotus flower blooming at Ueno Park's Sinobazu-no-ike pond in early summer. 'However, the frequency of that sound is approximately 9–16 Hz,' he writes. 'As we normally hear sounds within a frequency range from 20 Hz to 20,000 Hz, people were unable to actually hear the sound of the bloom of a lotus flower. But they loved and wanted to listen to that phantom sound. The experience was a kind of communal auditory hallucination.'

A prime listening site can be extraordinarily revealing. Minute actions click into focus. The clarity can slow pulse rate and perceived time. But loneliness may loom into view, also, and the deathly absence of significant activity. Like many old people, my mother kept a budgerigar. She found the bird a nuisance but its chatter and movement were a comfort. In 2000, a German publishing company released a CD of background noise that simulated the presence of a partner. *Nie Mehr Allein* (Alone No More) included titles such as 'A Shirt Ironed Hastily' and 'Finally, the Freezer Is Full Again'. If the budgerigar, the radio or the television seem too alien or technological a reminder of solitude for singletons, then the faint noises of steam from an iron or a fridge door opening and closing may prove more authentically human.

a queer silence

Listen. The word is too active, didactic, overloaded with authoritarian demands and the fallout from a million verbal fights. Listen to me, don't listen, shut up and listen, why won't you listen? Then maybe, why won't you hear me? Deeper than the surface of listening, where understanding meets (or refuses to meet) sensory input. In *John Cage's Queer Silence*, Jonathan D. Katz examines the political implications of Cage's compositional leanings toward silence, in particular the way in which his silence as a closeted gay man in the homophobic era of McCarthy and the cold war interlocked with an aesthetic that repositioned the cultural meaning of noise and silence.

'With the recognition that silence is coterminous with sound,' Katz writes, 'in that a silence exists as the ground from which sound springs and to which it ultimately returns, Cage finally developed a compositional strategy that favoured coexistence ahead of opposition. Silence preceded and exceeded sound and by so doing dissolved the binarism of sound–silence into a form of continuity. Through silence, the domination of one term over another simply dampened into quiescence.' Cage preferred conversational exchange to what he described as communication, or any other form of expression that attempted to impose an argument on a listener. 'One point of silence, then,' Katz concludes, 'is to dissolve the oppositional by freely allowing other voices to be heard.'

To fully allow, even recognise, other voices, is a skill contingent upon broadening the spectrum of what we regard as 'voice' within this vast resonant atmosphere in which we live. We hear, not just through the ears, as a conscious activity, but through the whole body, in a mixture of fully conscious, peripherally conscious and unconscious awareness. Hearing more like feeling: a multiplicity of impressions at the edge of perception. We hear space all the time, not just its echoes and foreground signals but also its subliminal undertow, the presence of atmosphere. In 1998, two Japanese physicists, Naoki Suda and Kazunari Nawa, discovered what are known as the background free oscillations of the Earth. This so-called hum is comprised of something like 50 pitches, ranging between 2 and 7 millihertz, way below human hearing and far too quiet to perceive. 'What's peculiar about the notes in the Hum,' wrote Robert Coontz in *New Scientist*, 'is that they have no obvious source. Not earthquakes, not nuclear explosions, nothing. The vibrations triggered by cataclysmic events fade away to nothing, but the Hum continues, regardless.'

The explanation? There are many, though a favourite was proposed by Naoki Kobayashi, a theorist at the Tokyo Institute of Technology. Kobayashi 'predicted that the Earth's atmosphere ought to excite free oscillations in the Earth'. The idea was taken up by Toshiro Tanimoto, from the University of California. 'In Tanimoto's opinion,' Coontz writes, 'the humming starts with drumming, the constant throb of fluctuating atmospheric pressure all over the Earth. When air pressure rises, the atmosphere presses down slightly harder on the ground or sea beneath it. When the pressure drops, the surface gently rebounds. In other words, the world is like a gong being constantly buffeted by countless soft rubber mallets. And at any given moment, some of them will be tapping at the right frequencies to excite the modes that make up the Hum.'

Another *New Scientist* article documents the hissing, crackling, popping sound produced by meteors and auroras. 'Reports of noisy meteors appear in the Bible,' wrote Harriet Williams, 'yet the cause of their bizarre sounds has always been a mystery. One person might hear the popping and whooshing clearly while another, standing just a few metres away, hears nothing.' Colin Keay, an Australian physicist, suspects that very low frequency (VLF) radio waves, a form of electromagnetic radiation, must accompany the meteor's trail. As Williams points out, radio waves are audible only if an object acts as a transducer, a kind of loudspeaker that converts the signals into audible vibrations.

'After some experiments in a soundproof chamber,' she writes, 'Keay found that all kinds of things can act as transducers. Aluminium foil, thin wires, pine needles or dry, frizzy hair all respond to a VLF field. The radio waves induce small charges in such objects, and these charges force the object to vibrate in time with the oscillating waves, effectively making them act like the diaphragm in a loudspeaker. Even a pair of glasses, he discovered, will vibrate slightly. And since they rest against the bones of the skull, glasses could increase an observer's chances of hearing VLF waves.'

At http://spaceweather.com, one mouse click unleashes an audio stream of sferics (impulsive signals emitted by lightning), tweeks (sferics that have to travel long distances through the dispersive medium of the ionosphere), whistlers (even more dispersed than tweeks) and other VLF radio sounds picked up by the Inspire VLF radio receiver at NASA's Marshall Space Flight Centre in Huntsville, Alabama. The selection of sound available for audition on this site includes 60-Hz VLF radio waves emitted by the power grid. A collection of crackles, distant echoing whistles, drones and interference, this atmospheric Babel is the source material of sound artists such as Joe Banks, aka Disinformation. Born in 1967 and based in London, Banks creates visceral sound works that are also literary in varying degrees, symbolically dense and thick with allusions to the histories of art and science. He has created pieces using high frequency radio band recordings of solar radio noise and electrical storms, filtered VLF harmonics of the 50-Hz ELF fundamental radiated by AC electricity, the acoustic decrescendo caused by intercepting the radio signal radiated by irregular alternating currents inside the internal circuitry of camera flashes and VLF band radio noise recorded in welding workshops.

In notes elucidating the barrage of sound heard on his *Stargate* release, Banks wrote: 'In January 1996 I tuned into a mysterious sound that appeared temporarily at about 4MHz. At that time I had no reason to suspect it wasn't some form of corrupted data broadcast. Its effect was so deeply hypnotic – sounding like a rumble and whoosh of rollers breaking across a vast beach, or a celestial choir intoning unending chords in chorus and response – that I recorded it anyway. In February, Ron Ham and Arthur Gee wrote an extremely informative article on Solar Radio Astronomy for *Shortwave Magazine*, describing a tradition of disciplined semi-amateur research reaching back as far as the 1930s ... Ron Ham recommends that observers stick to a strict observational routine – monitoring a chosen frequency for, say, three hours a day. In my case I was blessed with enormous luck. I immediately guessed from his description of solar noise storms' characteristic "seashore effect" that this was the phenomenon I had already heard.' *Stargate* does indeed sound like big waves pounding a distant shore, though the rollers break at a tempo few surfers would risk. Unsurprisingly, Banks is interested in psychological projection, the way in which information can be hidden in noise and the unpredictable consequences of discerning and extracting that information. Often grouped with so-called noise musicians, Banks seems to fit more easily into an informal, semi-clandestine and unorthodox tradition of 'disciplined semi-amateur research'. In his article, *Rorschach Audio: Ghost Voices and Perceptual Creativity*, Banks quotes Leonardo Da Vinci's well-known statement advising young painters to find inspiration in the staining of damp walls. He draws particular attention to the last sentence: 'In such walls the same thing happens as in the sound of bells, in whose stroke you may find every named word you can imagine.'

Susceptible to all kinds of subjective interpretation, the strange atmospheric frizz of VLF and other electromagnetic phenomena sounds similar, on the one hand, to electronic noise music; on the other hand to underwater, ultrasonic and electromagnetic sounds of various species – fish, marine mammals, aquatic insects, bats and plants – collected by specialist environmental sound recordists such as Douglas Quin, Bernie Krause, Hildegard Westerkamp, David Dunn, Michael Prime, Francisco Lopez and Chris Watson. Birdsong was once the norm in wildlife recording. Now it is easy enough to find sounds of crackling shrimp, melting ice, singing ants, pondweed, crabs falling from trees into water, geological rumbles, insects hidden under leaf litter in the Cameroon rainforest, vultures feeding on a zebra carcass, bats feeding in the lanes of Kent and in the caverns of New Mexico, and the tiny voltages produced by plants such as *Lophophora williamsii* and *Amanita muscaria*, amplified and used as control signals for battery-powered oscillators.

These remote, ghost zones, which are as much a part of our total environment as woodland or high street, seem to speak a language closely related to electronic sound or the drifting haze of nocturnal radio static. 'Soon afterwards,' writes W. G. Sebald in *Austerlitz*, 'when I mentioned the mysterious radio at breakfast, Austerlitz told me he had always imagined that the voices moving through the air after the onset of darkness, only a few of which we could catch, had a life of their own, like bats, and shunned the light of day.'

Thirty or forty years ago, recordings of the outer reaches of human perception would have been the research tools of zoologists and marine biologists, occupying the esoteric wing of an activity otherwise pursued by naturalists, birdwatchers or wildlife enthusiasts with a taste for audio recording technology. The contents of a 1977 issue of *Wildlife Sound*, the Journal of the UK Wildlife Sound Recording Society, included articles on the following subjects: peak programme meters; recording birds in Lebanon; customising a Uher tape recorder to facilitate its use while wearing gloves in freezing weather; a brief history of a recording location in England's East Midlands. 'Oh, to have been a tape recordist 100 years ago,' writes the author of the last piece, 'with perhaps only a horse and cart jogging over the cobbled roads to disturb the peace!'

Though doubtless sympathetic to those sentiments, Quin, Dunn, Krause, Westerkamp, Prime and Watson are all musicians rather than hobbyists or scientists. Most of them were raised on electronic music, improvisation, noise and the silence of John Cage. Between 1973 and 1981 Watson was a manipulator of electronics, tape and Vox Continental organ in the Sheffield band Cabaret Voltaire; in 1964 Krause replaced Pete Seeger in The Weavers, then pioneered synthesisers as one half of the Beaver and Krause duo. Inevitably, a recordist with this kind of background will contextualise their soundscapes within a wider history of experimental music and communication theory. 'Put simply, what we hear from other forms of life, and the environment they reside in, is information that is unique and essential about patterns of relationship in context,' wrote Dunn in his book, *Why Do Whales and Children Sing?* 'It is an experiential basis from which we can shape an understanding of the "integrated fabric of mind that envelops us."

'For example,' he continues, 'an important innovation of 20th century music has been the "emancipation of noise" so often associated with the composer John Cage. He and many other musicians have sought to expand the resources of music beyond the vocabulary of pitch and harmony that had previously defined it. Through the "musical" manipulation of the noises of everyday life they achieved an understanding of the meaning of these sounds as aesthetic phenomena, opportunities for a deepened awareness of the world we live in. Perhaps because of this contribution to art we can now understand the need to extend it further. The sounds of living things are not just a resource for manipulation – they are evidence of mind in nature and patterns of communication with which we share a common bond and meaning.'

a sense of foreboding

In December 2002, sound recordist Chris Watson produced two programmes for BBC Radio 4 on the subject of quiet and tranquillity. I asked him for his definition of the difference between the two. His e-mailed reply was lengthy, thoughtful and worth quoting in full: 'On location, to perceive what I may later regard to be memorable sounds, there are two significant characteristics: 1 Clarity & 2 Depth. Clarity being not coloured by other irrelevant sounds or interruptions. Depth being the ability to follow the sound, or its reverberation, into the distance. To be able to listen to the full envelope of the sound. Of course the paradox is that some sounds can convey clarity and depth even when played back or broadcast over the compressed mediums you refer to [television, radio, computers, etc.]. I'm fascinated by this, but can't explain it!

'My experiences of silence within anechoic chambers have felt like oppressive forms of sensory deprivation. In that silence, true silence, my ears and brain searched for a reference. I could "feel" my ears hunting for any sound to latch on to (this was perhaps rather like one's eyes darting across the ground to search for a fallen object). In the absence of external aural stimulus my hearing and brain seemed to turn inwards to perceive (or invent?) the sounds of my internal body mechanisms – pumping blood, thumping heartbeat and a characteristic hissing noise in my ears. I also felt an external "pressure" around my head. The experience was deeply unpleasant and two or three minutes was quite enough for me. Breaking the silence by speaking was not much help as all reverberations are absorbed and perspective is lost.

'Contrastingly, the quiet atmosphere of a place, location or habitat can be a revelation – a profound "presence" made up from the component parts. I tried to capture this real sense of place with my Touch CD – *Stepping into the Dark* – after experiencing several atmospheres that I felt had a tangible character.

'Some years ago I was working on a natural history film in Kielder Forest, Northumberland. Kielder is the largest man-made forest in Europe and I had microphones rigged and left fixed in many places. I had a vehicle pass and would often drive up and down the long shale tracks well before dawn to get into a recording position before first light. I had marked the entry point towards a particular microphone position by orange tape wrapped around the trunk of a tree by the track and several times I stopped, got out and gathered my recording equipment to set out into the dense deep blackness of the serried ranks of Sitka spruce. Coniferous forests have their own special sound. Any wind or breeze up across the canopy, through the pine needles, creates a low moaning tone which is modulated by the wind strength. On the forest floor the acoustic is dampened by the density of planting and a thick carpet of needles.

'I was used to this, however, and would usually set out into the forest full of anticipation for the recording prospects ahead. However, on several occasions, I would hesitate by the track and feel an overpowering sense of foreboding – something which I knew was irrational but nevertheless could stop me in my tracks. I would sometimes force myself to continue and start recording, at other times I got back in the car and drove further down the track where the atmosphere could be completely different.

'When I came to evaluate these recordings back in my studio I began to think that the sound of the forest in a particular place had a significant influence on my mood and I wondered if this mood or feeling could be re-created by replaying the recordings. Around this time I was also travelling around the world on film and radio sound trips so I started to gather what I thought may be likely recordings and solicit stories and anecdotes from local people and guides about their feelings for their "special" places and the influence of sounds. I found remarkable similarities of opinion from Iceland to Venezuela.

'Quietness is the key. In an undisturbed place where there is a layer, a reference, an atmosphere which we can rest our ears upon. These are usually harmonically complex and with a significant, noise free, low level, low frequency content. Other single sounds can impinge upon this layer, but if the dynamics are too great, i.e. loud, the effect is cancelled.

'These are not necessarily natural locations. A couple of years ago I was in a residential area of Havana making recordings in the street. I noticed at the time that the sound was remarkably "clear" for a city – then realised this was due to the absence of traffic noise – I could hear the sounds of children playing way down the street, also distant music and conversation in particular, which carried much more than usual and was not absorbed or lost to the muffled roar of engines.

'Quietness is rare, and precious, in Britain. Glen Affric in the Scottish Highlands is one of my favourite locations to record. There is a real presence in the glen and mountainside which is uncoloured by traffic noise or aircraft. I have recordings from the hillside of the wind blowing across the summit of The Lapaich, a distant mountain, some three or four miles away. "The sound of no sound" is something that we really have to listen to and for. Of course the wonderful thing about such sounds is that they are ephemeral and depend upon the weather for their existence. Hearing them is also an active process, perhaps rather like framing an image with a camera lens, our microphones or ears have to be positioned with care.

'Sounds at night can focus detail and attention. Sounds do travel further at night due to a layer of colder air being trapped near to the ground and man-made noise is also reduced, revealing otherwise prohibited locations. In particular, I enjoy atmospheres at night in wild places as they point up an exciting, secret world upon which we can eavesdrop, appreciate and enjoy, but not necessarily understand and I think that sense of mystery and awe is an important detail which is missing in much of our daily lives.'

There is a story of one peculiar duty required of the 18th century French rural peasantry, who were ordered to thrash the fish ponds of Finistère. Beating the surface of these waters maintained a tranquil silence for visiting Parisian aristocrats, who would otherwise be sorely disturbed by the incessant croaking of marsh frogs.

Audio atmospheres are mysterious; not just because much of their content may be invisible and implicit; not just because their cumulative effects come from elusive and under-researched phenomena such as pressure changes, infrasound, ultrasonics and other barely perceived sonic signals, aligned with subtle transitions in the acoustic environment; but because they are thick with imaginings, memories, utopias, foreboding. For the urban refugee, the desire for tranquility may be so neurotically pursued that any absurdity is worthwhile, even if it risks the possibility of revolution.

'There was a loud humming of insects in the garden outside,' wrote Yasunari Kawabata in his novel *The Sound of The Mountain* (*Yama no Oto*). 'It was past two. The humming was not the clear and distinct sound of bell crickets or pine crickets. It was blurry and ill-defined, rather. It made Shingo think of sleep in dark, dank earth.' This passage seems the perfect illustration of Chris Watson's observations on sound atmospheres and mood, the way in which a harmonically complex layer or reference allows us to 'rest our ears' so that the mind can travel without undue focus or purpose (in other words, daydream or relax).

Kawabata, who committed suicide in 1972, wrote beautifully about the darker side of such sensations. Embroiled in family drama, Shingo, the central character of *The Sound of The Mountain*, is beset by anxieties of old age, the imminent threat of losing one's bearings in the world. Moments of crisis, both trivial and profound, often arrive through a sound. When Shingo hears the temple bell ring at six in the morning, he knows he has woken too early, a common symptom of advancing age. A painful conversation is interrupted by the sound of pigeon wings: 'That moment a sound came from the heavens. To Shingo it was really as if he had heard a sound from the heavens. Five or six pigeons cut a low diagonal across the garden.'

Woken by a howling dog in the garden and the 'sound of wind and rain, like a raging sea', Shingo hears a roaring sound from deep within the storm outside. In panic, he wonders if he could be hearing a train pass through distant tunnels. A temple bell rings all day in celebration of Kamakura's seven hundredth anniversary. Shingo finds he cannot hear every stroke, so listens intently in order to make one stroke a focal reference for the ones that follow. Thinking 'how pleasantly quiet and relaxed it was, sitting in the breakfast room on an April Sunday, looking at the cherry blossoms and listening to the bell', he is surprised to hear his daughter-in-law describe it as an unpleasant, dark sound. The sound of the mountain is a sensation more felt than heard, a disturbance that might be dispelled by a shake of the head. No rational explanation can defuse the suspicion that death is coming and this rumble is its messenger. In the final line of the book Shingo is a victim of sound once again, though this sound is tangible and domestic: 'She apparently could not hear him over the sound of the dishes.'

A second electronic letter from Chris Watson relates a story of wind and its power to disconcert: 'I was up in Glen Affric at dusk in October trying to record the sounds of the red deer rut. I had set up my recording equipment on the edge of a clearing with the microphones pointing up the hillside. As the light faded the distant roar of stags rolled down through the forest and into the clearing. It began to rain. As usual I had heard the rushing sound of the wind blowing down the glen and across the canopy, but just at the point when the light was almost gone the wind changed. The effect was dramatic. The atmosphere changed very quickly, as did my mood and perception. I can honestly say that I felt something blow down that hillside and into the clearing – the quality of the sound changed, the deer seemed to stop calling and I felt the hairs on the back of my neck – what few I have – stand up. I packed up as quickly as I could and left. Over the next few days I went back up there to similar locations and made a series of successful recordings without ever feeling the same effects.' In his remarkably prescient book, *The Tuning of The World*, Canadian composer R. Murray Schafer gave an example of the overwhelming potential of this barely recognised undertow. An elderly woman had tried to commit suicide. A low throbbing noise was causing her distress, though nobody else could hear it. Eventually, a noise consultant was brought in. He heard nothing, yet made tape recordings anyway, and during analysis of the tapes discovered a strong peak signal in the 30–40 Hz range. Newspaper accounts of this result generated similar case studies from all over the country. The origin of many of these subliminal, profoundly unsettling sounds was pinpointed to power transmission lines. In other cases, houses and thin trees were amplifying vibrations ultimately attributed to the wind.

These low frequency vibrations, a health hazard for all those who live within their range, are reported all over the world. In 2001, a *Guardian* newspaper feature listed instances of incessant, intrusive hums in Largs, Scotland; Taos, New Mexico; Hueytown, Alabama; Rome, Preston, Blackpool, Norfolk and Bristol. The physiological effects of the hums can range from headache, chest pressure and nosebleeds to loss of short-term memory, nausea and violent vomiting. 'One sufferer in Bristol eventually committed suicide in 1996,' wrote Laura Barton, 'unable to bear the unrelenting noise.' The explanations for these hums are wide-ranging and inconclusive. They include pulse modulated radio transmissions from the Loran Long Range Navigation System, and extremely low frequencies (ELF) used in submarine communications. Operating at terrifying decibel levels and saturating vast areas of the ocean, the U.S. Navy's low frequency active sonar system (LFA) has been known to cause mass stranding and fatal trauma of whales in areas where the detection system was being tested. According to a *Los Angeles Times* report: '"I'm not putting my life on the line for endangered species," one Navy commander declared before a congressional committee. "Sonar allows us to keep our sons and daughters out of harm's way."'

There are archaeologists who believe that the disorienting effects of infrasound, standing waves and Helmholtz resonance, generated by noise created in certain acoustic chambers, may have been exploited in ancient rituals at megalithic sites (it has to be said that any Internet search for infrasound information haemorrhages bizarre claims from Nazi fetishists, alleged satanic child abuse victims and weird science addicts of all persuasions). Speculation and rumours about extreme sound have always been rife, though there seems no doubt that global sound levels increase continuously, both in forms we can detect easily and in cumulative damage that has no apparent source.

the boy with the tomato head

> 'There are issues of the spirit that involve longing and belonging which reverberate through all the work. I approach this lyric tradition through gazing; duration is an essential condition of gazing, it infuses all of the pictures that I take.'
>
> Thomas Joshua Cooper, interviewed by David Bellingham, *Source*, http://www.source.ie/issues/issues0120/issue14/ is14artthojos.html

What is a soundscape?

Like mindscape, 'soundscape' has more than a touch of the hippie about it and some soundscape recordists do speak in that queasy New Age language of 'heart songs' and 'totems' derived from C. G. Jung, Chinese Taoism and transcriptions of Native American oral literature. The word is clearly derived from landscape (and seascape) yet its lack of visual fixity suggests that imagination is harder at work. A live radio discussion on Resonance FM, hosted in summer 2001 by the Canadian plunderphonic composer John Oswald, raised an interesting issue about this difference between visual and audio 'images'. The other participants in this discussion included Michael Snow, Paul Dutton, Chris Cutler, Peter Cusack and myself. Oswald was talking about sampling fine slices from recordings made by other artists (Madonna, for example), then reconstructing ultra-complex swarms from these fragments into his own compositions.

Peter Cusack, an improvising musician and soundscape recordist, threw in a variation on this theme. He regretted the fact that it is impossible to make sound recordings that are the equivalent of photographs: in other words, audio recordings lasting 1/16th of a second, or thereabouts, that capture an entire scene (albeit sonic), and can then be seen in their entirety, in one glance, or perused in detail and at leisure. Cameras have been developed to allow a great deal of latitude in their use, which gives them the creative advantage over tape recorders. Life, captured within a frame, may be the starting point for photography, interrupted by mysterious transformations, ending again within a frame. This absence of instantaneous boundary around a tape recording pinpoints a significant difference between landscape, seascape and soundscape.

In the early 20th century, painters such as Kasimir Malevich and Alexander Rodchenko liberated themselves from this restriction of the painting as a window onto the world. Soundscape composition is a relatively new art form. Some of its struggles of self-definition are battles fought, won and almost forgotten in other media. J. M. W. Turner's *Staffa, Fingal's Cave*, may share certain characteristics with the sound of weather recorded by Chris Watson or the sound of waves recorded by Bernie Krause, but we can contemplate the painting for hours, a lifetime if we were fortunate enough to own it, or simply scroll across it, out of the corner of one eye, as we pass by on the way to something else. Representing one moment in time, the stasis of Turner's painting, or a reproduction of that painting, only transforms through the subjectivity of the viewer and the illusions of its surface. The paradox is that Turner's painting may have taken months of work to complete, yet can be scanned in an instant. Even a photographic seascape, such as Thomas Joshua Cooper's *A Quality of Dancing: St. Ives Bay and the Celtic Sea, Cornwall 2001*, a single photograph using slow shutter speed and extensive preparatory research, presents a similarly complex enfolding of durations.

The soundscape, on the other hand, may document a far greater sample of time, yet the unfolding of its documentary evidence enforces a duration. Sure, we can turn off the CD before it finishes, fast-forward to another section, walk out of the room and then return later, fall asleep or go back to the beginning before the end. Sure, the recordist can montage a number of recordings from different locations and dates, edit and process the material in post-production. But, still, to hear the entire recording we must listen through; then, once it ends, we return to that state we call silence.

As a pioneer in the theory of film sound, Michel Chion is a great help in clarifying the nuances of these differences. For example, he speaks of the very noticeable 'vectorisation in time' of aural phenomena. In other words, sound has an irreversible beginning, middle and end; it follows a sequential, to some degree linear, trajectory, even though there may be large volumes of depth and 'vertical' content packed into each microsecond. He also pinpoints the quicker perceptual capabilities of the ear over the eye. 'Visual and auditory perception are of much more disparate natures than one might think,' he writes. 'The reason we are only dimly aware of this is that these two perceptions mutually influence each other in the audiovisual contract, lending each other their respective properties by contamination and projection.

'For one thing, each kind of perception bears a fundamentally different relationship to motion and stasis, since sound, contrary to sight, presupposes movement from the outset. In a film image that contains movement many other things in the frame may remain fixed. But sound by its very nature necessarily implies a displacement or agitation, however minimal.'

Soundscapes tend to focus on the interest inherent in this displacement and agitation, though rather than compose or improvise a piece of music to explore the property, they frame a selective section of time and place through the act of pressing the record button. Clearly, there is more to it than that, and indeed the exact philosophy and ethos of soundscape recording becomes more vehemently contested as its attractions as a creative practice increase. To practitioners of disciplines such as painting, photography, film and video, some of these questions and arguments will be old stories endlessly rehearsed: the abandonment of the image frame as a window onto the world; the questions of whether documentation should be 'altered' or can aspire to art. But soundscape recording evolved predominantly from the practice of bioacoustic recording, so its tardy theorising emerges from scientific research rather than art. This concentrated on single species, usually individual creatures, or documented a habitat in order to locate and pick out individuals within the context of their local diversity in order to further a scientific understanding of communication patterns.

R. Murray Schafer coined the term 'soundscape' in 1967. 'The soundscape is any acoustic field of study,' he wrote in *The Tuning of The World*, then went on to examine differences between soundscape and landscape that I have explored above. The word soundscape appeared before this, however, in a series of pamphlets written by Schafer for teachers. These lectures, lessons and exercises were rich in suggestions of how to communicate new ideas about sound work and music. *Ear Cleaning*, published in 1967, included a lecture entitled 'The Musical Soundscape'. This was prefaced by a drawing, a kind of map (almost a fanciful computer desktop, before such things existed) depicting a 'cone of tensions', heaven and hell, the acoustic horizon and home, then beyond this cone, silence. This sense of music as a walk-through environment pervades many of Schafer's teaching techniques during this period. *The New Soundscape*, published in 1969, began with a question: what is music? Maybe this seemingly eternal conundrum sounds tired in the 21st century (though I hear the question often enough, after lectures and classes, during panel discussions and seminars), but in 1969, when almost every kind of music had been thrown into turmoil by forces ranging from politics and war to Zen and drugs, the issue was burning fiercely.

Schafer first admitted that any definition had become problematic. He relates the story of asking John Cage for his definition and Cage replied: 'Music is sounds, sounds around us whether we're in or out of concert halls: cf. Thoreau.' As Schafer explains, 'The reference is to Thoreau's *Walden*, where the author experiences in the sights and sounds of nature an inexhaustible entertainment.' Concluding this introductory chapter is another indication of Schafer's next move. He notes a contemporary shift in medicine from curative to preventative and suggests that a similar approach is needed in music. 'Observing the world sonograph,' he wrote, 'the new music educator will encourage those sounds salubrious to human life and will rage against those inimical to it.'

This proactive position aligned Schafer with the emerging ecology movement, for which Henry David Thoreau's 19th-century pursuit of a 'primitive wilderness life' was a profound inspiration. Schafer also coined terms such as 'acoustic ecology', 'schizophonia' (when sounds are heard divorced from their source, as on radio), and 'soundmark'. This last invention is perhaps the most interesting. One of the disadvantages of soundscape recordings when compared to other methods of documenting an environment is the lack of a historical perspective. 'We may know exactly how many new buildings went up in a given area in a decade or how the population has risen, but we do not know by how many decibels the ambient noise level may have risen for a comparable period of time. More than this, sounds may alter or disappear with scarcely a comment even from the most sensitive of historians. Thus, while we may utilize the techniques of modern recording and analysis to study contemporary soundscapes, for the foundation of historical perspectives, we will have to turn to earwitness [another useful neologism] accounts from literature and mythology, as well as to anthropological and historical records.'

He devised the term 'soundmark', a derivation from landmark, to describe 'a community sound which is unique or possesses qualities which make it specially regarded or noticed by the people in that community'. This established the conservationist agenda in Schafer's work, as well as seeding poetic and socially constructive links between soundscape and memory. In the late 1960s, Schafer founded the World Soundscape Project at Simon Fraser University, Vancouver, and in the early 1970s, members of the Project created a highly influential publication (a book and two LP records) entitled *The Vancouver Soundscape*. Here was the historical perspective otherwise missing from audio recordings. Statistics on the introduction of telephones mix with documentation of police signals, bellringing and muzak, photographs of sound generators such as steam trains, and written accounts of the noise of the Hastings Saw Mill Company or the spooky sound of the Point Atkinson foghorn, echoing under a sewing machine. The book concludes with a suggested soundwalk through a historic part of Vancouver, a guided tour past the whirr-click of Fleck Brothers' clock, the Western Electric neon light and the varying road surfaces by Young Iron Works.

Although Schafer is a vociferous conservationist, he finds noise abatement too negative to be a complete answer to problems of noise pollution and vanishing soundmarks. Similar conclusions are drawn by Emily Thompson in *The Soundscape of Modernity: Architectural Acoustics and the Culture of Listening in America, 1900-1933*. As she reveals, the variable boundary between noise and music was being mapped as much by legislation as by the Duke Ellington Orchestra or Edgard Varèse. Modernism brought efficiency in its wake. Thompson quotes William Strunk's dictum of 1920, from his *Elements of Style*: 'Omit needless words.' Sound was subjected to the same process of reductionism. One of the first landmarks in noise abatement was the persistent action of Julia Barnett Rice, wife of the publisher Isaac Rice. In 1905, Mrs Rice became so upset by the incontinent tugboat signalling that rocketed straight from the Hudson River into the Rices' capacious Italianate mansion on Riverside Drive and 89th Street, that she hired students from Columbia University to count the blasts. Almost 3000 were recorded in one night, the majority of them a high decibel equivalent of social communication among birds, and after two years of vigorous campaigning by Mrs Rice and New York congressman William Bennet, federal legislation was introduced forbidding all unnecessary blowing of whistles in ports and harbours.

Acoustic theory was in its infancy; machines were increasingly evident in both public and private space; music was entering a sustained phase of experimentation that deconstructed every aspect of its formation and reception. Like all students of noise, I find this period of sonic history thrilling, yet through patient analysis, Thompson perceives a more sobering theme. Ultimately, noise abatement was a failure – succeeding in wiping out soundmarks that were integral to the social flow of the streets, such as the cries of pushcart peddlers, yet helpless to stem the accelerating tide of motorised traffic. Julia Barnett Rice founded The Society for the Suppression of Unnecessary Noise in order to prevent audio disturbance near city hospitals, yet her intended benevolence 'would affect different classes of people in very different ways'. In 1907, barkers at Coney Island were banned from using megaphones by the commissioner of police. Thompson quotes the response of Pop Hooligan, the oldest barker on the island: 'What would Coney Island be without megaphones? How are you going to get a crowd to come in and see the boy with the tomato head and the rest of the wonders if you don't talk to them? I will see this Czar and make him abrogate his order.'

The real success in coping with noise was located within, rather than without. Architects decided that the future lay with cocooning. The emphasis turned to construction materials that could exclude the noise of modernity from interiors by manipulating private space, futuristic sepultural products such as Silentaire, Acousti-Celotex, Sprayo-Flake, 'Tomb' Brand Deadening Felt and the real grim reaper, asbestos.

As an art practice with a growing number of followers, soundscape recording is divided by the issue of sound ecology. Should a soundscape recordist be actively engaged in promoting a less 'polluted' sound environment? Or is this activity more aptly rooted in John Cage's famous question of 1958, asked in the third of his lectures called *Composition As Process*?: 'Which is more musical, a truck passing by a factory or a truck passing by a music school?' Unquestionably innovative, informative and influential, Schafer's approach to the soundscape now seems shot through with a personal aversion to urbanism.

The work of improvising musician and soundscape recordist Peter Cusack has been directly stimulated by the World Soundscape Project, though he questions certain aspects of their procedures. In particular, he feels that members of the WSP never asked people what sounds they liked or disliked, instead delivering an autocratic, frequently subjective and somewhat patronising verdict on noises bad for the health. This is true for the tone of their publications, though *The Vancouver Soundscape* does include the results of two surveys conducted among residents in the Vancouver area. Young people were asked to list the most beautiful and ugly sounds that figured in their lives. Among the ugly sounds are tyres skidding, gunfire, belching, and radio in a nature setting, which suggests that times have changed dramatically since the 1970s. Though they indicate an interest in the subjectivity of sounds, these surveys are inconclusive. Cultural and class differences can reveal widely divergent attitudes. 'Young people' might mean any age from 5 to 25 and beyond; as any parent knows, attitudes to sound and music will change at a dizzying pace at any given moment between those ages. What is clearly evident, however, is that people treasure certain atmospheric conditions as a 'perfect world' ideal and reject others as symbols of disorder, threat, boredom or inconvenience.

It was Cusack who drew my attention to the German philosopher Gernot Böhme and his writings on atmosphere. Böhme is engaged in developing what he calls an aesthetic theory of nature, an overview that goes beyond the split between nature understood either as natural scientific knowledge or artistic representation. In *The Atmosphere of a City*, published in 1998, he analysed the difference between a city's atmosphere and its image, exploring the way in which certain generators of atmosphere – odours, the acoustic dimension and life forms – contribute to a shared experience of urban living. He subtitles his paper, 'Acoustic Atmospheres', as a contribution to the study of ecological aesthetics. Böhme locates atmospheres as the 'in-between' between environmental qualities and human sensibilities. Atmospheres are most clearly felt as contrastive and ingressive experience. In other words, being surrounded by a barely noticeable atmosphere is too subtle to be experienced at anything higher than subliminal levels, but moving from one distinctive atmosphere to another can provoke a dramatic awareness of the transition, and the nature of each state.

'The discovery that music is the fundamental atmospheric art,' writes Böhme, 'has solved an old, annoying and yet inescapable problem of music theory, i.e. the question: of what does music's so-called emotional effect actually consist? In opposition to the helpless association theories and the theories that called upon fantasy to mediate, the Aesthetics of Atmospheres gives a simple answer to the question: music as such is a modification of space as it is experienced by the body. Music forms and informs the listener's sense of self (*das Sichbefinden*) in a space; it reaches directly into his or her corporeal economy.'

One of the ways in which we negotiate our environment is through a refined awareness of resonance and its atmospheres. This is a language based to some extent on emptiness: a constant monitoring of sound swelling and decaying, bouncing or falling dead within a series of enclosures both soft (the earth's atmosphere, a park), and hard (an office, a prison cell), open (a desert), relatively open (a valley), closed (a cinema) and claustrophobically enclosed (a cubicle shower), complex and resonant (a mountain range, a stairwell, a swimming pool), simple and absorbent (a bedroom full of soft, thick fabrics, an anechoic chamber).

I first met David Cunningham when he was a student at Maidstone College of Art in the 1970s. As a visiting lecturer I found his curiosity, energy and confidence inspiring. Later we worked together: I was briefly a collaborator within his pop group/not pop group The Flying Lizards, and as recording engineer, producer and muse, he was the third member of General Strike, the duo of Steve Beresford and myself that combined live improvising, songs and overdubs with a lot of studio processing. During the General Strike sessions, David's skill with delays – often created by looping ¼-inch tape – became a central feature of the music we were creating. During breaks (though these pauses were as much a part of the record as the playing and recording) we would sit uncomfortably on whatever served as chairs in his tiny meat locker studio in Brixton, talking about the great masters of studio echo: Lee Perry, Phil Spector, Joe Meek, Brian Wilson. Sometimes David would put on a 7-inch single like 'Summertime, Summertime' by the Legendary Masked Surfers, a Dean Torrence production that wanders lost in a fabulous maze of echo repeats and reverberation in its middle section. 'Maximal output from minimal input', he might call it now.

More recently he has written about the first Jimi Hendrix Experience recordings in London; how Hendrix arrived at the studio with his stage set-up, a wall of Marshall amplifiers. The engineer found that placing a microphone close to the amps caused instant overload, but instead of asking Hendrix to turn down the volume or use less amplification, he simply moved the microphone to the other side of the studio, 'so that those early records, 'The Wind Cries Mary' and so on, have that beautiful dense sound, the sound of many cubic metres of air moving around in a room. That sound and that engineer's decision have been a major influence on a lot of my work.'

This attraction to the synthetic mimicry of resonance, the structural potential of delays and the physicality of sound waves in enclosed space has evolved into a wider exploration of time, space and sound, and moved to the centre of his practice. The Listening Room is a series of installation works that ask people to listen to the space they are in. A microphone is connected to a noise gate (a device that can limit a signal, often used in recording studios to eliminate interference from a sound), an amplifier and loudspeakers in a highly reverberant room. Feedback between the microphone and loudspeakers builds up and resonates through the gallery, sounding the resonant frequencies of the space, which is in turn modulated by the movement of people around the space, atmospheric conditions, ambient noise and any environmental elements that disturb the air. When the feedback reaches a certain threshold, the noise gate cuts off the sound. The sound continues to resonate in the long reverberation time of the room, gradually decaying until it reaches a point below the threshold of the gate. The system switches back on and the process repeats.

The shifting pitches and consequent chords produced within this simple arrangement can be complex, since they are determined by a number of interrelated factors: the dimensions of the room, the location of the system and the time it takes for the sound to travel in three dimensions. As Cunningham says, this is not a simple equation. One source of this work was the recording session for The Flying Lizards' best-known record, 'Money', a single that was released in 1979 and subsequently became a top ten chart hit. The bass drum was recorded in a large concrete room and Cunningham's microphone cable was slightly too short to reach the drum. So the strange drum sound heard on the record is not a recording of a drum heard in isolation, but a recording of the drum activating the complex acoustics of a reverberant space.

Another source has been observations of complexity in natural phenomena and urban rhythms: 'I like to sit out on the roof of my flat in the middle of London,' he writes, 'and listen to the rich aural ecology of the city. It's a relief from the focussed listening of the recording studio. This city has evolved or degenerated to the point where the soundscape has a natural complexity, something that human instincts make our ears very comfortable with. An analogy of this pleasure would be with looking at a tree – you don't look at every branch and leaf individually but they're all there if you want to look closer; you can enjoy a very different sense of ordering (in comparison to a man-made artefact) just by recognising the generality of tree and the variations of the generality and the specific. The idea of trying to work with natural complexity in a musical situation interested and frustrated me for a long time until I realised that I'd been working with it for a long time. In sound, natural complexity is acoustic reflection, resonance, air moving in space and the generation of harmonics.

'It struck me that a human being may react to some discontinuity between what is seen and what is heard on an unconscious level, that there are more biological factors at work which inform us about the space we're in on more than one level of sense, that a disparity between a space and its apparent sound might have some effect on the inner ear akin to the balance mechanism, instinctual stuff – going back to some early human mechanism that tells you that the wall at the back of the cave has no echo which means that there's a very big animal there which will eat you.'

Appropriately, since Cunningham was taught by the late Stuart Marshall, who studied with Alvin Lucier, this reminded me of Robert Ashley's notes for the CD release of Alvin Lucier's *Vespers*. Lucier was the first composer to consciously explore the behaviour of sound and space in compositions that deliberately embraced science as well as art. He created an installation for sferics in 1981, for example, and the physicality of sound moving in space has been a constant theme of his work. *Vespers*, composed in 1969, is a piece that uses Sondols™, which are sonar-dolphin echolocation devices, to create an image of the performance space. The high-intensity clicks of the Sondols bounce off objects within a room and so accumulate into an assembly of sounds and their phantoms. Ashley talks about the problem (still with us to this day) of concert venues that compel an audience to face forwards, yet he disagrees with composers and musicians who lobby for changes in the design of halls.

'The deeper problem for composers,' he writes, 'and the reason the halls were built to present the music in front of the listener is that humans have learned over a long time to change position so that any sounds will come from the front, if this is possible to arrange, in order that the sounds can be located. Marshall McLuhan pointed out (even in the 1950s, when architects were being pushed to make performance spaces that didn't use the proscenium) that sounds from anywhere except directly in front are heard as a threat. We turn to face the threat. That is a rule of survival.'

reduced listening

Chris Watson and the Madrid-based ecologist, composer and sound recordist Francisco Lopez are engaged by the invisible and near-inaudible. 'Not only are non-biotic sound sources clearly prominent in many nature environments (rainfall, rivers, storms, wind),' writes Lopez in the sleevenotes of his *La Selva* CD, 'but there is also a type of sound-producing biotic component, present in almost every environment, that is usually overlooked: plants. They are also living organisms and in most cases – especially in the case of forests – what we call the sound of the rain or wind we could better call the sound of plant leaves and branches … Furthermore, a sound environment is not only the consequence of all its sound producing components, but also of all its sound-transmitting and sound modifying elements. If we are really listening, the topography, the degree of humidity of the air, or the types of materials in the topsoil are as essential and determining as the sound producing animals that inhabit a certain space.'

Lopez strongly criticises R. Murray Schafer's *The Tuning of The World*, describing the conception at the heart of the book as 'basically a "silencing", as if "noisy" were an evil condition in itself and also an exclusive feature of [the] post-industrial human-influenced world.' He is also critical of Schafer's judgemental notions on schizophonia, the sound detached from its source. Notorious for making listeners at his live concerts wear blindfolds, Lopez draws instead from the French inventor of concrete music, Pierre Schaeffer, and from Michel Chion's theoretical development of Schaeffer's ideas. Schaeffer believed that this possibility of plucking a sound from its original setting and then manipulating it as artistic material, free from associations or contextual surroundings, was the main achievement of the *musique concrète* techniques he pioneered in 1948. He described such sounds as *objets sonore*, sound objects that were the sonic equivalents of photographs, 'pieces of time torn from the cosmos'. Michel Chion describes Schaeffer's concept of 'reduced listening' – hearing a sound as sound, rather than listening for its cause or meaning – as an enterprise 'that disrupts lazy habits and opens up a world of previously unimagined questions for those who hear it ... reduced listening has the enormous advantage of opening up our ears and sharpening our power of listening.'

For Lopez, R. Murray Schafer confuses issues of health and environment with aesthetic judgement. In other words, certain sounds such as drones or machine noises are said to be bad for our health and polluting to the aural environment, simply due to an entirely personal opinion that they have no value as rich sound sources from the contemporary world. A case in point is the aeroplane, of which Schafer says, in *The New Soundscape*: 'No sound contains less interesting information than that of an airplane. Its only embellishment is the Doppler effect.' Of course, aeroplanes are a curse for those who live close to their flight paths. Their overall environmental destructiveness is symbolised, to some extent, by the calamitous effect they have on anybody unfortunate enough to lose sleep or general quality of life because of their noise and vibration. Those of us who fly frequently sign a devil's pact with this reality. But is it true to say that this is the least interesting sound in the world?

Japanese sound recordist Toshiya Tsunoda is interested in the properties of air, the way in which sound moves through yet also vibrates solid objects to produce a multiplicity of sensations, some of which are perceived indirectly, rather than directly through the ears. For the notes to his 2001

CD release, *Pieces of Air*, he writes: 'Our bodies are surrounded by air. Air fills space completely. But we are not clearly conscious of the existence of air in our daily lives. We notice air's existence somehow by the actions of vibration, heat and light. Air appears as a medium in our observation. Air spreads physical vibration into a space like a spring. Next, a time difference appears in the sound depending on the form of the space. Movement of this medium is greatly concerned with space and time. Moreover, it is also concerned with movement from past to present and from far to near. It is interesting to observe movement of this medium by physical vibration even without discovering its cause. We can find beautiful order there.'

Tsunoda often records by inserting microphones into pipes and bottles, so adding a haze of resonance, a dislocating distance, to sources that might otherwise be relatively ordinary or familiar: the seashore, or a gallery. For one of his recordings, he sets up two microphones in the middle of a field. A bird scarer bangs intermittently, its echoes describing an aural snapshot of the space. An aeroplane crosses the sky. We hear its approaching growl, lower and higher frequencies added, then subtracted as it passes, the sound reflections from the ground mixing with reflections from other objects and the Doppler effect of rising and descending pitch that finally rises again as the lower frequencies of the engine become less and less audible in the distance. At least two complex sounds coexist, both of them fluctuating in different ways, and concentrating on both simultaneously is not easy. To exercise reduced listening, Michel Chion insists that we must listen many times to a sonic object. Each time I listen to this aeroplane on my iTunes player, I hear new aspects to the sound. In fact, the low frequency is the last part of the sound to dissipate, but this was masked by the sensation of higher frequencies quickly ascending in pitch, a band of white noise that moves beyond the upper range of human hearing. 'Perhaps this airplane could be interpreted as tracing geographical features with its sound (like a sonar device),' Tsunoda writes.

Not the least interesting sound in the world then; rather a test of our desire, or lack of desire, to discover interest. The ear is an active medium, not just a hole in the side of our head that allows ingress to sound. Composer Maryanne Amacher has written about the tones that our ears produce in response to music. 'Produced interaurally,' she writes, these virtual sounds and melodic patterns originate in our ears and neuroanatomy. In fact, recent experiments at Johns Hopkins have shown that our ears continue to emit sound for a few seconds after death, establishing that our ears not only receive and absorb sound, but also emit sound (referred to by researchers as 'otoacoustic emissions').

Listening in quiet rooms, completely still, I find I hear sounds that are impossible to place. Faint rushing noises and gentle whistles. Are they inside, outside or a mixture of both? I find them curious and reassuring, as if the room is breathing. Could they be the first sign of tinnitus? I asked my friend Tom Recchion, a Pasadena-born musician and designer who suffers acute tinnitus during periods of stress and high blood pressure. In reply, he wrote: 'The first time I noticed the scream of tinnitus was early in the morning. It sounded like some work was being done in the neighbourhood and I was hearing the high pitched whine of the engine in some strange acoustic reflection through the air. It got progressively worse to the point where I couldn't stand being in the silence. I looked up the condition on the web and it said that it was caused by a myriad of things, there was nothing that could be done about it and in some patients it drove them to suicide or madness. As it got worse I could see how it could do that.

'There are various forms of tinnitus. There's a constant high pitch whine, a low rushing sound that's like a warm white noise, and a sputtering. I had the last two. It caused great confusion. When I went to bed at night and tried to relax it tended to get louder. The high pitched, sputtering, almost electric whine was the most unsettling physical condition I've ever felt. It sounded like a lot of the sounds that a lot of electronic composers are using now. Very fragmented and wavering, like a bad connection on a speaker or electric light.

'At its most severe I had no interest in listening to music, because I could hear the pitch right through the music. I felt very remorseful that the thing I loved the most in life might now and forever be impaired. In order to sleep I took to turning on a vibrating back massager and left it running on the bed all night. This masked the tinnitus enough so I wasn't focused on it.'

One possible cause of so-called subjective tinnitus – a sound that can't be heard by another person – may be the sounds of the brain at work. This theory proposes that many people can hear similar sounds at a similar intensity to tinnitus sufferers yet they accept these sounds or barely notice them. A tinnitus sufferer, on the other hand, can develop a conditioned response to the sounds that makes them unbearable. Silence, often highly valued for the memory of undisturbed peace, becomes unbearable, since this is when tinnitus creates maximum distress. Specialists who follow this theory believe that the condition can be helped by reprogramming the neuronal networks that selectively tune in to these brain sounds. Hearing is closely linked to survival. To cope with unwanted and irrelevant, though potentially dangerous, noise – the constant drone of cars in the city or the sounds of heavy surf at night – we learn to filter it out, subconsciously to relegate it to a safety zone. Tinnitus retraining therapy claims to be able to perform the same trick on tinnitus.

confronting the present

Soundscape recordings are themselves a substitute for memory. 'The prime goal of any recording is the creation of an *illusion* that creates an honest sense of place,' writes Bernie Krause. 'This may seem like a contradiction, but remember that the recording will never be the same as what you hear in the living soundscape.' One good reason for this is selective filtering. We hear what we want to hear, or need to hear. An Australian composer who combines digital electronics with soundscape recordings – Lawrence English – took me for a walk through rainforest close to his home city of Brisbane. At one point we stopped just to listen. I switched my minidisc to record and after some time was rewarded by the fabulous sound of catbirds – birds whose calls bring to mind images of babies being strangled or something equally horrible. Back in London I listened to the disc and was surprised by the loudness of motorbikes passing on the road nearby. The scene had been so tranquil that I focussed intently on sounds that were unfamiliar. The bikes I could hear anywhere, so I subconsciously reduced these to a minor irritant during my real-time listening; unless you prefer the roar of a Harley to the spooky wail of a catbird, my recording was pretty useless.

Like Toshiya Tsunoda, Jio Shimizu is a member of the Japanese WrK collective, a loose association of sound artists (also Minoru Sato, aka m/s, Atsushi Tominaga, Hiroyuki Iida), all exploring some of the more obscure aspects of wave phenomena, electro-magnetic interference and conceptual issues raised by the nature of audio transmission. One of the most elegant and eloquent WrK pieces is *050* by Atsushi Tominaga, exhibited in Gallery Kimoga, Tokyo, in 1997: two loudspeakers connected to a DAT player, each loudspeaker hanging face down over a pan of boiling water. Gradually, steam from the boiling water destroys the loudspeakers and corrupts the sound.

Jio Shimizu's *Insert Delay* (1996) is a cardboard box containing a cassette tape seated in cork and a mounted scroll of paper which unrolls to reveal sound spectographs. The sounds on the tape are repetitive, variable clicks (a mid-frequency click, in fact, for which there is no satisfactory word, so perhaps 'bumps' is a better description). These were created with the overdubbed sounds of a stylus trapped in the looped groove of a record. 'This tape was produced as art that should be played in the time and space of each individual who owns it,' Shimizu instructs. 'So, it should be erased, played or recorded at will. The gradual deceleration and acceleration in the running speed of the tape, wavering of the tape itself, as well as the conditions and after-effects, all form the overall creation. In the structure of the tape, the signals which have been played as sound are all from the past and at the point when we perceive these signals as sound, a "delay" has already been inserted.' The sounds on the tape are a memory of themselves, being an overlaid mechanical loop, and the act of listening to those sounds, altering them in any way or experiencing their involuntary alterations through fluctuations in the system, all constitute the insertion of delays (or layers of memory).

Significantly, Shimizu's use of the word delay suggests a musical meaning – an audio signal repeated to give the illusion of an echo – as well as all the temporal implications of repeated loops, work developing over time, even the delayed connection of a recording to its potential listening audience.

Phantoms on the threshold of perception, almost too elusive to grasp, masked by the sounds of daily life or blunted receptivity, permeate areas of contemporary sound work that are otherwise radically opposed in their philosophy. Much of the sparse, microscopic incident now common in new music, the concentration on resonance, inaudibility, inaccessibility, transparency and process, digital glitches, ghost voices, subverted mechanics and extreme bodily interiority, uncovers phenomena and layered meaning from beneath the hysterical onslaught of information, mediation and consumerism that the world has become.

Delivery systems are becoming more valuable than content. Never in the history of the world have so many delivery systems existed to transmit so much information. We can still send a message by carrier pigeon, of course, not that we fully understand how the bird finds its way, and we can still sing a folk song dating back hundreds of years, but these methods of communicating extremely specific and highly valued nuggets of information are now supplemented by a host of data pipes spurting (and ingesting, since digital interactivity promises to satisfy new levels of human desire) information of massively variable content. With these unprecedented, oceanic volumes of stuff comes a crisis of memory, the realisation that the tidal wave must be collected along with all the landmarks it has smashed into matchwood. Technological archiving becomes a locus of anxiety, since methods of archiving are vulnerable to the speed with which new data pipes are developed.

On 21 January 2003, as I was writing these pages, my friend and colleague Hugh Davies alerted me to a BBC website obituary, devoted to the little known electronic music composer Daphne Oram. Hers is a remarkable story. At the age of 18 she began working for the BBC as a sound balancer. During World War II, one of her responsibilities was maintaining the continuity of concert broadcasts from the Royal Albert Hall. She would have to listen to the feed of the live concert with one ear while simultaneously playing a recording of the same piece and listening to that in the other ear. If a bombing raid forced the live performers and audience to take cover, she would switch over to the recording so that radio listeners were untroubled by any break in the programme.

In 1957, she persuaded the BBC that the corporation should take an active part in electronic music. The first major broadcast to use new electronic, or radiophonic, techniques was *All That Fall*, a specially commissioned play by Samuel Beckett. Under the direction of Desmond Briscoe, *All That Fall* dispensed with naturalistic sound effects, replacing them with concrete sounds. From these early experiments, the BBC Radiophonic Workshop was founded, an in-house source of unusual effects that could be used not just for plays, but also for sound poetry (Ernst Jandl, Brion Gysin, Lilly Greenham and Bob Cobbing all recorded pieces for broadcast with the Radiophonic Workshop), comedy, science fiction, theme tunes, wildlife documentaries and any other genre of programme.

Daphne Oram was photographed in the early days of the workshop, wearing a fetching tweed dress and playing invented devices such as the mijwiz and wobbulator. Ultimately, she found the demands of producing background music too constricting and left the BBC in 1959 to create compositions such as the prophetic *Four Aspects*. She also developed Oramics, her system of converting pictures into sound by drawing on strips of 35mm film which was then read by photoelectric cells. Her work was brought to a halt by a series of strokes and she died in relative obscurity. Interest had been growing in her music; if her recordings can be edited and compiled into CD releases, there is every chance that she will achieve a posthumous following equivalent to the dedicated group of fans that has gathered around her colleague in the Radiophonic Workshop, the late Delia Derbyshire.

A number of e-mail comments were appended to the BBC obituary, most of them shocked that she had died, amazed at her pioneering spirit. 'The only equivalent I can think of today would be Björk,' wrote one correspondent. One, however, ignored the sadness of her later life and the innovation of her youth. 'If the archive of Daphne's work is held on 5.25″ or 3.5″ disk,' he wrote, 'I sincerely hope it's backed up on other formats as flopy disks [sic] are notorious for degrading in a depressingly short time. The custodians of this resource should look to make multiple backings on different media to minimise the risk of loss.' Without wishing to minimise the value of archiving or the very real problems posed by multiple formats, rapid technological change and obsolescence, the focus on resource seems to confirm our obsession with preserving the past rather than confronting the present.

ghosts   emanations   listening to the metal voices

'Against noises, my noise. And this noise pushes away all others, noises of the moment, from before, from the whole day, bringing them together through an extraordinary miracle into one perfect nothingness, complete relief.

As the night progresses and my self goes further into the sounds, under the kindly roof of darkness, friends, the feeling of friends being there that one keeps as a protection after they have left, the memory of encounters – of incidents that were important during the day, that for a moment had surfaced again as weak echoes – fade out, become scarce. They have stopped coming in.

I remain alone, abandoned by those close to me, now so far away.

No one, no one left.

Alone, my silence-breaker sails through the night.'

Henri Michaux, from *First Impressions* (1949)

Repeatedly, noise demands to be understood, or is this a misunderstanding of noise and its demand to be felt, which then becomes perverted into a quest for interpretation and explanation? When the noises of daily life are measured against a highly subjective moral scale, then 'old' soundmarks risk losing their meaning to sentimentality. As historian Professor Brian Harrison has pointed out, the hurdy-gurdies that were opposed as street instruments in the 1930s are now regarded as 'charming'. In Amsterdam for the Holland Festival of 2001, I joined the audience for a performance of Giorgio Battistelli's *Experimentum Mundi*. Battistelli conceived of this music-theatre piece in 1981 and has toured it around the world ever since. The premise is simple but novel: craftsmen and women from his southern Italian hometown of Albano Laziale are grouped on the stage with the tools of their trade. There are coopers, carpenters, a confectioner, flooring specialists, farriers, knife sharpeners, stone masons and cobblers, plus voices and a percussionist. As the piece progresses, stone paving is laid, a wine barrel is constructed, shoes are made, a wall goes up and spaghetti is cooked. The sounds of this activity and the actions constitute the surface of the work.

'To work with a tool, a stick or an iron bar is something that belongs to the collective memory of mankind,' Battistelli has said. 'These gestures and symbols are so deeply rooted in all of us, that people from totally different cultural backgrounds are able to find their own dimension, their own interpretation from this extract of human life.'

The opening sound (a sound of opening), was the cracking of an egg. Dough was kneaded, the blacksmith's fire crackled and for the first ten minutes or so I was charmed by the piece, its novelty and the harmonious chinking, hammering, sizzling, sawing and gossip that meshed so closely as a by-product of work. By the end, that sweetness had induced nausea. Sitting next to me, my friend Roland Spekle – curator, owner of the Barooni label and a seasoned judge of contemporary music – let out a snort of exasperation. 'So much for everything we learned from Cage,' he said. I felt he was right. After a time, I began to sense what it was like to visit one of the colonial expositions of the 19th and early 20th centuries, when 'native' peoples were put on show in replicas of their villages. Yet this was orchestrated, also, as if the workers were puppets. They seemed to be enjoying the experience (and why not?), even though, or even because, the natural rhythms of work – haphazard, rich in rhythmic complexity, repetitive, potentially maddening – were entrained within a score at once cute, predictable and reeking of avant-garde tokenism. These were genuine soundmarks (had we heard them *in situ*), though far from being an 'extract of human life', their role as a poetic echo of real graft had been pulled like a dead tooth. Through sentimentality, labour was trivialised rather than celebrated. Despite being a cross between Dylan Thomas's *Under Milk Wood* and Edgard Varèse's *Ionisation*, this was a composition that seemed no more edifying than any other theme park, constructed in the ruins of manufacturing industries, and staffed by the workers who once shaped their lives and communities around their work.

Michael Rüsenberg, a German soundscape composer who has released CD recordings of Cologne bridges and the sounds of Rome, has encountered this tension between soundscape as the artist's abstraction and somebody else's reality. In a lecture entitled 'Soundscape As an Aesthetic Category', he discusses a Hamburg-based project – Anticipating the Archaeology Of Sound – led by composer Asmus Tietchens. The idea behind this project is to collect the sounds of machines that have become endangered species. The spectre of Pierre Schaeffer's sound objects and reduced listening is raised once again: 'My friends in Hamburg make a superhuman effort to banish all aesthetic consciousness when listening to their recordings – and fail. Does this mean that I, who have no documentary purpose, should resist searching for musical forms in my own? This question remains to be dealt with. Nonetheless, I am convinced that once you accept the Cageian idea that noise can be music, you are caught in a trap. You hear noise with a musical ear, whether you are recording it or not!

'Three anecdotes to illustrate my point: on a trip to Chicago, we spontaneously went through an open door in Finkl's steelworks with the idea of recording. I was wearing head microphones that made it look like I was listening whilst I was in fact recording. One of the steelworkers was watching me, however, and since I was afraid that he might stop our activities and kick us out, I somehow managed to explain in sign language what I was doing. "You're recording the noise?" He laughed – and let us stay. At midnight in Rome, a street sweeper would almost have killed me when he realized I was recording him working. On this occasion, it was the language barrier alone that saved me. In Cologne, in an attempt to get permission to record inside a huge Autobahn-bridge, I waxed lyrical to the man in charge about the sound of the expansion joints. He replied as if I had made an obscene request: "Mr Rüsenberg, I am an engineer!"

'These three were pre-Cage – I am post. Noise to them is a by-product of their work – if avoidable, they reduce it to zero. My approach is that of an artist entering unknown territory. All that interests me is the by-product of the situation, not the situation itself. Absurdly enough for them, I actually saved these recordings for the concert, well knowing that there are other people like myself, notoriously hungry for sounds that are not part of their everyday life which they hear with a different ear.

'Don't get me wrong: I am not claiming that sound-objects as the soundscape-composer finds and transforms them are music per se. "A natural object cannot, as a matter of logic, have syntactical properties, whether it is a bird's 'song' or anything else." This is the voice of my favourite music philosopher, Peter Kivy (from *Music Alone*, Ithaca 1990). "However much bird 'songs' may sound like music, they cannot be music – unless, of course, we ascribe to birds a mental life comparable to our own, which few of us will want to do."

'So what do I do when I listen to the sounds of the real world and try to find a musical meaning in them? Kivy knows the answer, it is the "as-if" mode: "For to say we hear birdsongs as if they had syntactical properties is not to ascribe syntactical properties to them ..." And this is what distinguishes the steel worker from the soundscape artist and the soundscape listener: the "as-if" mode. Listening to the real world is the act of aestheticism in which we follow Hemingway, for whom we do not deserve to live in this world if we do not perceive it.'

'Let's face it,' he concludes, 'soundscape composition very often means bringing the noise into the concert hall.' This last remark reflects a real conflict of intent within the practice of soundscape recording. Within the text of a paper written for *Organised Sound: An International Journal of Music and Technology*, Hildegard Westerkamp took issue with Rüsenberg: 'If this is indeed what the soundscape composer does,' she writes, 'my question would be why and for what purpose?' She goes on to ask further questions: 'Is it not in fact the composer's responsibility to create a sonic environment with his or her composition that does not damage listeners' hearing, as much as it is the city planner's responsibility not to expose commuters to excessive noise? Is it not the soundscape composer's responsibility to act like an acoustic ecologist?'

To some degree, this debate seems predicated upon a misunderstanding, thanks to our old friend noise. There are massive noises to be found in Rüsenberg's *Kölner Brucken Sinfonie* but they are so exquisitely detailed, so shockingly sensual in their emergence out of discrete background, that they exactly conform to Gernot Böhme's belief that atmosphere is best appreciated when moving from one state to another. A bridge can be sensual even if the engineer can't hear it. If Westerkamp thinks Rüsenberg is a dangerously noisy fellow, she clearly hasn't heard much Merzbow, Masonna or Kid 606.

Westerkamp worked within R. Murray Schafer's World Soundscape Project in Vancouver, then kept its activities alive when the project had dispersed. Her own recordings, such as *Cricket Voice* and *Beneath the Forest Floor*, are beautifully dramatised evocations of an emotional responsiveness to natural soundscapes. She uses time-stretching on certain recordings – slowing them down to emphasise otherwise unheard characteristics of the sound – and so brings her own work into the same domain of noise occupied by Michael Rüsenberg. Noise, after all, can be quiet. It's a question of context.

Her paper for *Organised Sound*, 'Linking Soundscape Composition and Acoustic Ecology', is a passionate argument for the rationalisation of soundscape recording theory, a reluctant call for running a few fences around the unpatrolled anarchy of soundscape composition. Her belief is that soundscape composition can fulfil a political, activist role, creating what she calls a 'strong oppositional place of conscious listening' that works against 'widespread commercial media and leased music corporations, who strategically try to use the schizophonic medium to transport potential customers into a state of aural unawareness and unconscious behaviour and ultimately into the act of spending money. Rather than lulling us into false comfort, it can make use of the schizophonic medium to awaken our curiosity and to create a desire for deeper knowledge and information about our own as well as other places and cultures.'

Despite the interesting possibilities raised by her last point, this implicitly perpetuates some of the least edifying moments in R. Murray Schafer's theories, in which popular music is understood largely as the product of those manipulative money men at the top. In conclusion, she suggests that soundscape composition should have a didactic and moral purpose.

Westerkamp's belief that schizophonia can be used as a subversive method by sound artists as a strategy for reconfiguring meanings is borne out by works such as Bill Fontana's *Wave Memories*. In Trafalgar Square, London, this piece broadcast the live sounds of breaking waves from Cape

Trafalgar in southern Spain, masking the constantly circulating roar of cars and buses as they drove around Nelson's Column and creating the sonic illusion of silent traffic flow.

As for the question about the soundscape composer's responsibility to act like an acoustic ecologist, the answer from many such composers is a resounding no. How many artists build their practice around a consciously didactic, even authoritarian, purpose, or create works in the service of urban management? 'I don't belong to the eco-faction like Schafer,' sound artist Christina Kubisch told interviewer Christoph Metzger in 2000. 'It's too strident and pregnant with symbolism. But I think his approach is tremendously important. He was one of the first to place importance on simply listening ... In contrast to Schafer, I don't want to make demands on the listener in advance. I want to stir something that is already in him, something that can be carried further on an individual basis. I don't want to direct, it's not my nature. But why should I create works on the genuine and the fake, on nature and technology, if I didn't constantly concern myself with these issues?'

My own feelings may have been coloured by past rejections: in the early 1970s I contacted the recently founded magazine, *The Ecologist*, explaining my conviction that music, soundscape and landscape were closely interwoven; perhaps an article that investigated these connections might be of some interest. No, they responded; they couldn't see much of a connection between environmental conservation and sound. Then in 1978 I organised the Music Context environmental music festival at the London Musicians Collective. I approached the Noise Advisory Council to suggest some input. 'Thank you for your further letter about environmental music,' a man from the NAC replied. 'From the description and the example that you give the concept appears to be a little in advance of the Council's present preoccupations.'

alarm   prayer   collapse
            'I had no thought that night – none, I am quite sure – of what
            was soon to happen to me. But I have always remembered
            since, that when we had stopped at the garden gate to look
            up at the sky, and when we went upon our way, I had for a
            moment an undefinable impression of myself as being
            something different from what I then was. I know it was

then, and there, that I had it. I have ever since connected the
feeling with that spot and time, to the distant voices in the
town, the barking of a dog, and the sound of wheels coming
down the miry hill.'

Charles Dickens, *Bleak House*

Soundmarks are floating signs, not simply good or bad, attractive or
rebarbative, communal or divisive, hi-fi or lo-fi. A community soundmark can
draw people together or divide them, create harmony or spread panic. Think
of the scene in Akira Kurosawa's *Seven Samurai* when the tragi-comic
Kikuchiyo, played by Toshiro Mifune, hammers on the wooden alarm signal.
Though the villagers have hired samurai to defend them against bandits,
when the samurai arrive, they fear them, hide food and sake, captured
samurai armour and all the young women of the village. As the senior
samurai attempt to puzzle this out with the chief elder of the village,
Kikuchiyo takes direct action. The alarm sounds and everybody runs in panic.
Kurosawa colludes with Kikuchiyo in the scene, creating the excitement of
the first real clash of the film by mobilising the samurai and playing composer
Fumio Hayasaka's battle music. The irrationality of the mob rules for a
moment, then Mifune steps forward, laughing like a crazy man and banging
the wooden alarm with a mallet. You asked us here, he says, and then you
don't want us, but look what happens when you hear your alarm. So, the
false alarm is transformed into a powerful communal lesson.

Some Sunday mornings I wake up in a hotel bed in a European city where
church is still central to the meaning of the day. Richly impressive as it is, the
pealing of bells is a deafening, unwelcome assault on somebody who has
been working late into the previous night and besides, despite my love of
silence, I still get a gloomy Sunday feeling from cities emptied out by religious
observance. Community soundmarks and shared sounds can send
simultaneously different messages to different communities, provoke
unexpected reactions, open voids.

I am by no means the first to be annoyed by morning church bells. In
*Village Bells: Sound and Meaning in the Nineteenth-Century French
Countryside*, Alain Corbin writes about the bell sounded to mark the
Angelus, the prayers recited at 6.00 am, noon and 6.00 pm every day.
'Where temporal markers and rhythms are concerned, it was the web of

everyday sound that caused the most tension,' he writes. 'Few practices have aroused so much passion and fomented so much hatred as the daily ringing of the Angelus.' According to Corbin, secular bell ringing embodied a quite different concept of time to the sound of sacred bells. Waking up in the morning became desacralised. 'For more and more citizens what had been a sacred peal was now regarded as an unwelcome din,' he writes. 'At the same time, sleeping late and night life, given added luster by the routines of the elites and rendered more viable by improvements in streetlighting, acquired some of the prestige attaching to modernity ... What was at stake in all these conflicts was control of the community's biorhythms and the management of time allotted to toil and repose.'

In more recent history, the terrorist attack on New York's World Trade Center on 9.11.01 broadcast sounds and images that sparked polarised reactions among a global audience. Unlike the satisfyingly tidy impact and 'closure' of a Hollywood explosion, the sounds heard on television rolling news as the towers collapsed were fragmented, seemingly boundless, chaotic, resistant to understanding, intensely painful. In a way they have become soundmarks, since they were experienced live across the planet by a huge audience and their significance will roll on through history for who knows how long? Also broadcast globally, the visible and audible responses from those who saw the images and heard the sounds via television were a model of the divided belief systems that had led to the catastrophe in the first place: on the one hand, open mouthed disbelief, horror, inarticulate anguish and anger; on the other hand, exultant, whooping joy.

I asked Lee Ranaldo, guitarist with Sonic Youth, for his impression of the significance of sound on that day. Lee and his family were living in close proximity to the World Trade Center. This close, almost primal connection to the attack, as well as the aesthetic sense he has developed as a member of one of the most influential noise bands in the history of rock music (and I don't feel this is a trivial factor), make him a valuable witness to the sonic aspect of the event. 'I was in our apartment a few blocks from the WTC towers when the planes hit. The first plane's impact did not register as the event that it was. There are always loud booming sounds on the street here, and yet it seemed somehow more significant than the usual sounds of trucks rolling over big metal plates on the street, etc. A glance out the window confirmed many people looking up at the skies. Even after the TV reports of a plane hitting the towers the full impact of the day was not upon many of us in NYC. I went into the shower to get ready to take my son to his second day of school. If the first plane did not register as something completely out of the ordinary, the second certainly did. Even from inside the shower the sound of the sky ripping wide open followed by the explosive impact was without a doubt not the normal sound of a Manhattan morning.

'In spite of being so close, because our windows don't face the towers, we watched the entire thing on the television. At one point after both planes hit I left my family in the apartment and took the elevator up to our rooftop (eight stories up). I came out on the rooftop and rounded the shadow of a nearby building and there in my sight were the two towers, gaping holes and black smoke looming immediately over my head. A staggering sight. Within seconds of my sighting them – and this is my most vivid sonic memory of the day – there was a sound in the air like nothing I'd ever heard before, a giant roaring noise that I could not place or identify.

'My first thought was that more planes were attacking, coming in, but it was a sound different from that. I'm still trying to put my finger on how to verbally explain the latent sonic image of that sound in my mind's eye (or ear). In any case, concerned for my family, I rushed back inside and down to our apartment, arriving in time to witness the south tower crumbling on the TV screen, and moments later the black cloud of debris from it darkening our windows. It was the sound of the building about to fall that I'd heard – just the sound, for while it was in my view it was not in the process of crumbling just yet.

'It still chills me to recall those moments up on the rooftop. All told I may have seen the towers "live" that morning for a total of something under a minute, but the sight of it and especially that roaring sound just prior to the collapse of the first tower is imprinted on my memory. I almost hesitate to further describe it, as the experience I had of hearing it has been so qualified now by images of the buildings falling that I don't know if I can separate the sound as it exists in my memory from the images that now inevitably accompany it.'

the cork-lined room
Charles Dickens, hypersensitive to all the deep, treacherous and tragic-comic currents of atmospheres, wrote this in *Bleak House*:

'What's that?'

'It's eleven o' clock striking by the bell of Saint Paul's. Listen, and you'll hear all the bells in the city jangling.'

Both sit silent, listening to the metal voices, near and distant, resounding from towers of various heights, in tones more various than their situations. When these at length cease, all seems more quiet than before. One disagreeable result of whispering is, that it seems to evoke an atmosphere of silence, haunted by the ghosts of sound – strange cracks and tickings, the rustling of garments that have no substance in them, and the tread of dreadful feet, that would leave no mark on the sea-sand or the winter snow. So sensitive the two friends happen to be, that the air is full of these phantoms, and the two look over their shoulders by one consent, to see that the door is shut.

Think of Marcel Proust, living in his cork-lined room, sleeping during the day, writing at night. Solitude, isolation and retreat engender sensitivity, if that permeability to sensation is not clogged by obsession and loneliness; to live in the city is to accept and embrace a certain level of disturbance as part of the flow of change.

Though acoustic ecologists and those citizens weary of traffic roar, late-night parties, car alarms, construction, drunkenness and police helicopters complain about noise pollution, the sound of many northern cities is relatively controlled and, superficially at least, astonishingly uniform. Except for language differences, traffic density, specific sites that are unique to the locale (the Moroccan area of Brussels, for example), weather and the fine details of traffic signals, the sonic atmosphere of Toronto is not unlike Brussels, Glasgow, Copenhagen, Rotterdam or Reykjavik. In the southern hemisphere and the tropics, wildlife makes a sumptuously entertaining difference but subtract that and Brisbane loses a lot of its sonic individuality. Only by spending time in these cities will the micro-incidental differences fully emerge.

Then there are the notorious cities like Mexico City and Bangkok, where the volume (in both senses) of gridlocked traffic is almost beyond comprehension. In Mexico City, traffic cops at every intersection blow whistles so hard and so frequently that they look as if their eyes are going to burst. In Bangkok the throaty growl of two-stroke tuk-tuk engines adds harsh mid-range frequencies to the ominous drone that perfectly mirrors a leaden polluted sky. Ironically, these are cities that also reveal the most captivating, surprising soundmarks still surviving within chaos. This is an extract from *Sound Stories*, a collection of written soundscapes collected and published by the New Zealand sound artist, Phil Dadson: 'With a memory of the gigantic reclining Buddha image imprinted on my mind, I return to Bangkok to revisit Wat Po temple. Rather than roam around, I sit in contemplation of the Buddha, some 160 feet long, 40 feet high, and covered in gold leaf, resting on one elbow, the face peaceful, though not without irony. I'm struck by an unusual sound I can't place. Cascading pitches of watery, metallic voices, sort of bird-like, bell-like; sometimes clear sometimes blurred; close yet distant; golden but earthy; echoing and resonating throughout the temple. Later it layers with a burble of playing children nearby. After an hour or so of enchantment I set out to find the source. Along the length of the Buddha's back the sound becomes visible. 108 metal bowls line the wall, each a slightly different shape and size, supported at waist height in a ring of metal. For a donation, devotees receive a bowl of 108 tiny coins. They walk along the row of bowls, tossing a coin into each as they go, for good luck. The sounds are as random as the number and the action of the visitors, the pitches and rhythms equally surprising (108 inlays in mother-of-pearl, depicting the Buddha's life and virtues, are carved into the giant soles of his feet).'

In Australia I met Dadson after lecturing, amongst other subjects, about the effect of BBC Radiophonic Workshop sound effects on my childhood. This was a shared influence, since he had grown up in New Zealand listening to much the same material, along with shortwave transmission. Later, he sent me examples of his work, including the *Sound Stories* booklet. Having read his traveller's tale I was prepared for these sonic multiples of 108 at Wat Po, yet the complexity of the sound still surprised me.

From Bangkok I travelled north to Chiang Mai. Standing by a CD stall in the night market I heard a cover version of an Everly Brothers song, one of those dream songs that the Thais love so much, and nearby the high pitched frenzy of electronic noise. Most stalls were selling clothes, silk, knock-off watches and souvenirs, but one woman had chosen to specialise in toys that made the sound of birds. She was selling black plastic boxes that emitted loud trills, or the crowing of a cockerel, and little bird cages in which

tiny plastic birds sung an insistent, crazed high tweet. All of her toys were
working at the same time, all the time, like one of those adverts that proves
that really expensive batteries have a longer life than the cheap ones.
Underscored by the abrasive rattling farts of tuk-tuk taxis, this shrilling was
glorious and certainly a more humane option than the tiny songbirds sold
in cruelly restrictive cages at temple gates.

Wondering if she still (or ever) enjoyed the celestial fluting of birds after
such continuous immersion, I recalled a London performance by Alvin Lucier
of his *Bird And Person Dyning*, composed in 1975. Speaking to composer
Michael Parsons for *Resonance* magazine, Lucier explained the origins of the
work: 'That was a wonderful accidental piece. You know Igor Stravinsky said,
"I have all these happy accidents ..." But anyway, I got this electronic bird in
the mail once from somebody I didn't even know. It was a Christmas tree
ornament, and you simply plugged it in and it made this birdcall. And I was
just by myself in the studio and I had this idea to put binaural mikes in my
ears and to hear that bird, and to move my head and pan the sound of the
bird around in space. I had a mike in one ear and one in the other and I could
make the stereo image move by turning my head. So I started the birdcall and
I put the amplifier on, and I walked out into the room. And my volume was
a little bit too high and I started to get feedback, and before I could run to
the amplifier and stop the feedback I discovered that these beautiful
interference patterns were occurring between the sounds of the birdcall and
the strands of feedback. It was an accident. And so then I learnt to control
the feedback and to search for places in the room where the feedback is such
that it does cause these beautiful phantom images.'

In 2001 I was in Mexico City with Robin 'Scanner' Rimbaud, both of us
taking part in a festival of sound art. Feeling assaulted by the immensity of
the city, its noise and an overwhelming presence of police, soldiers and
private security guards, all armed with pump-action shotguns, handguns,
riot shields and hefty night sticks, we took refuge every lunchtime in a
mysterious though rather good Mexican vegetarian restaurant. Some tables
were laid out next to the office, its purple exterior and yellow interior nicely
highlighted by ultraviolet light. In the main room, diners were entertained
by a curiously distracted woman who played halting, disjointed medleys of
popular hits from yesteryear – 'Ebb Tide', 'What A Difference a Day Makes'
– on an out-of-tune upright piano. The melodies stretched and contracted
as she raced through sections in which she appeared to feel confident, then

picked carefully and slowly through passages paved with broken glass. On the streets we came across men playing huge barrel organs. Again, the melodies opened out and closed without warning. Many notes had strayed so far from their original tuning that they had grown comfortable in their new homes. Both of these 'found' sound events were like music heard in dreams and barely grasped, something that could not be composed or imagined except in sleep.

Deeper, buried histories within the urban soundscape are a feature of Scanner's installations. In 2001 he collaborated with American artist Mike Kelley for a work entitled *Ghosts* or *Dial M For Mother*. Together they recorded haunted places in Paris, locations 'loaded with an electrical presence' author Isidore Ducasse's apartment in Montmartre; the grave of Charles Gros, inventor of the phonograph; the interior of l'Eglise de la Sainte-Trinité where Olivier Messiaen played the organ. An engagement with the atmosphere of these sites begins with technologies that capture the unseen, or unheard: 'The theory is that somehow certain places may become impregnated by some subtle physical emanation, by the thoughts and emotions of those living and dying within them. An analogy can be found in the display of a physical medium, which seems to become surcharged with a psychic energy, from which phenomena doubtless radiate during the course of a seance. Recording using a thermal camera that allows one to tune into a particular temperature on the film and also a series of acoustic recordings in each of the locations, sometimes with the microphone itself connected but switched off, has allowed us to explore a form of "audio mirage" that can emerge from prolonged listening to an identical recording, where you almost begin to hear things not actually recorded on the original tape or disc. Somewhere beneath the surface we are finally revealing acoustic data and information, voices formed from the distortions in digital recording. It is in even the most subtle passages that one hears the most dramatic parts, the hidden shifts in detail and language we are searching out. A space will thus be orchestrated in which the audience can experience the essence of these voices from beyond, a densely orchestrated hiss of information.

'All of my works have explored the hidden resonances and meanings within the memory and in particular the subtle traces that people and their actions leave behind. The "ghosts" within sound and memory point to where I am currently propelling myself. Capturing these moments, storing them and redirecting them back into the public stream enables one to construct an archaeology of loss, pathos and missed connections, assembling a momentary forgotten past in our digital future.'

gored fig sacs

Towards the end of every summer, starlings invade the fig tree. They come in gangs, each assault crew a mob of quarrelsome assassins clothed in funeral drapes. Half-concealed in the aggressive leaf growth of the tree, they dart and stab, flashing quick glances left and right in a parody of nervous agitation. The chance passing of a predator capable of matching them is hard to imagine; their shrieking is ferocious, nature's equivalent of latter day free jazz when the point was to blow at the outer limits of volume and duration until all the energy in a room had been vacuumed into silence.

The timing of their arrival is as cruel as their manner. Many of the figs are close to ripeness but still woody and segmented. By the time they reach the point of near detachment from their host, a bulging capsule of vivid red succulence oozing white fluid at the tip, the birds have flown many missions. What they leave when they rise in a jabbering cloud and fly off is unspeakable: clusters of darkening sacs, hanging limp and empty like mutilated scrota, each one gored and decaying in a macabre reversal of the fig's more familiar image as ripe female sexuality. By autumn, the speared figs have shrivelled entirely. They drop from the tree, draping themselves around any plant or garden furniture in range, gradually hardening to a thin black prophecy of testicular retreat. Even to touch them lowers the temperature through its reminder of this annual beak violence.

In her book on Alfred Hitchcock's film *The Birds*, Camille Paglia describes the crows as 'Coleridgean emissaries vandalizing Wordsworthian notions of childhood'. The starlings in our fig tree radiate the aura of wild poets, drunk on fig juice, spraying dada sound poems and bird shit in all directions. Not too long before he died, Oskar Sala explained the reason why he had been commissioned to produce sounds for *The Birds* on his electronic invention, the Trautonium. In Hollywood, nothing was working. The film's composer, Remi Gassmann, had studied with Paul Hindemith and knew about the Trautonium. Hitchcock sent a scene from the film to Berlin, just to see if Sala could come closer to the effect that was needed. This was fear. Hitchcock wanted the sounds of the birds to frighten people. Fear came from the sound of electronics, matched by the sepulchral image of a crow.

I spend quite a bit of time in my garden these days. For a while, the garden became more important to me than my sound work, perhaps for some ominously menopausal reason, I thought in pessimistic moments. As it transpired, the creative and physical effort of creating a garden – as I did, going back to near zero, designing and planting a Japanese scheme in complete contrast to the permaculture jungle that rampaged through previous years – was well rewarded by acts of contemplation and minor revelation.

The significance of sound didn't entirely desert me during this period. On a fairly regular basis, though not regular enough for me to make a timetable to record it, a blackbird flies from the fig tree within my garden boundary to the large flowering crab tree just beyond the back wall. As it does so, it sounds a chattering alarm, and the audio drama of this short flight beautifully describes the modest dimensions of my garden plot – as well as mapping a compass point angle whose relationship to sunlight determines what I can plant where. Gradually I found myself making a link between this noisy spatial event and my developing thoughts about sound, so finding a way back into music after a period in which my feelings about sound seemed to be deadened.

Some months after creating the new garden I moved my studio and study into the recently converted loft in the roof. From this eyrie I can look out at the distant wooded horizon of Highgate and Alexandra Park in north London. Closer to home I can see directly into the treetops below. Wood pigeons often fly into the flowering crab, the ghostly flutter of their wings signalling their hefty arrivals and departures. Watching them swaying like oversize porcelain ornaments on the upper branches, listening to their soft calls, so much like the sound of an ancient Chinese clay ocarina, I'm reminded of Chow Yun-Fat in *Crouching Tiger, Hidden Dragon*, balancing with surreal grace in the branches of a giant bamboo forest.

This consciousness of spatial extent, directionality, interior and exterior, solar movements, wood, air, avian communication and the symbolic representation of nature represented within a Japanese garden, all delineated in the first place by a sound, brings to mind the underlying philosophical theory of Chinese and Korean classical music, in which individual instruments and musical compositions were seen as being equivalent to natural elements, points of the compass, political institutions, ultimately the order of the universe.

Also, I think of the Japanese term *shakkei*, which means 'borrowed scenery'. In other words, adjacent or distant scenery is incorporated as an integral part of the design. Toru Takemitsu wrote about *shakkei* as a musical device. A piece like *Arc*, for piano and orchestra, was strictly planned in advance. There were none of the chance elements of a *shakkei* garden, which includes outside features. 'Therefore,' he wrote in an essay called 'Dream and Number', 'my garden is closer to those at the Katsura Detached Palace or the Saihoji Temple in Kyoto. Actually, some of my works,' he continued, 'may resemble the *shakkei* in that natural sounds may be heard with the composed music. These works are close to the Shugakuin Detached Palace.'

My garden is Japanese to some extent – in its style, its features, its design and planting. The borrowed scenery is hardly inspiring. Beyond the flowering crab is a slab of brutalist red brick – sheltered housing that once featured in a television series called *Neighbours from Hell*. One of the residents, a young woman with a history of psychiatric problems, was playing her jazz records at slightly higher than audible volume and the neighbours demonised her for that crime. A powerful wall-mounted security light wrecks the nocturnal aspect, particularly when it's literally on the blink. Perhaps it keeps the real villains away but it destroys any fantasy I might secretly nurture of comparing my north London patch to a detached palace in Kyoto. That may not be so bad – I've visited wonderful gardens in Kyoto whose outer aspect is overshadowed by the most hideous 1970s municipal architecture. At least I don't play cassette tape lectures accompanied by shakuhachi music, out on the deck, the way they do in Koke-dera moss garden.

Such travesties are a long way from the evocations of quietude found in Japanese literature. 'The Tub Of Ashes' is a long renga-haiku poem – a form of collectively composed linked stanzas – written in 1690 by Basho and his followers:

> At the tub of ashes
> dripping sounds yield to stillness
> as crickets chirp
> in his lamp the oil grows low
> and autumn brings him early sleep

These lines encapsulate a familiar, though little explored, triangulation of sound, space, and memory. The sound is an absence of sound, that environmental sound of no sound that we call atmosphere. This was a time before water arrived on tap, before liquid detergent bottles sat in ranks on the supermarket shelves. Dishes were cleaned with ashes and in the hottest months the source of the water that dripped into the tub containing these ashes would dry up. A familiar sound is missing, though remembered, and so the evening heat is intensified. Crickets add to the soporific mood and sleep comes too easily to the subject of the poem. The compacted allusions to passing time and even decelerating time, along with spatial perspective and the changing seasons, maybe even a suggestion of advancing age, arise out of a few lines of verse that contrast domestic sound – the sounds of the household – with natural sound – the sound of the garden.

In my book *Ocean of Sound* I wrote about the *suikinkutsu*, a Japanese water feature that was relatively common in the Edo period from the 17th to 19th centuries. Only a few still exist these days and most are in private gardens. I encountered the *suikinkutsu* during my first visit to Japan in 1993, when I was touring with sound sculptor Max Eastley. Max and I were staying in Kobe, in the apartment of a sound recordist named Yoshihiro Kawasaki. As well as introducing us to the communal eating style of *shabu shabu*, Kawasaki-san played me his recordings of the *suikinkutsu* and showed me documents that described how it worked. Basically, the overspill of water from a *tsukubai* stone basin filters through stones onto an inverted ceramic pot buried underneath. The pot has a small hole in the top, or the bottom if you're imagining it the right way up. Water drips through at a steady rate and falls onto the reservoir slowly draining away at the base. The sound resonates within the internal volume of the pot but is obviously restricted in volume and diffusion by being buried under ground. Kawasaki gave me an introduction to a private garden in Kyoto – Zuishun-in – where a *suikinkutsu* was still functioning and so I had the lucky experience of hearing *in situ* one of the most rare, esoteric and ingenious examples of sonic technology that it's possible to imagine. Kawasaki-san copied a number of his recordings onto DAT tapes for me and I included an extract from one of these on the *Ocean Of Sound* CD that I compiled in 1995.

You can imagine this sort of thing being talked about on television gardening programmes as an unusual way to bring the mystic Orient into your suburban garden, but when I listen to these recordings I don't pick up any kitsch, New Age, Orientalist feeling. There is a paradoxical effect, calming yet uneasy. For a start, the sound is quite hard and metallic, and the intervals between drips are unpredictable. I find that this develops into an unsettling pattern: time is passing and its passing is marked, as by an egg-timer or loudly ticking clock, but each division of that time is unequal and random. Sometimes the drips are quick, sometimes they are very slow and none are very clear, since each one is coloured by the resonance of the chamber and the temporal extendedness of a splash. The pitches can't be second-guessed, either. There could be three basic pitches, roughly, but their order is programmed by the devil. The fact that the sound emanates from beneath the ground, from a hidden space, is quite disturbing. Natural springs are revered, since they denote a threshold, an opening into so-called earth energy, but the *suikinkutsu* has intimations of the invert aspect of that underworld, where dark things lurk. There are lavatorial associations, even; those ringing, incessant drips that evoke tiled bathrooms in Victorian hospitals or cinematic murder in the toilet, blood dripping onto a cold, white floor. At Zuishun-in I was given a bamboo pole to hear the sound better, though with the pole pressed against one ear and hearing the sea-shell effect of the bamboo's internal resonance mixed with the echoing drips, I found that this implication of demonic sound art became even stronger.

The notion of unpredictable temporal division is hugely important in music. When I hear the tube resonance recordings of Toshiya Tsunoda I'm reminded of the experience of listening through a length of perforated bamboo, but of all the music I know, the piece that seems to come closest to the *suikinkutsu*'s unpredictable division of time is Morton Feldman's *Triadic Memories*. Feldman's piano pieces could be described as a surgery of memory. Their organisation over lengthy durations is compelling, yet the divisions between notes, those absences we call silence, demand a huge effort of memory in order to retain a grasp of this unfolding structure. Feldman alluded to this in an introductory talk about *Triadic Memories*, given at the American premiere in 1982. He compared the performance style of pianist David Tudor, who could hold you in the moment, 'an accumulative effect of time frozen', with that of Roger Woodward, who, as Feldman put it, 'would find the quintessential touch of the work, hold on to it, and then as in one giant breath, articulate the music's overall scale.'

In his notes for the *all piano* CD set of Feldman pieces released in 2000, John Tilbury quoted the words of the late Cornelius Cardew, written in the early 1960s. 'Feldman sees the sounds as reverberating endlessly,' Cardew wrote, 'never getting lost, changing their resonances as they die away, or rather do not die away, but recede from our ears, and soft because softness is compelling, because an insidious invasion of our senses is more effective than a frontal attack, because our ears must strain to catch the music, they must become more sensitive before they perceive the world of sound in which Feldman's music takes place.'

... imagine ...
reading   a   book
written

like   this

andbeinggripped

     by
     every

word

Most of us have read, or attempted to read such exercises in fractured prose (some written by John Cage), but how many of them do anything other than float away from our attention, then sink like paper boats on a pond? This is one illustration of the achievement of Morton Feldman. Soft as iron, his works dismantled narrative to the point of dissolution, stretched and punched holes in the fabric of time, yet they have the power to hold the interested listener in a concentrated state more commonly associated with the unfolding of a mystery.

There is more than one way to tell a story. Anybody who ever attempted to compose or improvise a sustained piece of music (or prose) will know how difficult it is to write with such sparseness and precision. How many notes? Why this one and not that one? How to move from one sound to the next? In the end, with so much swelling silence, why bother to make sounds at all? When Feldman first showed John Cage one of his compositions, Cage asked, 'How did you make this?' Feldman answered, 'I don't know how I made it.'

The question (and the echo of its bewildered response) resurfaces through every moment of Feldman. The success of much of Feldman's work depends upon musicians making decisions about the details of the piece without asserting any tics and clichés of individual expression. As Feldman wrote in the notes for a Mainstream label recording of *Durations*, composed in 1960–61: 'After several years of writing graph music I began to discover its most important flaw. I was not only allowing the sounds to be free – I was also liberating the performer. I had never thought of the graph as an art of improvisation, but more as a totally abstract sonic adventure. This realization was important because I now understood that if the performers sounded bad it was less because of their lapses of taste than because I was still involved with passages and continuity that allowed their presence to be felt.'

From this point of view, Tilbury represents an ideal. His work in the improvisation group AMM operates within this hinterland of 'sonic adventure', striving for a kind of anonymous yet vivid clarity. Sounds can emerge and interpenetrate, apparently through a process of being allowed life and autonomous momentum by the musicians, rather than being forced into existence, then bent into or out of shape to fit. Feldman described this as 'project[ing] sounds into time, free from a compositional rhetoric that had no place here'. Touch is critical – the rejection of exaggerated gesture – and Tilbury refers in his notes to the most esoteric fingering technique used in playing the ancient Chinese *ch'in*, a zither with seven silk strings. This touch, called *ting-yin*, used only the bloodstream to alter the timbre of a note. A further step can be added to that extreme. In his 8th-century commentary on the Chuang-Tzu book, Chêng Hsüan-Ying wrote: 'Even the most skilful zither player, if he strikes the *shang* (note) he destroys the *chio* (note), if he vibrates the *kung* (note) he neglects the *chih* (note). It is better not to strike them at all: then the five notes are complete in themselves.'

Feldman presents specific problems of interpretation. His work is a meditation on memory, sounds carrying the listener into a state in which variations of sounds and repetitions of phrases that have gone before have the effect of rubbing out their predecessors. Painters illuminated the elusive for Feldman. Pianist Mats Persson illustrates this with a story about the artist Cy Twombly's meeting with Feldman in Rome, in connection with the premiere of his Samuel Beckett opera, *Neither*. 'Twombly was to have a direct influence upon Feldman's music,' he writes, 'and it can be seen as a prime example of how the hypersensitive Feldman not only registers visual impulses but transforms them into his very own. Working on large canvases, Twombly starts by sketching delicate lines in oil colours, pencil and chalk. The lines are then covered by thin layers of white paint that partly hide and veil the contours and figures, making them seem as if emerging from a mist. This is where Feldman gets the idea of letting the right pedal remain depressed throughout the whole of such piano pieces as *Triadic Memories*.'

Paradoxically, the effect of this erasure that takes place in the mist of sustain is cumulative, yet any conventional idea of development is far less important than the sense of being absolutely in the moment of present time. The sound itself is beautiful, an oscillation between fragility and strength that never threatens for even a second to fall into the banal prison of audiophiliac, New Age beauty. Captured in acoustic space, the notes hang and disperse in an air that becomes cloudy with fading sound. Muted and soft-edged, they are located at exactly the right distance to make us feel we are sharing the space with the piano.

Feldman believed that he was fortunate to be taught piano by two anti-disciplinarians. Instead of being restructured through rigorous practice into the code of professional pianistics, he was allowed to indulge his compositional ideas and develop a love of sound. 'I was instilled with a sort of vibrant musicality rather than musicianship,' he once wrote. Although the early works reveal some traces of the angularity, dynamics and continuities typical of the 1950s, by the time he came to create pieces such as *For Bunita Marcus*, *Palais de Mari* and *Triadic Memories*, Feldman was alone in his explorations. Continuity was the air itself. Washed by infinitely subtle gradations of tone that linger after the echoes of repetition, the room becomes silent sound, the memory of sound and the future of sound.

everything you need from the ships and the ice cream

A number of sound theorists have stumbled upon references to the *suikinkutsu* in recent years and found this consciously temporal aspect of its design extremely relevant to the study of sound imagery and psychology. Michael Forrester, a psychologist at the University of Kent, wrote a paper called

'Auditory Perception and Sound As Event', in which he quoted Tadahiko Imada, writing about the *suikinkutsu* in the *Soundscape Newsletter* of 1994.

Imada was in fact quoting from the published papers of a musicologist, Naoka Tanaka, who offered some theories on the appeal of the *suikinkutsu* to its original audience. Can we use the term 'audience'? Probably not. I should point out that my lavatorial image of the *suikinkutsu* sound is not entirely inappropriate. One thing I learned during my visit to the Kyoto garden was that the *suikinkutsu* was sometimes constructed close to an outside toilet. After using the toilet, a person would wash their hands with water from the *tsukubai* basin, then, a little while later, hear the dripping progress of that water as it fell, drop by random drop, onto the enclosed reservoir below. Delayed perception, along with the embedding of the listening process into biological necessity and practical hygiene, are commented on by Tanaka. 'While looking at some of the garden plants and stones,' she wrote, 'and while listening to the voices of the birds and the whispering of the wind in the trees, the *suikinkutsu* contributed its quiet sound later. The result was that people forgot their ordinary time sensations, little by little during other visits in the Japanese-style garden. However,' she continues, '*suikinkutsu* is totally different from the other classical arts (e.g. the Japanese tea ceremony and the art of flower arrangement) in that it is just one aspect of Japanese daily life, closely related to the human sensory organs and physical movements or daily actions like washing hands and gargling.'

What Michael Forrester has to say in the lead-up to this example is interesting. One of the subjects he broaches is the relationship between sounds and their significance in our emotional lives. He talks about certain sounds, or sound conglomerates, becoming lodged in memory as markers of security: 'the sound of family moving about the house after I'd gone to bed giving me a sense of security and belonging', being one example. Such memories linger. They can exert a powerful sense of centredness, or perhaps push open a door within a darkened mind, offering a faint image of escape.

In *Austerlitz*, W. G. Sebald writes of hearing a radio programme about Fred Astaire: 'Astaire's father, who according to this surprising radio programme came from Vienna, had worked as a master brewer in Omaha, Nebraska, where Astaire was born, and from the veranda of the Austerlitz house you could hear freight trains being shunted back and forth in the city's marshalling yard. Astaire is reported to have said later that this constant, uninterrupted shunting sound, and the ideas it suggested of going on a long railway journey, were his only childhood memories.'

During an interview with Björk, in May 2002, I asked her if she could think of one of these soundmarkers. She responded immediately, even though we had been discussing a completely unrelated subject prior to this question: 'When I was a child I was brought up with all these hippies, which was very wild and very exciting for a child. But I did have these weekends with my grandparents, that in the long-run, have proven very healthy! My grandfather used to take me on Sunday mornings to the harbour and we used to look at the ships and eat ice cream and never used to think that was very important. I realised a few years ago when I was put up in some fancy hotel in Switzerland on a morning off, I had a walk to the lake and I heard the boat noises and had an ice cream. I felt I was in heaven and I was really living large. I thought it was because of the five-star hotel I was staying at, but actually that had nothing to do with it. No emotional feeling of having everything you need came from there. It came from the ships and the ice cream.'

Encouraged by Björk's quick answer, I asked others. Giving a lecture during my Visiting Research Fellowship at the London College of Printing, I asked students on the sound design course if they could recall such emotional markers. Pia Gambardella, a sound artist and one of the editors of *Noisegate* magazine, gave me this example: 'Whenever I hear the sound of church bells, it reminds me and takes me straight back to moments in time when I was small, vividly to the time every summer I'd travel to our family house in a small village in the south of Italy where we would visit my grandparents for our holiday. When I hear church bells ringing it reminds me very much of that time with all my family, lots of people around, everyone together. The sound gives me a secure safe feeling, but also very sad, the sound always makes me cry. The bells always seemed to be ringing, a very particular hollow ring, the church being below us a little down the mountain, every quarter hour, Mass, on feast days the bells would ring all day long, interspersed with cannon fire which ricocheted around the mountains in the valley.

'Lying in my bed in the bright sunny mornings, the bells ringing every quarter hour. I'd have the white sheets completely over my head stopping the flies tickling my face; there were so many flies in my room, buzzing around my head, with the church bell ringing every fifteen minutes.'

Maybe a latent or active curiosity about sound, emotions and psychology helps certain individuals to focus more clearly on their memories. A sound installation by Pia Gambardella – *Listen With Mother* – shows ultrasonic and radiographic images of a foetus. Her interest lies in prenatal conditioning: how are we influenced by the sounds we hear before we are born?

Equally, we might ask how the aesthetic sense and career decisions of later life can be influenced by childhood experiences of sound. Leading a seminar for theatre students some years ago, I asked them to recall a significant sound event that had made them really conscious of sound at an unusually heightened level. Most looked blank. Two volunteered experiences very readily. One man talked about being in the middle of London, then flying to somewhere remote and on that same day, standing on the summit of a mountain, awed by the shattering silence.

Discussing the examples given, we discovered that both volunteers had grown up within Quaker families. Despite studying together, neither of them knew this about each other. During their childhood they had attended (with some discomfort and embarrassment at the time) Quaker meetings, a uniquely informal type of 'service' in which Friends can stand up and speak when they wish. There is no structure prearranged for these contributions. 'To a newcomer, the meeting may seem "silent",' explains a Quaker Faith website at members.tripod.com (complete with intensely irritating sacred music that plays on every page), 'but in reality it is an experience of intense listening ... sometimes no audible word is said, but we are together refreshed and washed clean by the fountain of living water. Sometimes one Friend will deliver an inspiring sermon ... sometimes a Friend will be compelled by the Spirit to speak something that seems to make no sense, only to learn later that it was a divine answer to someone else's need.'

A Sunday lunch in February 2003: talking about the Friends Reunited website and a CD produced under their brand, a collection of songs from the 1980s selected by all the thirtysomethings who miss their teenage years. The conversation moved on to less accessible sonic memories. Andrew remembered the sound of a lightbulb, a faint ping shortly after being switched off at bedtime, and the feeling of fear that could build up in the dark just from the shock of that tiny, mysterious sound heard through darkness and silence. Eileen remembered a time in her childhood, staying on her grandmother's farm in County Down, Northern Ireland, and hearing silence for the first time in her life. After growing up on a London estate, this silence was loud and weird, she said, and even now the quiet of the countryside can stir this unsettling memory. Cathy recalled the silence she heard for the first time in her home in

Cork, in the Republic of Ireland, growing up within a big family, then one day being alone in the house for the first time and feeling frightened by absence first of all, then by a slow awareness of the voices spoken by the house: a creak, a tap, a rustle, a groan.

Not markers of emotional security, then, or proof that silence is good and noise is bad, but three versions of anxiety kindled by quiet, all of them nervously sharing the mixed emotions of being alone. How long do these sound memories last for a person with no special interest in music, I wondered? Since my mother is the oldest person I know, I asked her. She was born in 1912; one of her first memories is the sound of Zeppelin bombing raids during World War I. 'The Zeppelin sound was a drone,' she said. 'It wasn't loud like the planes you have now. My mother would hide us under a big wooden table and put saucepans on our heads. My father worked at night – he worked as a supervisor on the tramways so he wasn't there. You waited till it was over. I don't think they had any warnings. You just took cover when you heard the noise.' Like the others, she remembered quiet with disquiet: 'I remember as a child, lying in bed at my grandmother's thatched cottage in Long Parish in Hampshire. I slept in a room where the thatching was right near me. The roof sloped and you had to mind your head. I heard sounds in the thatching and I was frightened. It was a frightening sound to me as a child because I didn't know what it was – a mouse, a bird, I didn't know. It was quiet. When we got back to London I hated the pavements. We didn't have pavements at Long Parish. My grandmother cooked on an open fire and we drew water from the pump.'

If the sounds of quiet caused anxiety and the noise of war caused fear, strange emissions from new technology were a source of wonder: 'We didn't have radios in those days. We had crystal sets and when we put the wires together we got very excited. You just heard a noise, you didn't hear voices. I also remember being really thrilled when I first heard the ring of a telephone in the house. It was the first time anybody had spoken on the telephone.'

As Forrester points out, the act of remembering these emotional soundmarkers, which are so central to a developing sense of self, reproduces sets of related images and associations that go far beyond the raw audition of sounds themselves. So, the term 'audience' is not particularly useful in this context unless we use it as an indication of the divided self, a state in which we acknowledge the observer in us and become the audience of our own personal drama. This raises problems particular to the simultaneity of external and internal sound, sound heard from outside our bodies but playing in our heads. As Forrester suggests, 'What is inside and what is outside becomes unclear, an observation which should remind us that to listen is not the same thing as to hear in a passive sense. We can then ask, how are we to conceive of sound as event.' And as he points out, using research into auditory geographies, those of us who grew up in North American or European culture tend to prioritise the visual. 'Even our labelling of sound events emphasises the nature of the object making the sound,' he writes, 'rather than the phenomena. For example, as a description we are more likely to say, "the bell sounds", rather than "the sounds bell".'

The more we delve into this, the more we realise that our language is embedded with a spatial, rather than time-based, orientation. Despite a powerful emotional commitment to sound events, our relationship to sound can be perplexed, ambiguous and uncertain. Sound invites us to understand a strange mixture of phenomena, often complicated by the characteristics of an audio transmission system. Perhaps in the end, the critical point is how to listen and remember. Then we can learn how to unpack these habitual behaviours and buried dreams. Cornelius Cardew's insight into the softness of Feldman's music helps us to understand this a little better – the way in which having to strain to catch the music is part of the process of entering his sound world. Similarly, Naoka Tanaka's analysis of the *suikinkutsu*'s time delay as an agent of temporal forgetting is another example of transformation affected by subliminal triggers.

This brings me back to the blackbird in my garden, making its brief but noisy journey from the right-hand side of my listening field to the left, from a landscape in which I have some control to a landscape controlled to a faltering degree by my local council. The sound of this bird moving through these overdetermined spaces – symbolic, emotional, social, political, geographical, seasonal and botanical – is now lodged in my memory and triggers profound emotional reactions. These reactions have their source, or some of them, in the increasingly problematic signification of terms such as audience, time, space, memory and performance within the context of sonic arts. To some degree, as Jean-Luc Godard has said, or as a character in one of his recent films has said, technology has replaced memory.

Film director Atom Egoyan's installation, *Steenbeckett*, addressed this issue. Shown in London in February 2002, the work was based on Samuel Beckett's dramatic monologue, *Krapp's Last Tape*, in which a man celebrates his 69th birthday by sorting through boxes filled up with old tape recordings. Egoyan gives an example of him listening to a tape made 30 years before and hearing his 39-year-old self commenting on a tape he had just finished listening to, a recording made 10 years before that. 'With this passage,' Egoyan wrote, 'a man listening to his younger self commenting on his even younger self – Beckett is able to express the central paradox of personal archiving technology; its ability simultaneously to enhance and trivialise experience.' Egoyan's installation dealt with the transitional moment of history in which we now live, in which analogue technologies such as film and magnetic tape are being displaced by the digital. As he put it, with Krapp's tape recorder, 'something was expressed about the profound nature of the way that memory, experience and desire could find a conscious and material manifestation'. To simplify even more, a strip of tape passing through the playback head of a tape recorder, threatening to unspool as it comes to the end of its reel, is analogous to the memory of a life threading through the space and time of the world, then unspooling into nothingness.

The fact that music is a displacement of air, a periodic vibration, a movement of sound waves, always raises the ambiguity of what is being said when words such as time, space and memory are used in isolation. Digital technology can take away the space, or the air, from music production, though I'm not sure I'm as pessimistic as Godard in thinking it takes away memory entirely. Like Atom Egoyan, I'm a practical person. In the same way he no longer uses a Steenbeck to edit film, I no longer use analogue tape. Other than those times when I'm sorting back through boxes of tape, like wearish old man Krapp, delving into the archives for the purpose of resuscitating past music for a new audience, I record on minidisc, onto CD, or directly onto the hard disk of my computer. Then I work on the sound files, burrowing into their imaginary space microscopically, transforming them from raw material into a sketch, a fragment moving towards a composition, even a finished composition.

In one sense this is comparable to the practice of composing music by writing notation on staves, building a composition by remembering or imagining sounds and their organisation, then documenting by purely visual method the information needed to bring that remarkable feat of imagination to life at some time in the future. Just as a performance or interpretation of a score will almost inevitably diverge from a composer's intention, what occurs in the space of my imagination, let alone my memory of that process, is not the same as what takes place in the virtual space of my hard disk. And in another sense, it's completely different. My music is actually in there, in the computer – ones and zeros – lurking in virtuality and activated simply by one keystroke rather than waiting in attendance on the formation of a human ensemble or soloist sufficiently skilled to render a page of manuscript into coherent sound. I love this aspect of digital composition and at the same time regret it. Recently I was composing a piece in this way. At one point in the afternoon I threw open the loft window, recorded a random chunk of the world outside, then incorporated this into my composition. It's a technique used in the past by film makers. Dziga Vertov did this at the Radio Centre in 1930s Russia, throwing open the window to connect with the voices of ordinary people and their audio environment. The Indian director, Ritwik Ghatak, did something similar, mixing uninvited noise from outside the cutting room into the overall sound of the film in order to create more richness and a different perspective. You might say this is a version of the *shakkei* principle, the creative deployment of borrowed scenery. The effect is to introduce space and air, chance and memory into an otherwise claustrophobic world.

During the same visit to Berlin in which I had seen the trance musicians from Brazil, I was taken to an Akio Suzuki installation by my friend Werner Durand. At the very top of a steep flight of worn steps in an old disused church tower, the Parochialkirche, the piece seemed to barely exist. A thick bamboo, maybe two metres long, was suspended horizontally from the roof. In this cold stone emptiness, there seemed nothing to do but push the bamboo, gently encouraging it to revolve in a circle, and this revolution generated the tiniest high pitched sound as small wireless microphones hidden inside the ends of the bamboo made feedback conversations with an unobtrusive tuneable FM radio receiver on the floor.

Throughout his life, Suzuki has used simple means to illuminate the subtle properties of sound. 'In 1988, I held an event called Space In The Sun,' he has written, 'the aim of which was to spend an entire day listening to the sounds of nature. I created a special space for this event in the mountains of Aminocho near Kyoto – two parallel walls of sun dried bricks which produce a unique echo effect similar to the famous "roaring dragon" walls at Toshuga Shrine in Nikko. I sometimes revisit this space, located right on the meridian, and I am touched by how time and weather erosion are gradually causing it to fade into its surroundings.' Suzuki has spoken about 'becoming the listener'. In 1976 he created an installation called *Howling Objects* at Minami Gallery in Nihombashi, Tokyo. The principle was identical to the piece created in Berlin decades later: wireless microphones inserted into freely revolving paper rolls; surrounded by FM radios, the microphones produced a delicate feedback as they passed into the range of the radios. 'I think of Minami Gallery as being the start of all these works using a certain material,' he told Nobuhisa Shimoda in a 1993 interview for *Sound Arts* magazine. 'Compared to European-style music that was developed to allow everyone to hear the same thing simultaneously, the flat situation you have in a gallery enables people positioned in various places around the room to hear a variety of things. That's what gets me excited about doing a performance.'

Then in February 2002 he performed at the School of Oriental and African Studies in London. What Suzuki does so well with modest means is to create a listening state, a condition of receptivity to the circularity of human breath and motion, sending audio signals into space, then absorbing the psychoacoustic map of that space back into the body. Now living in rural Tango, on the Japanese coast, Suzuki has developed a form of sound art over the past 30 years that combines improvisation and instrument building with speculative archaeology and a deep sensitivity to natural process.

In the unprepossessing environs of the Brunei Gallery lecture hall at SOAS (lectern, wood panelling, corporate flower arrangement) he began with two small stones, clicking them together, slowly turning in a tight circle, changing the pitch of one stone by opening and closing the cup of his hand. Of all resistant materials, stone combines the most vivid capacity to articulate spatial echoes with the richest delicacy of tonal subtlety. Suzuki offered this evidence without the slightest trace of didacticism, enacting a personal ritual in which micro gestures can imply macro conjectures.

All of the sound makers he used were enriched by a personal history. In conversation during short intervals between the music he revealed that his mother used to strike two flints whenever he left the house. Such sounds have significance as rites of purification – their origins embedded in an animistic time when nature was full of spirits and the explosive impact of two hard surfaces could drive away wicked intentions. After the stone percussion, he played a stone flute. An *iwafue* stone flute played later during the concert had been passed down to him by his father. A replica of an earthenware flute dating from the early Yayoi period, 2,300 years ago, duplicated the flutes excavated in abundance from prehistoric sites in the Tango area. From the available evidence, Suzuki surmised that these were used by female shamans; with his experience as a player he has discovered techniques for sounding these flutes that confound the scientific conclusion that they have a limited range.

After playing a folksong on flute from Yae-yama island, Okinawa, he explained the linguistic theory that archaic expressions can survive in remote locations long after they have passed out of common usage in metropolitan centres. Could this also be true for melodies, he wondered? Then came the Analapos, two cylinders connected by a long spring. This invention of his requires the participation of a volunteer from the audience (Suzuki is witty enough to allow this phrase its fullest showbiz implications). The woman who claimed the job performed her passive task of holding one cylinder while at the far end of a stretched spring Suzuki sang into the other.

As if calling across far mountain passes, one vocal note would still be fading as the other began. This arcane art lay somewhere between ventriloquism, acoustic measurement and the otherworldly mirliton utterances of mask ceremonies. Even though I spent a fair amount of time in my youth kicking amps fitted with spring reverbs, just to hear the explosive echo from inside the box, not to mention performing with the UK doyen of spring music, Hugh Davies, I felt spellbound by Suzuki's command of this mysterious device.

Suzuki has described his performances as a case of the emperor's new clothes. Some members of his audiences suspect that a kind of magic is going on. Their rationality challenged, they try to see behind the simplicity of his sound work – the tools and techniques he uses – and instead find themselves experiencing a revelation.

Question time after this rare London performance, entitled *The Sound of Mogari*, illustrated this odd phenomenon very nicely. Using the declamatory, authoritative voice, a professorial male insisted that one of the stones that Suzuki was using to make music must be hollow. He also seemed to think that the naturally reverberant, voice-resonating Analapos was battery operated. Contradicted on both counts, all he could do was splutter about the unbelievable marvels he had just witnessed. Collapse of stout party.

Suzuki has converted these strong memories into sound work now meaningful in a far wider context. Yamataka Eye, vocalist with Japanese band The Boredoms, wrote this note for a CD collection of recordings rescued from Akio Suzuki's tape archive: 'Your physical environment is just so vital,' he says. 'So when I read Akio Suzuki talking about the mountain behind his home, his Firefly Cage studio, playing at the lakeside and so on, I was sighing with pure jealousy. I imagine how happy he must be, being able to play with sounds like these, on a lakeside with fireflies flickering around him.'

whoaoaoagh   whoaoaoagh

In the spring of 2002 I was recording tugboat horns on a stretch of the river between the Thames Barrier and the deserted Millennium Dome. This was speculative background work, preparatory recording for a commission to compose a piece for the Thames Festival in late summer. The way the horns articulated the spatial complexity of the area with their echoes was fantastic – a near instantaneous sonic analysis of reflecting surfaces that the eye would be unable to grasp without architect's drawings, large-scale maps and aerial photographs. The tugboat business has been shrinking, of course, since the development of containerisation and the declining importance of the Port of London. Only a few companies have survived out of a once thriving trade, and from the way they talk about it, it's easy to see that the sound of the horns is as meaningful to lightermen as any other aspect of their work. The individual signature and powerful volume of each blast speaks for their diminishing space, both on the river and in the wider economic world, and so it suggests pathos and pride at the same time. I liked the fact that one skipper had strung CDs on a line along his tug. The flashing of sunlight on the silver discs keeps seagulls away, he told me. I wouldn't want to suggest that there was any hidden agenda of digital music versus the natural world but you never know.

In August I was introduced to Peter Duggan, now turning his company's river skills to a variety of strange jobs, including towing the firework barges of Groupe F whenever they mounted a spectacle of fire on the Thames. Something of a Bob Hoskins lookalike, Duggan had worked on tugboats as a boy. Now nearing retirement, he took me on board *Revenge* at his post-apocalyptic junk yard, sailing through the Thames Barrier to tranquil Barking Creek, all the while lamenting the lack of working boats on the Thames, the agreeable quiet of the scene and the incursions of city workers from the money trade whose overpriced riverside apartments had replaced wharfs once piled high with sugar, timber and bacon. Those same yuppies, he said, now complained about the noise of barges bumping together during the night in the same way that townies who move to the country complain about the early morning crowing of cockerels. I asked what a tugboat siren meant to him.

'We all come from east London. What you got to put out your brain is that east London wasn't a yuppie area like it is today with all these fancy houses you see. There wasn't none of that. It was a complete working river – men rowing barges, tugs, watermen, unloading ships. You never had the conveyor belt to unload a sugar ship. We used to have to bring barges down alongside. The cranes would unload them in sacks, across the barge on a corrugated walkway. They'd have a couple of sacks and tip it up.

'Everything today is different. So hundreds and hundreds of people worked in the dock system. Watermen, lightermen, stevedores, their living come by way of here. When you think you had the Dominion Monarch going in there, ships of that nature, they employed lots of people. Old year out, new year in, they'd all be laying out on the buoys here where the stevedores'd be unloading. It was a tradition, old year out, new year in, that they blew their horns. They blew their horns all over the place. We used to – well, my mother did anyway – we used to open all the windows and doors, they used to go out and listen to it. It was a ritual. It was a sound that brought a sort of pride to you.

'These ships were all around you. They were outside your door. The building used to reverberate with the noise – whouagh whouagh whouagh – and you'd hear a big liner that'd supersede all the little ships. You can imagine the stoker down there years ago, half-pissed where he's been on the plum pudding, stoking the fire to get enough steam up to blow the whistle for ten minutes. You can imagine it. You'd hear all different kinds of whistles, you know? Whoaoaoaogh. Rattle the place. Whoaoaoaogh.'

This seems to me to be a perfect illustration of a lost soundmark: a spectacular acoustic event, an informal yet significant ceremony that marked the passing of the old year for a community that has now dispersed or vanished. The first act of federal noise legislation passed in New York as a result of the well-meaning lobbying of Julia Barnett Rice would have prevented it, which should serve as a warning against any excesses of haste or enthusiasm in the suppression of noise. Unlike the Armistice Day silences, all preserved in their nothingness, this apparently glorious cacophony of boat sirens seems to have escaped technological memory, though further research might prove otherwise.

During my first recording foray among the fiercely dedicated tugboat fraternity I had looked around the company office of Cory Environmental. Pinned to the wall I found an old map of the Thames and the fingers of its tributaries that reach beyond London. The River Lea was shown, running northwards through Hackney Marshes to Waltham Abbey, then Waltham Cross, where I grew up, and out to Broxbourne, where I attended school in my teenage years. As a small boy, travelling on the steam train that connected Waltham Cross to the cavernous arches of Liverpool Street station, I would stare out of grime-smeared carriage windows at the East End slums and bomb damage of Bethnal Green and Stepney as we rolled past, shocked by visible ruin and decay.

On the office map I noticed the munitions factories at Enfield Lock and Waltham Abbey marked on the yellowed map and suddenly remembered the sound events that had punctuated my childhood. Explosions. Boys tend to like explosions and I certainly used to enjoy the way their distant force ripped through the suburban equilibrium of Waltham Cross. I never asked too many questions about them, then forgot them until that moment in the offices of Cory Environmental. This was a subject my father would have warmed to, but in one of those horrible ironies that haunt the relationship between children and their parents, he died before I could raise one of the few topics that might have brought us closer.

My mother was rather vague, being less interested in ordnance. The husband of a friend of hers once worked in one of these factories but he had died too. She discovered that the main source of the explosions was a place called the ERD, or Environmental Research Department, where her friend's husband had worked on projects so secret that he refused to speak about them, even to his wife. Apparently, people trying to grow tomatoes on nearby allotments complained regularly when the windows of their greenhouses were blown out. A local vicar joined forces because the stained glass was suffering but it seemed his own church bells were causing the damage (a classic conspiracy scenario, by the look of it). I tried a web search and began to discover the importance to the area where I grew up of the Royal Small Arms Factory at Enfield Lock, where leg irons for Australia were once manufactured, and the origins of the Waltham Abbey ERD, traceable back to the private powder mill of a Mr Walton, purchased for the Crown in 1787.

Everything from drinking laws and railway stations to the founding of the Enfield Highway Co-operative Society had been shaped by this business, it seemed. Now I think about it in more depth, I realise that some of my fascination with sound and space has its origins in those distant bangs. Their emotional resonance, carried on waves of physical resonance bouncing off all those newly built suburban houses, was deeply connected to their ominous significance for all the adults around me, still trying to recover from the shattering effects of World War II. The factory siren that marked lunchtime, another powerful soundmark of my childhood in the 1950s, was the same siren that had sounded the alarm and all-clear for air raids during the Blitz. To me this was all new – just interesting sounds – but to anybody more than ten years older than me, these sounds were the equivalent of an official denial of the freedom to forget, an attenuation of the soundtrack to war.

Sometimes these deep childhood memories need more than one catalyst to bring them out in the open. Peter Cusack's compilation CDs have stimulated some of these thoughts. For his anthology called *Your Favourite London Sounds*, he asked hundreds of people a question: 'What is your favourite London sound and why?' The answers were many and various: some famous, like Big Ben or the 'Mind the Gap' announcements at Bank underground station (is that different to the same announcement at Waterloo?); some social, Dalston Market or a club queue in Hoxton; some very personal, such as 'Michelle's phone message'; some the universally shared soundmarks of 'post through letterbox' and 'key in door'; some selected with the idiosyncratic ear of the musician, such as drummer Charles Hayward's choice of the Deptford Grid electricity sub-station at the edge of the Thames, a saturating drone washed by waves from the river. 'I like the way you can walk through the overtones,' Hayward says, 'and I especially like the strange conjunction of that and the sounds of the river, and the sounds of people walking through the pebbles.'

Other sounds have a distinct air of cinema futurism (now pastism, perhaps?): disembodied announcements echoing in public space; polyglot languages overheard on the transport system; impersonal reminders of heightened security in the beleaguered city; ageing machinery grinding toward obsolescence, its tortured wails a taunting reminder of our financially draining dependence on clockwork history. A fondness for sounds like this has been nurtured, to some extent, by an imagined aesthetic developed since the 1960s in the dystopias of films such as *Blade Runner* and *THX1138*.

'One of the surprises to me,' says Cusack, 'was how considered people's answers were. For the most part the question was taken seriously. Another surprise was how detailed and specific answers were. I found this especially encouraging. It has been said in soundscape circles that because of ever increasing noise we are losing the ability to hear. I think this is nonsense. We may find it pretty difficult to talk or think about sound but we certainly hear it, including the details within all the noise.' Evanescent and thick with layers of substance and deep meaning, sounds are difficult to describe, which is why so much music criticism resorts to the material that surrounds sounds – social context, politics, mysticism, biography, trends, money, gossip – rather than discuss sound itself.

Yet sound is possessed of a sensuality, a resonance, a pathos, that stirs people deeply. Sometimes we have to look to the most extraordinary writers to find a satisfactory account of sound at work within the turmoil of humans. This is James Joyce, writing in *Ulysses*:

> 'Besides how could you remember everybody? Eyes, walk, voice, yes: gramophone. Have a gramophone in every grave or keep it in the house. After dinner on a Sunday. Put on poor great-grandfather. Kraahraark! Hellohellohello amawfullyglad kraark awfullygladaseeagain hellohello amawf krpthsth. Remind you of the voice like the photograph reminds you of the face. Otherwise you couldn't remember the face after fifteen years, say. For instance who? For instance some fellow that died when I was in Wisdom Hely's.
>
> 'Rtststr! A rattle of pebbles. Wait. Stop.
>
> 'He looked down intently into a stone crypt. Some animal. Wait. There he goes.'

And this is Marcel Proust, from the first page of *The Way By Swann's*: 'I would ask myself what time it might be; I could hear the whistling of the trains which, remote or nearby, like the singing of a bird in a forest, plotting the distances, described to me the extent of the deserted countryside where the traveller hastens towards the nearest station; and the little road he is following will be engraved on his memory by the excitement he owes to new places, to unaccustomed activities, to the recent conversation and the farewells under the unfamiliar lamp that follow him still through the silence of the night, to the imminent sweetness of his return.'

My choices of sound for Cusack's CD were emergency sirens heard in the distance at night and swifts – the ones that wheel over the rooftops in my road every summer. The country name for swifts was devil birds – easy to understand, since they behave, and sound, like demons or sprites unleashed from a bottle. The swifts make a distinctly spatial sound (as do the emergency sirens), their high-pitched screaming drawing a dizzying map of air and obstacles, and its arrival and departure provokes seasonal nostalgia, the consciousness of cyclical regeneration, bloom and decay. A Cusack CD of sounds, stories and people from the Lea Valley, east London – the title of which is *The Horse Was Alive; The Cow Was Dead* – also reminded me of incidents from my childhood: playing on the marshes by the River Lea, laying coins on the Liverpool Street to Cambridge railway line and listening for the approaching train, walking along the tow path with my mother to Waltham Abbey, where we would visit the cattle market and I would be terrified out of my wits by the screaming of pigs, the crush of farmers, the close proximity of horses, cows and bulls.

Also, I realised that a book I had read earlier in the year – *Playing with Water* by James Hamilton-Paterson – had nudged the memory of these explosions without fully dislodging them. *Playing with Water* is an amazing, beautiful book, an account of Paterson's life in the Philippines, some of the time spent living completely alone on a deserted island. The use of home-made bombs by fishermen unlocked memories of explosions and music for Paterson. Hearing the explosions of distant fishing expeditions unleashed a Mozart sonata in his head. 'It is a tune I have not consciously heard in decades,' he writes, 'something released from childhood like a trapped pocket of prehistoric air returning to circulation from the heart of a smashed flint ... suddenly with a rush an entire memory comes back of Mozart and detonations and bright sunlight. Once again, it seems my present life on this curious island has evoked a private past.' The memories go back to Canterbury, and a summer when he and his friend Howard played Mozart duets on the piano and constructed an endless series of bombs from cordite, sodium chlorate weedkiller, .303 cartridge cases, clay, gas pipe, toilet paper, magnesium powder, ether and granulated sugar. 'That summer rang with tunes and bangs,' he recalls. 'I can still remember the music we played, though. On distant, piano-less Tiwarik it suddenly all comes back, summoned from the attic of memory by explosions.'

For me, it's similar, but in reverse. During my web search, skimming through a tedious Ministry of Defence document on the management of defence, I was pleased to discover that departmental conservation groups in certain areas of past munitions production have converted old ammunition boxes into nesting sites for barn owls and other species of birds. They even provide a picture of an owl, perched happily on a box inscribed with army lettering. This transformation of memory brings me back neatly to that blackbird, traversing my garden from fig tree to crab and back again. Anybody familiar with Japanese gardening will know that these are not strictly appropriate plantings. The flowering crab is out of my control, being *shakkei* and controlled by the local council, but the fig could have been uprooted in the same spirit of callous determination with which I took out the apple tree that shaded everything and never gave more than three worm-riddled bits of fruit a year. It seemed a crime, though: to take out a fig tree, particularly one that provides ripe figs for breakfast in the late summer and then, as a bonus, offers a week of chaotic noise as those starlings disembowel the top layer that I can't be bothered to pick.

That was where the significance of this insignificant blackbird lay, I realised with a grinding slowness that is typical of personal awareness. The fig tree was planted by the Greek Cypriot family from whom I bought the house, 14 years before. They had fashioned their own little Mediterranean oasis with grapes, figs and jasmine, then finally fled cold London and headed back to Cyprus. Gradually, over the years, I slashed, burned, uprooted and replanted until it was all gone. Only the fig tree is left to provoke memories of my history in this house. The flight sound of the blackbird serves to remind me of promising beginnings, happy events, catastrophes and survival. It's also a sonic minidrama, immensely attractive to somebody fascinated by sound moving through space. I can now think of many instances in my past and present work where this consideration has been uppermost, though I hadn't really appreciated its importance until now. The garden led me to an awareness of the bird flight ... sound to event ... which led me back to the garden, which led me finally to those violent bangs ... event to sound ... travelling over long distances to enliven my suburban boyhood. Not everything is explained by this circuitous, quite modest revelation, but as old man Krapp discovers during the review of his personal tape archive, the smallest insights mean a lot.

3 Moving through sound

As my mother was hearing German Zeppelin airships drone over the roofs of Tottenham in north London, the first telephone to ring in her house, the inarticulate noise of a radio sparked by the crossing of two cat's whisker wires, this space in which memories were hidden and phantoms lurked was undergoing a bombing raid of its own.

After Albert Einstein, Sigmund Freud, Max Planck, Marcel Duchamp, Pablo Picasso, Kasimir Malevich, Thomas Edison, Guglielmo Marconi, Alexander Graham Bell, the Lumière brothers and Georges Méliès, Jules Verne, the Wright brothers, Raymond Roussel, Kurt Schwitters and all the other explorers and inventors of collapsed space, mental space, flattened space, traversed space, invented space, invalidated space, captured and transported space, space-time, outside becoming inside and inside becoming outside, space could no longer be easily understood, negotiated or trusted. What to do, other than hide under a table, wearing a saucepan?

From railways to digital information, this disappearance of space has been a progressive and rapid process. 'The representation of the modern city can no longer depend on the ceremonial opening of gates,' writes Virilio, 'nor on the ritual processions and parades lining the streets and avenues with spectators. From here on, urban architecture has to work with the opening of a new technological "space-time." In terms of access, telematics replaces the doorways. The sound of gates gives way to the clatter of data banks and the rites of passage of a technical culture whose progress is disguised by the immateriality of its parts and networks.'

Virilio might have added shopping to the factors that erase or conceal gateways. In Berlin's Ostbahnhof I wander around like a fool, searching for station platforms, tracks, trains, just the faintest evidence of railway activities would do. For some minutes, all I can find is Pasta Pizza, Internet Café, a pharmacy, a chocolate shop, sandwich bars, instant Asian food, an exhibition of venomous snakes, a flower shop and a dozen other manifestations of the *Bahnhof* lifestyle.

Two of the most significant breakthroughs of 20th-century audio art were essays in movement, which seems less a coincidence than evidence of Futurism's ideological presence in technological arts. In 1948, Pierre Schaeffer composed *Etude aux chemins de fer*, a montage of shunting and train whistle sounds recorded at a Parisian railway depot. Then in 1961, Max Mathews, director of Bell Laboratories Acoustical and Behavioral Research Center, developed a program to synthesise sound and created the first fully synthesised piece of music, a disembodied robot vocalist singing 'Bicycle Built For Two' over a jaunty waltz that anticipated the vocoded motion studies of Kraftwerk's 'Trans-Europe Express', the voracious forward motion of PacMan and the global rush of Afrika Bambaataa's 'Planet Rock'. A visit to Bell Labs by Arthur C. Clarke led to Stanley Kubrick transplanting this idea into the distant future. By 1968, the release date of Kubrick and Clarke's *2001*, the bicycle was floating in space, its synthesised though plaintive 'Daisy, Daisy ...' gradually winding down in pitch and speed (rocket volition decelerating to a baby's crawl) as HAL the computer was deprived of its artificial life.

There are clear links between searches for audio phantoms and the literature of supernaturally perceptive flâneurs and wanderers such as W. G. Sebald and Iain Sinclair; the discovery of inexplicable landmarks and useless objects (so-called Thomasons, named after a baseball player whose career in Japan was a notorious failure) concealed within the city and documented by artist Akasegawa Genpei; the psychogeographic cartographies of the situationists. In 1956, Guy Debord wrote about his concept of *dérive*, the practice of drifting through the city according to chance, discovering the microclimate of unknown areas.

'One of psychogeography's principle means was the *dérive*,' wrote Sadie Plant in her book *The Most Radical Gesture: The Situationist International in a Postmodern Age*. 'Long a favourite practice of the Dadaists, who organised a variety of expeditions, and the surrealists, for whom the geographical form of automatism was an instructive pleasure, the *dérive*, or drift, was defined by the situationists as the "technique of locomotion without a goal", in which "one or more persons during a certain period drop their usual motives for movement and action, their relations, their work and leisure activities, and let themselves be drawn by the attractions of the terrain and the encounters they find there". The *dérive* acted as something of a model for the "playful creation" of all human relationships.'

sound place   kotatsu top musician   but no music

> 'Perhaps we should be happier in our cities were we to respond to them as nature or dreams; as objects of exploration, investigation and interpretation, settings for voyages of discovery. The "discourse" that has shaped our cities – the utilitarian plans of experts whose goal was social engineering – has limited our vision and almost destroyed our cities. It is time for a new vision, a new ideal of life in the city – and a new, "feminine" voice in praise of cities.'
>
> From *The Sphinx In the City*, Elizabeth Wilson, 1991

Finally, I managed to find the trains and the platforms in Berlin. In a record shop called Gelbe Musik, a meeting place as much as it is a treasure trove of the sonically curious and intriguing, I bumped into Akio Suzuki. His English is not very comprehensive. Whenever anybody asked him if he knew a particular CD or had heard of a certain artist he would smile and say, 'I'm very local man.' Local, that is, to his house by the sea in Tango, Japan. For the Sonambiente Festival, held in Berlin in 1996, Suzuki created a piece called *Otodate*, or in English, *Sound Place*. Simply, he walked the city, then painted a symbol – a white circle enclosing two ears that also look like feet – at any spot where he discovered an interesting sound. These were marked on a Berlin map, so an *Otodate* tour of the city would ignore tourist landmarks like Checkpoint Charlie, the Brandenburg Gate and the Reichstag, and instead discover distinctive soundmarks.

'When living in the city we have no relationship with echoes,' writes Shin Nakagawa in the Akio Suzuki exhibition catalogue, *"A" Sound Works Throwing and Following*. 'When I was young I would enjoy shouting aloud and hearing my voice come echoing back to me when I went exploring in the woods with local children in the mountain forests of Okayama Prefecture, where my grandmother lived. However, nowadays I do not have the courage to face a high-rise building and scream "Hello". Nevertheless, that bears no relation to Suzuki. He goes in search of echoes no matter where; both in the forests and in the heart of the city. Rather, he goes to listen.'

'Walking through sound' is an increasingly common phrase, an indication that sound work is now perceived as the emission and reception of signals within a diffuse environment, rather than the construction of sound blocks erected before passive listeners. Many people now conduct large parts of their lives in electronic spaces that have no location. Unique, chaotic areas of cities are demolished and replaced by rationalised urban renewal. Evidence of globalisation is everywhere. Shopping is king. Corporate capital invades public space with its brands, exerts private control and turns leisure into a commercialised, touristic mimicry, or mockery, of the *dérive*.

To move through the city without any clear aim, capturing dispersed sounds on the fly, registering the fluidity and chaos of an urban audio dynamism that evades bureaucratic and commercial control; this is closer to the strange invisible space that now overlays the physical dimension, an absorption into the collective drama of random events and behaviours that flows through the streets. A refusal to be swept up, disembodied, separated from physical space or collective history.

Journal de Tokyo is a CD, released in January 2003 by Yuko Nexus6, a journalist, electronic composer and media and visual arts lecturer in Nagoya. I hear her album as a diary (this old-world word – album – is more likely to be used in reference to a collection of photographs these days, rather than a CD) written by a person unafraid to combine imaginative ideas with observations, documentations, personal reflection and the untidy clash of erasures, lost moments, errors and accident. We hear various voices, male and female, French and Japanese, the squeal of tape running fast forward or reverse, abrupt cuts from one ambience to another. Audio glimpses of spaces, as if somebody slid open a screen, silently closing it before the view can be understood. Ordinary sounds of the city – a baby's cries, a street violinist, cars, public announcements – are cut from random moments, then framed to sound rich and magical. A pause, then the ticking of a clock. Repeated actions are heard, type unknown. Tiny repeated fragments from the introduction to a record ('Theme from *A Summer Place*', I would guess). The faint residue of earlier recordings.

So is this a diary? I asked her. Exactly, she replied. When she was younger she used a cassette tape of her father's favourite Beethoven to record music she liked. He was furious. Now she uses the same method, recording a session with a friend, then recording over it so that only fragments of the original can be heard, like writing secret thoughts with a confidant, erasing them, writing again to conceal the erasure even further. What might be infuriating in heavier hands is absorbing and cute. There seems some parallel with the photographs of Hiromix and the Japanese girl photography trend of the 1990s: disposable cameras, snapshots of everyday life and its accessories.

Yuko's work comes from small, private gestures yet suggests many connections outwards, into the social sphere and public space. Hypnotic little musical loops, happy sounds for toys with short attention spans, are overlaid or interrupted by extracts from language instruction records. I ask her whether she dislikes the atmosphere of concerts. After all, she had written about another musician called Pirami, who calls her music 'happy experimental': 'Once a month she invites sound creators to a Kuwareco Night party at her house, which among other things has led to the discovery of a group of high school home tapers. What Pirami does is light-hearted and positive. Although she loves contemporary music, she confesses, "I've never had an enjoyable time at any of the contemporary music concerts I've been to." For one reason or another they all felt too much like "concerts" and although there were always lots of "different" people, there were never any young women the same age who looked like they'd be interesting to talk to ... There is no question that the number of young people enjoying sound without any preconceived notions is increasing. New and interesting sound isn't coming from concert halls, it's coming from the small apartments of young women like Pirami, and the possibilities are endless.'

Maybe concerts are redundant? 'Actually I like concerts,' she replies. 'Concerts mean small venue and small audiences, though. I like performance art, so I'd like to involve "performance" in my play. "Performance" means some gesture, reading, talking, walking, playing with toys, etc. Maybe I don't like "MUSIC" – MUSIC makes pure, perfect small world. Of course I like to listen to MUSIC, to be addicted in the musical world, but I can't make MUSIC. So every time I try to mix something else into my music. Sounds, errors, and whatever. I like something strange very much.'

She describes Pirami as a *kotatsu*-top musician. A *kotatsu* is a small table fitted with an electric heater underneath. A *kotatsu* futon lies over the frame of the table and drapes down to the floor, then the tabletop sits on the futon to keep it in place. 'The days when synthesisers and computers were the prized possessions of a limited number of universities and other institutions are over,' she writes, 'and instead, these items can be found cluttering the tops of *kotatsu* in small boarding houses in these same areas ... So it seemed to follow that contemporary computer music can be composed, performed or a CD recorded in any room with a *kotatsu* (actually, it doesn't have to be a *kotatsu*).'

The image is cosy, reminiscent of somebody sitting up in bed playing an acoustic guitar, though the gap between this scene's informal domesticity and the professional production capabilities of a modern computer, probably hiding enough processing power to launch missile systems or run the infrastructure of a small country, is breathtaking.

field trips

Born in Texas in 1939, composer Max Neuhaus transformed an early love of showy swing band drummer Gene Krupa into a brief but distinguished career as percussionist to the avant-garde. Others have done the same and it's not so surprising; Krupa would print formidable lists of struck and scraped objects on his LP covers. For better or worse, his manic soloing popularised the idea that drummers could make music without the rest of the band.

For the 1970 release of Karlheinz Stockhausen's *Zyklus*, solo for percussion player, the piece was realised in two individual versions, one by Christoph Caskel, the other by Neuhaus. The composition had originated in 1959, created as a test piece for the Kranichstein Music Prize for percussion players, held in Darmstadt. According to Stockhausen's notes: 'The piece is written on 16 spiral-bound sheets of paper; there is no beginning and no end; the performer may begin on any page, but must then play a cycle in the stipulated page-sequence; he stands within a ring of percussion instruments and during the performance turns a full circle – in terms of the principle positions he takes up – either clockwise or anticlockwise, according to the direction in which he reads the score.' According to which direction is taken, the performer will sense a movement either towards freedom or determinacy. Where the extremes meet, the dualisms of static and dynamic, or purposeless and purposive, are supposed to break into each other without the critical point being noticed.

By the time *Zyklus* was released, Neuhaus had abandoned his career as a percussionist to set out on a more radical approach to these issues of movement through sound space, latitude for the interpretation of the performer (and listener), and the dualism of freedom and determinacy. Between 1966 and 1968 he 'performed' six versions of a piece called *Listen: Field Trips Thru Found Sound Environments*. People would show up expecting a guided tour, a lecture or a performance and instead have their hand stamped with the word 'listen', then be led by a silent Neuhaus around some urban site of sonic notability: Consolidated Edison Power Station at 14th Street and Avenue D in New York City, Hudson Tubes from 9th Street to Pavonia and the New Jersey Power and Light Power Plant in South Amboy. Later he conducted more of these audio tours in Canada.

In 1974, Neuhaus came across a triangular grating on a traffic island halfway across Times Square in New York. Beneath the grating was a subway ventilation chamber and Neuhaus decided that this should be the site of a permanent sound installation. Having spent time at Bell Labs making sound generating electronic circuits, he created a sound, connected it up to a nearby traffic light, then in 1977, finally lowered it down into the ventilation chamber. If the wires were disconnected by maintenance workers, Neuhaus would put on a hard hat, erect some cones and patch them back in.

The piece was an event you either heard or you didn't and the only way you could hear it was to stand directly overhead. There was no sign to flag the fact that art was happening or give out the name of the artist if, by chance, you walked across it. The sound art equivalent of that ventilation breeze that lifted Marilyn Monroe's dress, Neuhaus's secret installation survived until 1992, the same year that the Times Square Business Improvement District was formed to clean up the neighbourhood. As is often the way with urban renewal, the initial purge is rescinded once the makeover is complete, when selected eccentric and risqué items may be reintroduced in a more tasteful context. Marshalled into action by dealer and art collector Christine Burgin in 2002, a coalition of the Times Square BID, Dia Art Foundation, MTA Arts for Transit and an impressive army of business interests including Condé Nast, Bertelsmann, Inc., and New York Marriott Marquis pooled their considerable resources to reinstate this modest soundmark.

'Repeated walks, circuits, attempts to navigate – to get to the heart of the labyrinth – proved frustrating. There was no centre. The geometry had been botched, the alignments twisted to flatter false imperatives: the money lake.'

Iain Sinclair, *Lights Out for the Territory*

Compositions sourced from the urban soundscape can be traced back to the Italian Futurists and their celebration of industrial and military noise, or experiments like *Wochenende*, or *Weekend*, created in 1928 for German radio by a painter and film maker named Walter Ruttmann. Remarkable for its time, the piece depicts a weekend through the use of sound; regrettably, its linear, episodic parade of voices, machine noises, cuckoo clocks, sirens, bells, whistling, car horns, pigeons, brass bands, laughter, geese, cat, dog, drinking songs and yawns is a dull suburban procession by comparison with the multidimensional visual works of Marcel Duchamp, Man Ray and Kurt Schwitters that pre-date it.

Although individual noises still create the temptation to make soundscapes, recordings of sound walks (either footsteps through the real or journeys pasted together in the digital domain) now attempt to find some sense in the surreal juxtapositions, sonic mazes, illuminations and deserts of the city. Utopias are out of the question; only a mapping of chaotic, fluctuating conditions is possible, a research trip into instability. As artist Tacita Dean says of her Berlin Project, created for radio: 'Most of the sound was recorded in Berlin except for the odd bit of voice recorded in Kent. It was around a man, Robert Steane, known as Boots, who was in Berlin as a boy. His father (English) was a silent movie star in UFA who broadcast for the Nazis and was prosecuted for treason after the war. It's a rambling narrative based on *A Dialogue between the Body and the Soul* by Andrew Marvell: sounds of air (soul) – a wind storm at the beginning, a Hoover, even a fart in the ladies loo in KDW, versus sounds of body – footsteps etc. The narrative is totally guided by sounds of the city. I recorded everything. Nothing is archive, i.e. a Zeppelin did fly over the house. I realise it takes some explaining but suffice to say for this one, I really struggled and in the end recorded hours and hours of sound and found the "narrative" from the sounds.'

Narrative can be a story without closure, a story without beginning or end or surface development. In 1998, record label owner and sound recordist

Eckhart Rahn released a CD called *Pachinko In Your Head*. Rahn made his recordings in the Aladdin Pachinko Parlour of Shinjuku, Tokyo, where the bored, the restless and the addicted play pinball as if trapped in a hell whose lack of purpose is amplified by its intensity of light and noise. 'What you hear on this disk,' he wrote, 'is the natural sound of a multitude of steel balls working their way through a multitude of Pachinko machines. When there are 1,000 or 2,000 machines operating simultaneously, there could be somewhere near a million balls in circulation.' He draws links between this endless repetition and permutation of miniature patterns, and 20th-century music, art and science developments such as minimalism, noise, Dada, chaos theory, Futurism, *musique concrète* and indeterminacy. 'Advanced chaos theory,' he writes, 'leads us to believe that seemingly random events – when encountered in very large numbers – establish a new order of predictability if not beauty and symmetry. When listening to *Pachinko In Your Head*, an imaginary rhythm appears to be emerging from the chaos of interfering sounds, sometimes when concentrating but occasionally only when not concentrating.'

Drawn by the mania, others have returned to Pachinko's relentless downpour of clattering steel balls and barely fathomable layers of electronic melodies. Kobe-based singer Haco released 'Pachinko Mandala' in 2000 under the name of View Masters. I asked her where the sonic attraction lay. 'I like it that each acoustic space is different in each Pachinko parlour,' she replied. 'This includes the sound of the machines (ten or more of the same model machine often stand in a line, which sometimes produces sound similar to Terry Riley-type minimal music), the background music that is played over the loudspeakers, and the announcements of the day's winners. A million steel balls being shot into and spat out of each machine makes a fantastically chaotic noise. It's a bit similar to filtered pink noise waves. The steel balls create a feeling of "mass" and "speed". Of course, the players at the parlour are just keen to play and apparently experience a "high" of some kind. Personally, I don't play. I just listen and record the space secretly for between 20 and 40 minutes. It's a kind of urban meditation.'

A Haco performance can be an engaging interaction between voice, simple objects and lo-tech electronics, a world away from the depersonalised, machine environment of the Pachinko parlour. In fact, there is no contradiction. Her 'Bugfield' performance piece uses two contact microphones to pick up and amplify the oscillating sounds from a computer's internal electromagnets. The piece ends with Haco inserting a blank CD-R into the drive, setting in motion the computer's most agitated and complex sound emissions. 'As we surf the waves of the drastically changing society we live in,' she wrote in *Improvised Music In Japan*, 'we also come into contact with primal aspects of the landscape that remain unchanged. "Sound", under these circumstances, seems to function as a reflection in a mirror (= the viewer).'

I asked if she felt that this way of working was an entry point for 'small' people (small in the sense of being a private individual lacking great financial or political power) to develop an alternative relationship to forbiddingly complicated technology manufactured and distributed by vast and remote corporations. 'After the performance, some people said they had never imagined how fantastic the CD-R drive sounds,' she replied. 'The most interesting thing about the concept is that people attempt to "convert ideas" with the "ear", not with computer software, and not with "*onkyo*", sound resonance materials. My interest is not only focusing on a minimal idea – for example, playing with a sine wave or an oscillator – but examining a wide range of viewpoints – for example, sounds in ordinary life or bird's eye views with the ear, by zooming in and out on the observed object with sound.

'In this project, I try to approach "popology" by emitting sounds that everybody makes when they use a computer. Commonly, people simply ignore or fail to notice sounds like the CD-R drive, but by trying to train the spotlight on such anonymous sounds, I hope the audience will change its ideas about sound. In my performance, "Bugfield", the computer is used to encourage a different focus regarding the computer. Stereo bugscope is very simple and works not only with a computer, but with any other electromagnetic device.'

From Toronto, electronic composer and *sho* (Japanese bamboo mouth organ) player Sarah Peebles included a more distantly recorded Pachinko track on her 2002 CD *108 – Walking Through Tokyo at the Turn of the Century*. 'Even the Pachinko parlour's wall of sound reveals distinct songs, shapes, recurring themes and momentary spaces,' Peebles writes, 'when examined closely through the looking glass of digital signal processing.'

Her CD began as part of her working practice, an expedition to collect samples of individual sounds which could then be processed in real time within the computer using the MAX/MSP program. Later she realised that at a subconscious level she was hearing each sonic event as part of a continuous sound map. 'Tokyo is a megalopolis without a centre,' she writes. 'Rather, it is a city with several large centres. The space between sounds in Tokyo can be (physically) spatial, periodic (having periodicity) or cyclical, or all of these. Music emanating from mini-speakers in front of shops comes into and out of focus as one walks toward the evangelist (who is pre-recorded, emanating from a loudspeaker on a pole on a corner) on the way to Shinjuku station. The timbre of his voice changes as one walks through the area; it is "filtered" essentially by the air – which includes the temperature, humidity and pollution of that moment – and the reflective or absorbent surfaces of bodies in motion, cars, bicycles, and buildings.'

'The "sound chaos" that fills Sarah Peebles' ears is somehow unbalanced compared to the sound chaos of a western culture,' Hiroshi Yoshimura has written in notes accessible through the CD website, 'yet that is why it is an accurate perception of the Tokyo soundscape itself. What I mean here by unbalanced is that the Japanese, through culture or habit, are accustomed to sensing the tranquility through the din or even creating noise to find tranquility.' He describes this as a culture of relative listening, also giving the examples of Carl Stone and Christophe Charles as two other electronic composers who work in this way.

Christophe Charles was born in Marseilles in 1964 and now lectures in Japan. I met him in Tokyo in 2000 and saw him perform at the Heights Gallery concert that seeded the first ideas for this book. Usually his pieces are sampled from soundscapes, then processed in the computer. His music can give the listener the sense of being in the middle of a crowd yet screened from the haptic presence of this reality. The effect is like gazing at a complex scene, peering directly into the pale low sun of winter and being dazzled by the light.

I asked him about his working methodology. 'I am mainly working with sampled sounds,' he replied. 'The best music to me is that of the environment, as we hear it here and now. I think of human music as an extension of this environmental music, and I like to cut and paste the environmental sounds I hear together with other environmental sounds, in order to create new sound spaces. Therefore, digital sampling techniques are very useful as it is possible to cut quite precisely ($1/1000$ sec.) and to filter the sound samples in many ways. From one sound I can keep only one part in time or in timbre, one frequency from its spectra. From the moment the sound enters my computer it becomes digital data, then I can transform it into text, images, light, etc, and transform it again from text, images, light, etc. To me all these are filters.

'Of course I could keep the sounds as I first hear them, they are beautiful enough, but I think of the filter itself as another kind of sound, and filtering is to me mixing the original sound and the filter. The sound and the filter "adapt" to each other, and their interaction creates mostly unforseen results which are often amazing. The task is then to distinguish what can be kept and what is not worth keeping. My standard for keeping/throwing away is mainly based on what I understand as being "new", that is, what has not been discovered yet. I want to avoid the trends of the moment. My method to achieve this is to listen to a lot of music and listen hundreds of times to the sounds I produce. The ones I keep are those which are still interesting after having been heard many times.'

In pieces such as *Deposition Yokohama, Deposition/Radical* and his collaborative soundfile exchange with Markus Popp, *dok*, there seems very little gravitational pull towards a centre. The music has a dispersed quality, successive clouds of varying density that move around the listener like floating dust, tree blossom blown in the spring winds or harder gusts of rain. For Charles, the use of the word 'deposition' suggests a dethronement of authority, a power shift away from administration and control. There are random elements in the operations of the computer in processing these sounds sampled from life, processes that also depose some degree of the composer's authority over his own work. I asked him if any of his work could be described as generative.

'I have done some pieces', he answered, 'where the computer would choose the samples and the combinations of parameters of the filters attributed to these samples. For each sample played there would be a new combination of, for example, 16 parameters. In that sense there would be almost no repetition of a same combination: the computer chooses a value between 0 and 128 for each of the 16 parameters, which provides a rather large scale of variations.

'But I understand "generative" not only as a music in which sound combinations would change constantly, but as a music which would never give all of itself at once; a music where it would be always possible to hear new things, even from the same recording which doesn't change, a music which is impossible to remember completely. This kind of music is possible when its structure is complex enough, and in a way, unforseeable. It can be quite simple in its production, like the piece of Kosugi Takehisa, "Microphone", which uses only a sheet of paper and a microphone, but which produces ultracomplex sounds and intervals between sounds:

> MICRO I
> Wrap a live microphone with a very large sheet of paper.
> Make a light bundle. Keep the microphone live for another
> 5 minutes.
>
> T. Kosugi (1964)

'This piece uses amplified sounds of paper and their reverberation through the space where the piece is performed. It is a kind of aesthetics to keep the material simple, but I see no reason for not using a very complex material which can be obtained by dense combinations of sounds. This can be achieved by 1000 people performing together like in the compositions by José Maceda. It can also be achieved by a computer.'

the urge to disappear

In 1999 I walk into a public library in Whitechapel, east London. At the desk I am issued with a Discman, a CD and headphones. In exchange I give a credit card as security. After pressing start on the CD player, I hear the voice of Janet Cardiff in the headphones, guiding me to a specific shelf in the crime fiction section of the library. I can hear some ambient sounds from the library – people moving across the hard floor, hushed voices – yet already I feel unsure whether these are part of the CD recording or happening as real-time events. Cardiff guides me through dim corridors, their dull municipal paint peeling in long strips like the dead skin of a burns victim. I am inside her head, she is inside mine and we are both inside the stories of many books. I think of something said by artist Susan Hiller, in conversation with Mary Horlock: 'The effect of so many voices all speaking at once is something like the sense I have of the vast sea of stories we live within, and the option to listen to individual stories is a choice left to viewers as they wander through it.'

Janet Cardiff hurries me now. Somebody is signing out a book, leaving the library; we have to follow. I don't question why. I have placed myself in her hands, inside her voice, pulled along by the compulsion of her work.

We walk along Brick Lane, past the sari shops, past the vague blur of vivid sweets, pungent scents and vivid music, into bleak side streets where a sense of threat enters the narrative – footsteps approaching from behind – and again there's that uncertainty about their location from within the artist's story or my own story, right here on this street with which I have no familiarity.

I am leaving myself behind. My radar, the detection system that alerts me to safety and location, seems to be switched to low intensity readings because I am in three places at once: inside Cardiff's urgent narrative which unfolds like an old-fashioned crime novel; in step with her voice of guidance, which safely walks me over dangerous roads, along narrow pavements and secret alleys; then in my own sense of the here and now, thinking about her work and the ideas it stimulates, observing the strange juxtapositions of Dickensian London and the upsurge of services aimed at the financial sector, what Iain Sinclair calls the 'money lake'. To be directed and informed by this voice is a noirish feeling and parental at the same time. I respond as a parent, having guided my child across roads enough times; simultaneously as a child, my small hand in my mother's hand. Then as a child again, I think about the noir voice, a voice-over, maybe Veronica Lake or Barbara Stanwyck, drawing me into darkness. Confused, I follow like a lamb.

The sclerotic artery of Commercial Street is negotiated without injury as we step, hand in hand, head in voice, towards Liverpool Street Station. We cross Bishopsgate and she asks me to sit for a while on one of the benches that look across towards Spitalfields. Look at that person walking past, she says, and indeed there is a person walking past. Of course, this area is hardly short of people walking past at any time of day but the operations of chance at work here are still fascinating. We sit in church quiet, which allows me to regain a better grasp of who I am and where we have been together, then end inside the transparent cathedral of Liverpool Street Station, gazing down from the street level balcony at the purposeful scurrying below. Something operatic plays on the headphones, which may be a touch overstated, too much like a 1990s television advertisement for insurance, but then again, the end is definitely an end.

Born in Canada in 1957, Janet Cardiff now lives in Lethbridge, Alberta. Making these kind of pieces, it's not easy to be prolific. They demand the right context, a unique engagement with the setting and a one-to-one relationship with each collaborator, who in other circumstances we would call the audience. Along with *The Missing Voice (Case Study B)*, as experienced above, her other pieces include *In Real Time*, created for the Carnegie Library of Pittsburg, *A Large Slow River*, set in Oakville Galleries, Gairloch Gardens in Oakville, Ontario, and *Forty Part Motet*, based on *Spem in Alium*, composed by Thomas Tallis. For the latter piece, forty separately recorded voices were played back through the same number of loudspeakers, all of them placed strategically through the performance space. Writing about this piece, Cardiff said: 'When you are listening to a concert the only viewpoint normally is from the front, in traditional audience position. With this piece I want the audience to be able to experience a piece of music from the viewpoint of the singers. Every performer hears a unique mix of the piece of music. For the audience to be able to move throughout the space in the ways they choose they are able to be intimately connected with the voices as well as hear the piece of music as a changing construct. I am interested in how sound may physically construct a space in a sculptural way and how a viewer may choose a path through this physical yet virtual space.'

terror and beauty

During the second half of 1999, American composer Stephen Vitiello was a resident artist in New York's World Trade Center. The Lower Manhattan Cultural Council had been offering a residency programme for several years, allowing painters, photographers and sculptors to set up temporary studio space on the 91st floor. Then in 1999, this programme expanded to include media artists.

'I had read Alan Licht's article on Maryanne Amacher,' writes Vitiello, 'where she spoke of her residency at the New England Fisheries. She had mounted microphones over the water and had a sound feed permanently running into her studio. I borrowed that idea, with the intent that I would open my studio windows, mount a set of microphones outside and have constant access to the sound outside the building – to listen to and process. I was awarded the 6-month residency but didn't know until I moved in that the windows were sealed shut and were triple thick glass, shutting out all unwanted sound from this picture-perfect real estate.

'My studio had been the former home of a Japanese investment firm which had gone out of business in the Asian economic crash. I set about the task of working out how to get the sound from outside the studio to the inside without being able to open the windows. I tried all sorts of microphones and looked into lasers. Finally, a friend introduced me to some very inexpensive, commercially available contact microphones. With some extra amplification and tweaked e.q. [equalisation], I was able to get sound. The first that I ever heard come through was church bells. It was chilling and so liberating. In retrospect, I think the fact that the windows did not open made the project successful. I had the task of bringing in what we were denied. The second filled in the void – allowing an emotional, physical connection to the view that was otherwise impressive but also flat. The airplanes and helicopters, the storm clouds, the movement of the building, suddenly had presence. The terror and beauty of being that high up became much more real.

'I captured sounds with the contact microphones, as well as with photocells. Bob Bielecki, an engineer friend, came up one night. We were talking about the way that the view changed at sunset. The buildings seemed to disappear, being replaced by the ghostly lights in windows, on the river, the red and green tracking lights on the wings of the planes. He wired up some tiny photocells for me, that were usually used in electronic equipment such as light meters. When wired to an audio cable and pointed through a telescope, at the lights, we were able to hear the frequency of some of the lights as a sound frequency, thus listening to the lights. The lasting image I have of working in the studio is of sitting alone at night, with a pair of headphones running though my mixing board and out to two contact microphones taped to the window. The microphones became a stethoscope through which I could listen to the pulse of the building.

'With my original proposal, I expected to take those sounds and manipulate them in real-time performances. During my residency, I recorded several different kinds of sound – windy days, planes and helicopters, traffic, the building swaying after a hurricane – but almost never found an effective way or reason to process the sounds. There was nothing that I could do or wanted to do to "improve" them or make them more musical.

'After the buildings were destroyed, I thought I should put the tapes away. The reality of what had happened made any use seem trivial or potentially disrespectful. Two weeks after September 11, I was asked to speak at The Kitchen, along with several other artists, on our experiences of working in the World Trade Center. I played the recordings with some

Rolf Julius
Sound reflections

hesitation. The response from the audience was very strong and direct. They felt that I had to share these recordings, as this was a way of listening to a building that could never happen again. I was then invited to present the piece as part of the Whitney Biennial. The Whitney specifically wanted a 5.1 surround presentation. I met with an engineer who introduced me to a high-end processor that successfully stretched the stereo signal and played it back from 5 discrete speakers, plus subwoofer. The feeling is that you are standing in the midst of the building as it sways and creaks with moments of wind and a plane passing.

'While that residency and project had a very strong influence on my work, I haven't made a habit of recording the city, or a focus on 9–11 as subject matter. One attempt to address 9–11 was made in a concert at The Cartier Foundation in Paris just last week, January 2003. The concert was programmed as part of an exhibition curated by Paul Virilio, on the concept of Accident as a cultural, post-technological phenomenon. I was told that Paul wanted me to use my World Trade Center recordings in the concert.

'Rather than focus on those sounds, I got a recording of 9-11-02, when a moment of silence was observed in NYC and Washington. That moment of silence is filled with the anxious clicks of journalists' cameras and wind whipping the microphones and audience. We (a duet with Scanner) started the performance with that recording, and gradually began to stretch it, slow it down and try to re-inhabit that moment, re-presented to an audience caught under the hanging sculpture of Nancy Rubins, made up of a collection of crushed and burnt airplane parts.

'In general, my work has continued to relate to architectural spaces, to site-specific projects, looking to capture the feeling of spaces through sound and to create spaces to replant some of these sounds. Depending on the context, sounds may go through vast forms of digital or analogue manipulation. Others, remaining relatively pure, or as much as a digitally captured recording can hope to be pure, remain a form of truth.'

ghost in water   bomb silence

'Takemitsu's music is a kind of fundamental landscape for my spirit. Both his sound and his quietness are the voice of our generation's spirit, who have experiences of overcoming the conflict between the Western and the Japanese.

'In my high school days, I listened to his music for the first time. It was very, very impressive because his music is neither the classical music (in the Western style) nor the Japanese folk music. Every sound and silence in his music was drawn from our real life. We live in a modern Japanese society. We need not the European style expression, nor the Japanese traditional style. We are able to have our original style after Takemitsu.'

Mikako Mizuno (composer and musicologist)

Of all the chilling exhibits in Hiroshima's Peace Museum – a shredded school uniform, melted glass bottles – the object that most affronts a humanist perception of how the world should work is an upright piano. A pattern of shadows is fixed into its wooden carcass, this withheld light a permanent memory of one instant on one day in 1945 when the flash of America's atomic bomb burned brighter than the sun. 'Our ancestors cut off the brightness on the land from above,' wrote novelist Jun'ichiro Tanizaki in 1933, 'and created a world of shadows.' He deplored the progressive forces that were flooding electricity into Japan's old world of muted tones, of materials that blotted up sound and light. After U.S. A-bombs eradicated Japan's imperial ambitions, Tanizaki's aesthetic of shadows took on sinister new meanings.

For Toru Takemitsu, born in Tokyo in 1930, the old world of Japan carried a burden of hard, shameful memories: the war, the emperor, the catastrophic trajectory of Japanese nationalism and militarism, a culture of enforced patriotism that repressed the consciences of many people. 'Because of

World War II,' wrote Takemitsu, 'the dislike of things Japanese continued for some time and was not easily wiped out. Indeed, I started as a composer by denying any "Japaneseness".'

During the war Takemitsu lived with an aunt who played the *koto*, yet traditional instruments such as the *koto*, *biwa*, *shakuhachi*, *sho* and *futozao shamisen* were almost as obscure and mysterious to him as they were to foreigners. A 19th-century traveller named Isabella Bird described the *shamisen* as an 'instrument of dismay'. For different reasons, Takemitsu took a similar view until he heard *gidayu-bushi*, the hyperintense, clattering music that accompanies *bunraku* puppet theatre.

Takemitsu scored for *biwa* for the first time in his music for a film entitled *Nippon no Monyo* (Japanese Patterns). Directed by NHK documentary film maker Naoya Yoshida in 1962, this black and white short reveals strong mutual influences moving back and forth between film and music languages. Visually, the film explores Japanese visual aesthetics and the close correspondence between forms found in nature and their highly stylised representation and abstraction in designs found on clothing fabrics, lacquer ware, sliding screens and architecture. Chrysanthemums transform into overlapping semicircles, a repeated sea of waveforms, then into water and bird flight. All of these mutations are echoed by electronic distortions of *biwa*, percussion and *koto*.

In the same year he used *biwa* in his score for director Masaki Kobayashi's 1962 film, *Hara-kiri*, then in 1964 for the 'Hoichi the earless' section of Kobayashi's *Kwaidan*. In 1967 he composed *November Steps* for *shakuhachi*, *biwa* and orchestra, a landmark in confrontations between alien music systems and technologies, yet he continued to write about Japanese instruments in a tone that vacillated between awe, curiosity and frustration. From this ambivalence flowed the insights that led Takemitsu to create *musique concrète* without being aware of Pierre Schaeffer, then opened him to the Zen-inspired philosophy of John Cage.

> Then Hoichi lifted up his voice, and chanted the chant of the fight on the bitter sea – wonderfully making his biwa to sound like the straining of oars and the rushing of ships, the whirr and the hissing of arrows, the shouting and trampling of men, the crashing of steel upon helmets, the plunging of slain in the flood.
>
> From *The Story of Mimi-Nashi-Hoichi*, by Lafcadio Hearn

Takemitsu was fascinated by the limitations of instruments such as the *biwa*, a loosely strung four-string lute fitted with only four or five frets and struck with a huge triangular plectrum. He speculated on the reason for such a huge plectrum and was led to the concept of *sawari*. With its loose strings and minimal fretting, the *biwa* defied quickness, melodic complexity or tonal purity. 'The major characteristic that sets it apart from Western instruments,' wrote Takemitsu, 'is the active inclusion of noise in its sound, whereas Western instruments, in the process of development, sought to eliminate noise. It may sound contradictory to refer to "beautiful noise", but the biwa is constructed to create such a sound.'

The large plectrum, like a sharpened hammer, is appropriate to the creation of 'beautiful noise'. The entire instrument is difficult. The player must focus on single sounds, their subtle variations, the silence that precedes them, the decay of the note into nothingness. An examination of *ma* – the Japanese word signifying an interval in time and space – is essential to an understanding of *biwa* repertoire and the work of Takemitsu. As critic and writer Donald Richie says, interviewed for Charlotte Zwerin's 1994 film biography *Music for the Movies: Toru Takemitsu*: 'Emptiness is not there until something is in it.' As for *sawari*, this describes a part of the neck of the *biwa*, then extends its multiple meanings into aesthetics by denoting touch, obstacle, even menstruation. 'For me there is something symbolic about this,' Takemitsu concluded. 'The inconvenience is potentially creative.'

This sensitivity to the continuum of noise–sound–music–silence might have drawn a less complex artist into conservatism, the lure of unspoiled nature, and tradition's shadow world. But Takemitsu's generation had been forced into political rebirth: As a Marxist, Kobayashi continually returned to anti-authoritarian themes in his films and Takemitsu searched for ways to reconcile the ubiquitous signs of modernity in postwar Japan with those elements from the past that could be retrieved from the taint of militarism. Takemitsu first looked to European composers for inspiration: Debussy, Ravel, Berg and Olivier Messiaen (described in an article entitled 'The Passing of Feldman, Nono and Messiaen' as 'my spiritual mentor'); later the more contemporary Americans: Cage and Feldman. Memorably, he described Feldman's short-sightedness, his need to be close to the manuscript pages as he wrote: 'Whenever I hear his music I think of its tactile quality, of his ears "hearing" the sounds.'

Although Takemitsu tends to be summed up, sometimes dismissed, as a composer of calm, beautiful music, one of his most important realisations came from the smell, the sweat and the noise of public transport. 'One day in 1948 while riding a crowded subway,' he wrote in *A Personal Reflection*, 'I came up with the idea of mixing random noise with composed music. More precisely, it was then that I became aware that composing is giving meaning to that stream of sounds that penetrates the world we live in.' Feeling isolated at that time, both from other composers and people in general, he experienced this epiphany as a potential release from the falseness in art. The urban soundscape led him to wish for a more direct relationship to the people around him. 'It came to me as a revelation,' he wrote. 'Bring noise into the realm of organised music.'

In 1951 he co-founded the Experimental Workshop in Tokyo. The group, including composers Hiroyoshi Suzuki, Keijiro Sato and Joji Yuasa, would have been called Group Atom but for understandable objections to the word 'atom' by one of the members. By 1955, NHK (Japan Broadcasting Association) in Tokyo had founded its own recording studio, the same studio where Karlheinz Stockhausen later created *Telemusik*. Also in 1955, Takemitsu began composing tape and *musique concrète* pieces such as *Vocalism Ai*; *Relief Statique*; *Sky, Horse, And Death*, and *Water Music*. The piercing aerial pitches and sudden percussive shocks of *Sky, Horse, And Death* made a link between the qualities of Japanese instruments such as *hichiriki*, *sho*, *biwa* and *shakuhachi*, and the radical new possibilities of transforming concrete sounds offered by magnetic tape and studio processing. Created for a radio drama in 1954, the piece is shamanistic in its imagery and intensity, anticipating Takemitsu's work in cinema through the wildness of its dramatic movement and spatial contrasts, the mercurial sensations of realism that burst through a forest of otherworld sounds.

Not all of Takemitsu's collaborations were deadly serious. *Vocalism Ai* was a magnetic tape piece for two voices, one male and one female, both repeating the Japanese word *ai*, or love, in a variety of intonations, speeds and pronunciations. The piece was used in a very cute, very 1960s animated film by Yoji Kuri. Yet emotion and the voice had the deepest possible significance for Takemitsu. As a 16-year-old student, he was drafted to the mountains to help with the construction of a food distribution base. The war was in its final year and, in those desperate times, only martial music and patriotic songs were allowed. One day, secretly, a student draftee played a record of a French chanson. Takemitsu was so moved by this moment of poetry that he decided, if the war should ever end, he would dedicate his life to composing music.

sound of yourself

> 'Much speech leads inevitably to silence. Better to hold fast
> to the void.'
>
> Lao Tzu, Tao Te Ching

'In performance,' Takemitsu wrote, ' sound transcends the realm of the personal. Now we can see how the master shakuhachi player, striving in performance to recreate the sound of wind in a decaying bamboo grove, reveals the Japanese sound ideal: sound, in its ultimate expressiveness, being constantly refined, approaches the nothingness of that wind in the bamboo grove.' This recalls the philosophy of the remarkable flute player, Watazumi-do Shuso. Born in Kyushu in 1911, Watazumi-do abandoned Zen Buddhist training, claiming it was too restrictive for his breath. Instead, he devised his own techniques of physical and spiritual exercise, using flutes made from unusually long, thick lengths of bamboo and playing in a style that was not so much music as a form of self-awareness. 'So in that sound you have to put in your balls, your strength and your own specialness,' Takemitsu said. 'And what you are putting in then is your own life and your own life force. When you hear some music or hear some sound, if for some reason you like it very well, the reason is that that sound is in balance or in harmony with your pulse. And so, making a sound, you try to make various different sounds of the universe, but what you are finally making is your own sound, the sound of yourself.'

Some of Takemitsu's most powerful film scores were constructed around the sound of flutes, suggesting the twisting of emotions, a shrill tortured spirit breath caught in a sea of howling winds and dragged back to its source. At the first sight of Lord Ichimonji, the doomed King Lear figure in Akira Kurosawa's *Ran*, Hiroyuki Koinuma's *shinobue* flute shrills the urgent warning cry of a bird that forsees imminent catastrophe. In Shiro Toyoda's *Illusion of Blood*, Iyemon Tamiya, a feckless bastard ronin (masterless samurai) played by Tatsuya Nakadai, gives his wife poison. As she writhes in pain, face horribly blackened and swollen, hair falling out in clumps,

Takemitsu's sparsely orchestrated score of dissonant strings, flutes and crashes (perhaps produced by dropping objects onto the strings inside a grand piano) reaches beyond music. What we hear could only be a tempest breaking down the wall between human reality and the ghost world. Rhythmically unpredictable, proceeding as a series of shocks, this bitter noise merges with the squeaking of rats.

In Kobayashi's *Kwaidan*, the strangled wail of the *shinobue* shatters visual silence, merging with the barking roar of a snow blizzard. In *Onimaru*, Kiju Yoshida's melodramatic 1988 version of *Wuthering Heights*, Takemitsu begins with *shakuhachi*, strings and lush brass voicings reminiscent of Gil Evans; wind and the scream of rats and crows sweep them away; as the narrative plunges deeper into inhuman misery, so the score narrows its scope to a meteorological rumble, interspersed with sparse *koto*, solo *shakuhachi* or electronically treated alto flutes, often falling silent in deference to a threnodic moaning landscape of wind, water and haunted birds. Even the horses seem to be mouthpieces for demon tongues.

Takemitsu's music was so suited to ghost stories and dramas portraying conflict between duty and individual conscience because it gave the illusion of emanating from a source midway between nature and culture. His score for Kobayashi's *Kwaidan* is an introjection of this ambiguity. The first story in this quartet of supernatural tales, *Black Hair*, takes place in a well of silence. The story begins with a door swinging open and shut. Voices and ambient sounds are withdrawn apparently at random. Takemitsu's score is sound, yet its displaced relationship to the action we see on screen – almost a sound effect, almost music – plunges the viewer into an anxious and hopeless dream. The sound seems to take place in another dimension, another place, some alien time zone a few beats away from any human pulse, yet it shares space with the evidence in front of our eyes. Concepts such as artificial, human, natural and supernatural are poisoned by doubt.

One of the main sound sources for this section of the film was wood: wood torn apart, ripped with knives, snapped in two. A masterless samurai leaves his wife to better himself, remarries, then runs into a wall of disillusion and remorse. Returning home he finds his wife waiting for him, happy to be reconciled. He sleeps with her, then in the morning finds he has been sleeping with a desiccated corpse. Ruined by his abandonment, she had died long ago. 'The splintered soundtrack is violence of his interiority not merely represented – as if we are in his head,' wrote Philip Brophy in *How Sound Floats on Land*, 'but of his interiority materially externalised. Through the psychotic disynchronisation engineered by the inversion of spatio-temporal parameters, we experience his sonic hell.'

'The fear of silence is nothing new,' Takemitsu wrote. 'Silence destroys the dark world of death.' The samurai stumbles through his collapsing house, pursued by his wife's hair (now a disembodied thing with a will of its own), his feet plunging through rotten floorboards, timbers falling as he leans on them. Sometimes, the heightened and distorted wood noise represents this physical decay; at other moments it serves a more ominous purpose of accentuating his realisation that he has stepped through an invisible curtain into the dark silence of the spirit world. The story ends with the samurai staring at his own crazy ghost reflection in the water of the *tsukubai* basin.

> 'Just after eight in the morning Takuya looked up from his desk, his attention caught by something distant, yet quite audible. It was a strange, almost rending sound, as if a huge piece of paper had been violently ripped in two. Seconds later a palpable shock wave jolted the air. His subordinates all sat stock still, looking bewildered. No enemy planes had been reported in Kyushu airspace, and the sound they had just heard was clearly different from anything they had yet experienced.'
>
> Akira Yoshimura, *One Man's Justice*

Silences were a common feature of films made by the postwar generation. Dissent was impossible during the war years, yet their silence was broken only by the devastating impact of two atomic bombs, explosions so far beyond any known experience that they eradicated normal human communications and rational speech.

In Shohei Imamura's *Black Rain* we see a dog trotting along an empty street, whining in the heat; people chat happily on a train; a tea ceremony is in progress somewhere on the outskirts of the city. Takemitsu's ominous strings overlay a terrible silence; then, like a rupture in universal law, the atomic blast turns life inside out. In Kobayashi's *Samurai Rebellion*, set in

1725, there is a puzzle. Why was the gentle, personable Ichi accused of striking the feudal lord, expelled from the castle and forced into a marriage with the son of Isaburo Sasahara, played by Toshiro Mifune?

Finally, she whispers her story to her husband. We see the incidents she recounts, but the action unfolds within an acoustic void, a silent play wrapped in the atmosphere of dream or distant memory. Voices are heard in this silence, then the scene is broken down into still shots, cut as savagely as the gun battle timing of violently struck *biwa* and percussion. When Ichi slaps the lord's smug new mistress, we hear the first two slaps, then the third is silent. Sharp woodblocks and *biwa* fill that absence but in a different time, as if we have fallen into a time slip. *Samurai Rebellion* begins with drums and woodblocks, a dramatic thunder cut visually by angular, abstracted shots of architectural patterns such as roof tiles. The first scene shows Isaburo testing a new sword on a straw dummy. Again, there is silence. Focus moves from the edge of the blade to Mifune's face and back again, a blurring of humanity and purpose underscored by heavily filtered sounds that have lost all recognisable definition.

A plunge into sound, talk stopped by immersive totality, also signified an ambiguous intoxication in postwar modernity. Even Akira Kurosawa, whose films are renowned for their bold editing, taut narratives and intensively written scripts, was prone to slip into sonic dream when lost in the city. *Stray Dog*, released in 1949, is the story of a policeman whose gun is lifted from his pocket during a bus ride. Mifune plays the cop and his frantic search for the stolen weapon trails us through the dangerous chaos of Tokyo's *demi-monde*.

In one notable sequence, Mifune walks through the yakuza-dominated black market of Ueno. The summer heat is intense, a central theme that intensifies the eroticisation of the city. We feel a sense of disorientation as one image dissolves into another, one district merges with the next, and Mifune (or his double, shot from the waist down) moves through a striking tour of popular songs, a cross section of Latin, Hawaiian, French and Japanese–Cuban exotica that reflects the urban soundtrack of Japan during this period of U.S. occupation.

Following a conversation in which musicologist Shuhei Hosokawa and I discussed this scene, I asked Hosokawa, an authority on Latin music and musical exotica in Japan, if he might add more detail to the musical background. 'On the scene of Mifune's wandering around the black market,'

Hosokawa responds, 'I freely quote Yuichiro Nishimura's *Kurosawa Akira: Oto to Eizo* (*Akira Kurosawa: Sound and Image*, Rippu Shobo, 1990, Tokyo, pp. 76–77). The soundtrack of this scene consists of a collage of 12 tunes including a Chinese Latin-like piece made in the 1930s for a talkie film but also popular in Japan since then; "Tokyo Boogie Woogie", recorded in 1948; "The Moon in Colorado", an American prewar song; "Roses in the South"; "*Koi no Manjushage*", a Japanese tune from the late 30s; "*Bungawan Soro*", an Indonesian piece famous during the wartime; "The Serenade of Dorigo", a semi-classical violin piece; and "Hoffmann's Boat Song" by Offenbach, known in Japan since the 1910s.'

Eventually, the music gives way to the environmental sounds of trains and rain – we see Mifune speaking to people but hear train sounds rather than voices. Finally, the film wakes up from this dream, and to dialogue, with the sounds of machinery. This montage of music, concrete sound and image is far longer than we expect such a sequence to be. 'It is so long,' Donald Richie wrote in his study of Kurosawa, 'that one expects summer to be over and autumn begun by the time it finally stops.' But anomalies and inconsistencies in film are perhaps more needed now than they were in 1965, when Richie first wrote his book.

Stray Dog was based on a true story and inspired by the style of detective novelist Georges Simenon. What Kurosawa seems to be attempting with this sequence is an atmospheric distillation of the entire film. The speech that precedes the interlude is telling. The woman who stole Mifune's gun gazes up at the night sky and says, 'Oh, look, how beautiful. For twenty whole years I've forgotten how beautiful stars can be.' The claustrophobia of the film – its characters caught in manoeuvres of survival – is momentarily prised open to admit a view of the world, an appreciation of sensation, that is otherwise denied. In a similar way, the sequence that follows partially liberates the viewer from verbal language for a limited time.

The score for *Stray Dog* was composed by Fumio Hayasaka, Kurosawa's musician of choice up until Hayasaka's death in 1955. His assistant was Masaru Sato, who took over as composer when Hayasaka died from tuberculosis during the filming of *Record of a Living Being*. Twelve recorded songs were edited into the sequence, with each record physically marked to show the exact spot where the music would come in. Technical limitations precluded any possibility of matching music cuts to film frames. In his monumental study of Kurosawa and Mifune, *The Emperor and The Wolf*, Stuart Galbraith IV investigated the technical difficulties of creating the sequence, an indication in itself that Kurosawa was sure of what he was doing: '"There was no tape at that time," said Kurosawa's longtime script supervisor, Teruyo Nogami. "The first day of dubbing didn't go very well so we stopped and decided to try again the following day. Mr. Kurosawa went back to the waiting room but the soundman, Mr. Fumio Yanoguchi, didn't join him there, even though Mr. Kurosawa waited a very long time. When he went back to the dubbing room, he found Mr. Yanoguchi crying by himself. I guess he was completely exhausted from all the complex dubbing work."' Shuehei Hosokawa draws attention to the contribution of sound recordist Ichiro Minawa, who worked for Kurosawa as well as inventing the stomping and roaring sounds of *Godzilla*. In another black market slum scene, in *Drunken Angel*, Kurosawa wanted a specific part of a recording of the 'Cuckoo Waltz'. Minawa had to put the needle on the record at the exact spot. 'Don't you think that Minawa's skill was anticipating today's DJs?', Hosokawa asks.

Even in period costume dramas, Kurosawa was happy for Hayasaka or Sato to use rhumbas, mambos and anachronistic instruments like electric guitar or baritone saxophone (in Sato's case, heavily influenced by Henry Mancini) alongside Japanese traditional music. At the same time, he searched for authenticity in sound effects. Galbraith quotes an anecdote told by script supervisor Teruyo Nogami. Kurosawa suggested that a sword cut should have a sound, so Ichiro Minawa experimented by slashing at large cuts of pork and beef and recording the sound. Eventually he found that the most satisfying of these aural wounds came from assaulting a whole chicken stuffed with chopsticks.

Kurosawa's views on sound were very clear. 'Ever since the silent film gave way to the talkie,' he said, 'sound has interfered with the image – and at the same time this flood of sound has become largely meaningless. That is why the director must be very careful – because a motion picture must be the most effective combination of both image and sound. Cinematic sound is never merely accompaniment, never merely what the sound machine caught while you took the scene. Real sound does not merely add to the image, it multiplies it.' In fact, sound film had been strongly resisted in Japan by the *benshi* storytellers who narrated for silent films from behind cinema screens. Once talkies were established in the early 1930s, film became one of the most important media for introducing the musics of Cuba, Argentina, Hawaii and other exotic locales to Japanese audiences.

Other Kurosawa films – *Drunken Angel*, *Ikiru*, *High and Low* – feature less extreme examples of the *Stray Dog* tour through urban soundscape. 'Kurosawa, working with recordist Wataru Konuma,' writes Galbraith, 'does an excellent job integrating ambient sounds with Hayasaka's music [for *Drunken Angel*]. The neighbourhood may be crawling with yakuza and pollution, but it is still bustling with activity. Music emanates from rundown dance halls, as buyers and sellers haggle, stores pitch their wares through distorting loudspeakers (still prevalent in the Japan of today). The integration is so complete that Okada [the yakuza character played by Reizaburo Yamamoto] plays (on a guitar) his own motif.'

In *Ikiru* (*To Live*, released in 1952), the dominance of ambient sound over dialogue happens twice: once when the dying Watanabe, played by Takashi Shimura, decides to sample forbidden pleasures in the company of a writer of cheap novels. Again, the sequence is lengthy at nearly 15 minutes (imagine if Jack Lemmon's visit to a strip club in *The Odd Couple* had lasted for that long). The two of them stumble from Pachinko parlour to jazz club, mama-san bar to dance hall, piano bar to strip club to ballroom. In the course of this night crawl through the city we hear Pachinko machines, French chanson, boogie woogie, strict tempo ballroom, a 1920s love song, Latin exotica, mambo, American pop songs, the car horns of a traffic jam mixing with fragments of piano heard from a club, then finally the sound of trains. What we feel is the emergence, or re-emergence, in urban Japan of a life that the nationalists sought to destroy: decadent, brash, foreign, yet full of life.

The second scene takes places after Watanabe learns he has terminal cancer. 'As he wanders the streets oblivious to everything around him,' writes Galbraith, 'there is no sound at all, yet behind him are the flashes of welding at a construction site. As he crosses the street, there is a sudden burst of traffic noise as he's nearly run over. The effect puts us inside Watanabe's mind and emotions, which Kurosawa does again and again throughout the film's first half.'

Years later, Kurosawa used this powerful technique in *Ran*. Takemitsu scored only two films for Kurosawa: *Dodesukaden* in 1970 and *Ran* in 1985. Very few ambient sounds are heard during the climactic, brutal battle scenes in *Ran*. Kurosawa simply shows the nightmare of war as a progression of violent acts, a chilling silence surrounding what we see, enveloped in Takemitsu's hugely moving orchestral theme. Kurosawa could be stubborn about music. During post-production on *Kagemusha* he fell out with Masaru Sato. The replacement, Shinichiro Ikebe, composed the kind of score Kurosawa had been demanding, which turned out to be a dreary string of martial clichés. For *Ran*, Takemitsu had wanted to score the battle scenes for voices only, a threnody of cries that would convey the human agony of war. Kurosawa wanted Mahler. Of course, Takemitsu was a more determined person and a far more talented composer than Ikebe, yet finally even he capitulated to one of cinema's most gifted tyrants. The final result was breathtaking, yet Takemitsu continued to wonder what the emotional effect of those battles might have been if only screams and cries had broken the silence.

perpetual flux

Takemitsu's 1948 epiphany in the subway convinced him that contemporary music was self-enclosed within the systematic rigour of its own language. His incorporation of concrete sound and urban noise was an effort to reach out to people who heard these sounds as part of their daily lives. Although his concert music was delicately coloured, subtle, filled with challenges by its apparent lack of conventional form, his strongest film music was created for a cinema of violence, eroticism, cruelty, horror and emotional precipices. Working with many of the most interesting postwar directors in Japan – Nagisa Oshima, Masaki Kobayashi, Susumu Hani, Akira Kurosawa, Shohei Imamura, Masahiro Shindoa, Kon Ichikawa and Hiroshi Teshigahara – allowed him the opportunity to explore the dramatic impact of genre dislocations, anachronistic juxtapositions, stylistic borrowing, gorgeous melody, extreme noise, alienation and shock.

'Toru Takemitsu was an avid film fan,' Masahiro Shinoda told me. Takemitsu scored a number of Shinoda's films, including *Double Suicide*, *Gonza the Spearman*, *Samurai Spy*, *Banished Orin* and *Petrified Forest*. 'I heard him once say that he had seen as many as 300 films in one year. I believe what fascinated him most about film was his keen interest in the overlap of real sound and the soundtrack along the sequence of the film. The rustling of silk, footsteps, the opening of a *shoji* sliding door, and notes from musical instruments – they were all "music" for Takemitsu. Even before musical instruments make sound into "music", there were sound sources, and such sound could turn into "music", or turn into "film/images". One of his utmost requests to me when I was shooting the film was to record every sound at a shooting site with the most scrupulous care.'

'Why do I write film music?' Takemitsu replied to interviewer Peter Grilli in *Music for the Movies*. 'It's because movies have erotic elements as well as violence. I don't like things that are too pure and refined. I'm more interested in what's real. And films are so full of life. Sometimes, working on a concert piece by myself, as the excess is gradually stripped away it becomes increasingly pure, but that is not really interesting. Something pure only becomes interesting when combined with something coarse. Writing music is like getting a passport – a visa to freedom, a liberty passport.'

His collaboration with film director, ceramics artist and *ikebana* master Hiroshi Teshigahara lasted from 1959 until 1991. The music composed for these films ranged from harsh prepared-piano scrapes and thuds, and ravishingly pretty Fender Rhodes jazz piano, to eerie drones, romantic strings, accordion and even a Burt Bacharach influence. For *The Ruined Map*, Teshigahara's 1968 film about the city as desert, samples of Elvis Presley's 'I Need Your Love Tonight', torn in gouts of tortured noise out of a landscape of shuddering, groaning drones, are intercut by Takemitsu with Vivaldi's *Violin Concerto in C Minor*.

Elvis Presley's voice had been sampled for an electro-acoustic composition even earlier than this. Working on electronic and computer music at Bell Labs in the early 1960s, composer James Tenney created a piece called *Collage #1* which reshuffled the sexual energy data of Presley's 'Blue Suede Shoes' through a system of IBM punch cards. In the collision of histories in his meeting of Presley and Vivaldi, Takemitsu anticipates sampling philosophies explored much later by composers such as John Oswald, John Wall and Christian Marclay – the collapsing and subversion of memories. There is an acceptance of change and decay in this, the idea that a body will grow old, eventually merge with earth, air and water. A concert piece, pop song or jazz tune will change according to the ensemble that plays it, the nature of the room, the fashion of the time, technological developments, the mood of the players, the response of the audience. The same recording can sound radically different when heard on the radio, an expensive sound system at home, a powerful sound rig in a club, on television with a video clip, from an MP3 downloaded from a dubious site on the Internet, in a shop selling clothes, in a noisy bar or a quiet restaurant, or from the overspill of somebody's headphones.

A song strongly associated with a particular singer – 'My Baby Just Cares For Me' by Nina Simone, for example – weathers with age and becomes almost artless. Performances of the song deteriorate over time as the singer's voice crumbles to a ruin, but there are compensations for this loss of youth and technique: an accumulated weight of biographical experience (at least a part of which is known to the audience), an overwhelming sense that nature is taking over from artifice.

This is something like the Japanese concept of *sabi*. '*Sabi* grew out of the Heian admiration for lovely things on the verge of extinction,' wrote Thomas Hoover in his book *Zen Culture*. 'By the medieval period this curious attitude was extended to things already old, and so entered the idea of *sabi*, a term denoting objects agreeably mellowed by age. *Sabi* also brought melancholy overtones of loneliness, of age left behind by time. New objects are assertive and striving for attention; old, worn objects have the quiet, peaceful air that exudes tranquility, dignity, and character.'

Takemitsu's score for Hiroshi Teshigahara's film *Rikyu* evokes political intrigue and the clash of values lying at the heart of the story, yet at the same time expressed the simplicity of 16th-century Zen Buddhism, the feeling of steam evaporating in the stillness of the tea ceremony.

Rikyu is about a historical figure, the tea master Sen No Rikyu. Born in 1521, his clear vision of Zen values systematised the rules of the tea ceremony. In *Rediscovering Rikyu and the Beginnings of the Japanese Tea Ceremony*, Herbert Plutschow uses Evan M. Zuesse's ideas of confirmatory and transformatory ritual as a tool for greater understanding of the different modes of tea. During times of peace, tea tended to be confirmatory in its mirroring of social and political order, with participants practising it to 'affirm class belonging and allegiance'; in times of crisis, the ceremony was more likely to impose equality on the participants, so aiming for a transformation of conflict into peace.

As Teshigahara's film makes clear, Rikyu was forced to compromise under the patronage of the shogun Hideyoshi, a volatile and dangerous man of strident tastes. Rikyu was his tea instructor as well as his political go-between, and the film begins with a scene that introduces the ways in which these two men expressed their contrasting strengths of will. Rikyu cultivated morning glory, an imported European flower. Hideyoshi comes to see the blossoms one morning but Rikyu has picked them all before he arrives. Furious, Hideyoshi crawls into the tea house to find one bloom standing in the alcove. At that moment, Takemitsu's music pierces the silence like a cluster of delicate shoots bursting through a forest floor.

'This preference of one over many is typically *wabi*,' wrote Plutschow, 'the small is better than the one, one better than many, little better than too much, the subdued better than the extravagant, something short-lived like a morning glory better than something that lasts forever, depth better than superficiality.' Rikyu believed more in *wabi* than *sabi*. '*Sabi* can still encompass snobbery,' wrote Hoover in *Zen Culture*, quoting lines from a poem by Rikyu, illustrating the *wabi* idea of deliberate restraint:

> How much does a person lack himself,
> Who feels the need to have so many things.

Another scene in the film shows Rikyu supervising the firing of a tea bowl, its radiant scarlet heat transforming to black as the bowl cools. Rikyu insisted on simple black tea ware, despite pressures from Hideyoshi to use more gaudy, ostentatious colours. Eventually, Rikyu was forced to commit suicide by Hideyoshi, an ending that seems to have been about both politics and the organisation of time. 'As the uncontested leader of the nation,' writes Herbert Plutschow, 'Hideyoshi wanted tea to express and confirm the new social order and for it to change from a transformatory to a confirmatory ritual. Under radically different political and social situations, Hideyoshi wished tea to adapt to these new conditions, something the old and conservative Rikyu may have resisted. Hideyoshi's attempt to control tea may have brought him into conflict with Rikyu's wabi ideals, as exemplified in Hideyoshi's preference of red Raku tea bowls while Rikyu preferred the black ones. Rikyu wanted wabi tea to survive as the nation's egalitarian ritual, despite pressures for the ritual to reflect the new socio-political order.'

Hiroshi Teshigahara died in April 2001. During his rich and varied life he had become head of the Sogetsu School of Flower-arranging, founded by his father, and organised many events in Japan, including performances by John Cage and Merce Cunningham. At the Sogetsu Arts Centre in April, 1960, Takemitsu played his tape piece, *Water Music*. Realised in that same year by Takemitsu and recording engineer Junosuke Okuyama, the piece electronically manipulates water sounds. As a verbal adjunct to the piece, Takemitsu explained that the sight and sound of flowing water made him think of Taoism, the Chinese system of thought described by Joseph Needham in volume II of his *Science and Civilisation in China* as 'a naturalistic pantheon, which emphasises the unity and spontaneity of the operations of Nature'.

'I may have received some influence from Voltaire's thought,' Takemitsu added. 'My image of tao is not a continuous road but just dots.' This is how the music sounds: particles of sound that knock and rub against a volume of emptiness. 'For this occasion [at the Sogetsu Arts Centre], one of Teshigahara's oldest friends, the Noh actor Hideo Kanze, was enlisted to dance, which, as the critic Kuniharu Akiyama points out, was not so strange since the amplified sounds of dripping water came through like a Noh drum,' wrote Dore Ashton in her book, *The Delicate Thread: Teshigahara's Life in Art*.

Woman of the Dunes (*Suna no onna*), released in 1964 and nominated for an Oscar in 1966, was perhaps the most enthralling and enduring collaboration between Takemitsu and Teshigahara. Based on a novel by Kobo Abe, the film is essentially a meditation on freedom. Abe's book tells the story of a teacher who takes a short holiday to pursue his hobby of studying and collecting insects. At the end of a hot day he is offered accommodation by villagers who live among sand dunes near the sea. He is lowered down into a deep pit, occupied by a woman living alone, then finds himself trapped there, perhaps for eternity. To some extent this is a study in torture, but also an examination of the conflicts between a Western-style bureaucratic, materialistic, analytical life and a more Taoist acceptance of universal order.

At a deeper level lies a contemplation of form, a subject close to Takemitsu's heart. 'Without the threat of punishment there is no joy in flight' is the aphorism that precedes the novel. 'Certainly sand was not suitable for life,' Abe wrote. 'Yet, was a stationary condition absolutely indispensable for existence? Didn't unpleasant competition arise precisely because one tried to cling to a fixed position? If one were to give up a fixed position and abandon oneself to the movement of the sands, competition would soon stop.' In the same way that these geological ruminations led Abe immediately to the biological and social, so musicians were beginning to ask similar questions and apply them to notions of authority and organisation in sound.

Abe's novel is alert to the significance of sounds following the sudden reduction of sensory input that falls upon his central character: 'He could hear the sound of the wind sweeping over the edge of the hole, the lisp of the shovel cutting into the bed of wet sand, the distant barking of dogs, the faraway hum of voices, trembling like the flame of a candle. The ceaselessly pouring sand was like a file on the tips of his nerves.'

Teshigahara projected the peculiarities of this story into the convergent sensuality of cinema, focussing microscopically on the texture of sand and skin, the movement of insects, the sensory impact of wind and heat. Surfaces are eroticised; rationalism and the bureaucratic order of modern life are pitted against animism and the inexorable rhythms of nature, these transformations and oppositions echoed by Takemitsu's granular, eerie musical score of sudden distorted shocks and attenuated, fibrous tones: music as skin tones.

Teshigahara and Takemitsu move fluidly between abstraction and narrative, the multiple echoes of sound and image. At the very beginning of the film we see only black. What we hear is the clatter of trams, whistles, tannoy announcements. Following the black comes a succession of images created by Kiyoshi Awazu: line drawings, like contour maps, the official stamps, seals and thumbprints of bureaucracy, calligraphy; from Takemitsu, harsh distorted noise blocks, suddenly the faint ambient sounds of a city, a sudden thick fur ball of a chord, wood striking wood in an echo chamber. Then we see the teacher climbing dunes that fill the cinema screen, folded and rippled by oceanic wave forms, blown in thin nets of capricious smoke. As Kobo Abe described it, 'the antithesis of all form'. Takemitsu's cue for this entry into sand is played by a small ensemble of flute, oboe, harp and glockenspiel and strings. The sliding glissandi of the strings recall the traumatic, enveloping clouds of high pitches typical of music composed by Krzysztof Penderecki, György Ligeti and Iannis Xenakis during the same period of history.

As the teacher lies back in a rowing boat becalmed in sand, thoughts and memories trickle through his mind: all the corroborating documents – the identity cards and employment certificates – needed for a proper existence in the modern world, then disputes with his wife. Talk and mechanisation begin to fade. Temporary erasures of verbalisation are an aspect of this flexibility – the world hovering in balance between nature and culture, rationalism and instinct, freedom and structure, word and absence of word, sound and silence, the shifting of the sand, perpetual flux.

In 1998, I asked Teshigahara to note down some impressions of collaborating with Takemitsu. 'In the jobs we worked together we never pre-arranged anything,' he wrote. 'At the rushes stage he looked at what I had shot very carefully until he collected all the sounds to complete the finished work. He spent all of the time with me. He checked not only his music but also meticulously checked the sounds recorded for the film – for example, the actor's words and concrete sounds. There are so many different sounds in a film, but he checked every single one and would say, "we can scrap this noise and hear music here", or vice versa. Also, we tried to mechanically process the concrete sounds.

'For my films, he said it took him a long time to decide what type of sound we would have, or what type of instruments in some cases. For example, the sound of sand in *Woman of the Dunes*, or the mountain of coal in *The Pitfall*. These films revolve around material elements more than narrative, so it was difficult to balance those elements with the use of actual sounds.

'In *The Pitfall* we made the sound with two prepared pianos against harpsichord, or in *The Face of Another* we used glass harmonica. To decide on the glass harmonica apparently took him a month, but the process was enjoyable and once it was decided the composing went very smoothly.

'With *Rikyu* he looked at the rushes very carefully and said there was no need to colour it with sound. I thought he might do just the minimum of cues but he ended up doing 24. I think he tried to execute it with simplicity. He used Western antique instruments, like viola da gamba and portative organ. During the historical period in which *Rikyu* is set these instruments were believed to have been brought into Japan by missionaries and performed by them. So if that is true, Rikyu the tea master might have heard them, which is interesting.

'Our first collaboration was my first documentary, *José Torres*. In 1959 I met an upcoming controversial boxer called José and I interviewed him for four days continuously. I was confident that I had captured everything about him but as I was so excited I wasn't able to shoot it calmly and objectively. I was looking forward to having music added. I asked my editing team for ideas and Takemitsu was suggested. I had heard about him so I gathered my courage and spoke to him. He saw the rushes and took it on straightaway. He was very excited by it. The music is based around jazz and the popular feeling is that it was his major film score. He always denied it, but the music is full of lyricism and pathos. The sound flowing out of him had a good blues feeling. In that film, the sound of the boxing and the music blend into one. There's no waste. It's perfect.

'I always trusted his work and expected new challenges. I think he expected the same from me. Of all contemporary composers I like his compositions the best and he knew that. Our friendship was always work-oriented but he came to see a performance of his works that I had organised after he had been in hospital. We worked together until very late over dinner and drinks and he showed a tremendous interest in all the projects we discussed. Most of my films used his music and his music had become a vital element of my work. I'm badly affected by the loss of my closest partner.

'Takemitsu didn't care about categories. He always responded to the beauty of music with great sensitivity. That's why he was able to create his own world. He wrote with more freedom for his film music than he did for his normal compositions. His use of Elvis Presley and Vivaldi in *The Ruined Map* was one example. Also, the prepared pianos in *The Pitfall* fits in very well with the rough scenery of the destroyed coal mine, the characters walking over coal lying in the road and feeling it underfoot.

'He said that film music should be something that should neither explain the pictures or accompany them. He used many different elements to provoke musical ideas and then matched the score to the pictures. He tried to create a self-contained world that ran parallel to the images yet fused them together. I felt at one with the way he worked. Our collaboration together was continually exciting.'

Takemitsu described the form of his own music as a walk through a garden. In such a garden, the sudden appearance of Elvis Presley practising karate beyond the fence would come as no surprise: just the *shakkei* principle of borrowed scenery in action. 'I love gardens,' he wrote. 'They do not reject people. There one can walk freely, pause to view the entire garden, or gaze at a single tree. Plants, rocks, and sand show changes, constant changes.' In other words, a sound work can be traversed, scanned through varying modes of perception, appreciated from different viewpoints and time frames. His perception of time and continuity in relation to musical form was a part of this, a recognition of time's circularity. He admired the modalism of Miles Davis, Wayne Shorter and Gil Evans, citing George Russell's tonal theories, his comparison of Ornette Coleman and John Coltrane solos to the flow of the Mississippi River.

'My music is something like a signal sent out to the unknown,' he said. The sound gardens that he constructed could be sensual and calming, sparkling with firefly showers, vibrating with the vibrant greens of soft mosses, austere, geometrical and symbolic like the Kyoto dry gardens of Daisen-in, Zuiho-in and Ryogen-in. But all Japanese gardening is symbolic. Takemitsu knew this, knew also that the philosophical principles quietly governing the shaping of artificial nature could be applied to the shaping of sound. The results could be the same: a transformative ritual.

Many taboos constrained the design of an 11th-century garden. Takemitsu was a modern man who had felt the shock and ensuing silence of the atomic bomb. There were dark places within his sonic gardens, spirits lurking, ghosts of all the tragedies of the century, places of haunted weather. 'My music is composed as if fragments were thrown together unstructured, as in dreams,' he wrote. Peter Grilli, writer and co-producer of *Music for the Movies*, has quoted Takemitsu's last thoughts, written to friends a few days before his death: 'Don't worry about me. I will get a stronger body as a whale. And I want to swim in the ocean that has no west and no east.'

silence within noise

Put a crayfish in an aquarium and then add a turtle and in no time at all, the turtle will have eaten the crayfish. In this situation the crayfish seems to be heading for extinction. It's a little bit like the bat and the moth. The bat is able to detect the moth just by sending out high frequency sounds until it hits a flying object of the right dimensions. Moths should be extinct but they're not. They have an answer to the bat – ears that can detect ultrasonic signals – and when they hear squeaking they go into a routine of unpredictable loops and dives.

A crayfish defence system depends on the tiny hairs that cover the surface of its body. They function in much the same way as the hairs inside the cochlea of a human ear, detecting extremely faint, almost inaudible sounds that may be a hungry turtle. The odd part of the story is that these hairs won't work if there's too much silence. Put a crayfish in a silent aquarium, add a turtle and it gets eaten, but add some random background noise to simulate the crackling and popping we can hear on underwater recordings made with hydrophones and the crayfish escapes. This is called stochastic resonance. Aural white noise or visual white noise can help both humans and crayfish to distinguish the event they want to see or hear. The randomness of white noise allows more possibilities of a very faint sound wave finding another wave with which it can resonate and so be reinforced.

Strangely enough, Takemitsu anticipated this discovery, writing an article about the artist Odilon Redon in 1980. 'We hear white noise as one sound,' he wrote. 'However, by further processing we create new sounds. But the importance of comparing white noise to traditional musical sounds is the realisation that through white noise we reach sounds inaudible to the human ear – part of which I intuitively call the "river of sound".'

from a distance

In January 2003, I am sitting in the Berlin apartment of sound artist Rolf Julius. Looking around me, I can see the new technology of iPods and computers. In an adjacent room, many rice bowls, stones, tiny loudspeakers and heaped pigments of gorgeously vibrant colouration cover the floor. In photographs this humble set of tools can look like divination bowls, jellyfish, esoteric medicinal powders and cooking spices, flower petals floating in tidal pools, surrounded by marine life.

Through a small loudspeaker, quiet sound will agitate the powder. 'The music should sound grey,' he told his musicologist friend Shin Nakagawa when they were discussing a work called *Grey*. 'The sound was just a low, monotonous buzzing sound; there were no clues there that might lead us to the conclusion that it was "grey". He pointed to the grey pigment that was placed on top of the speaker, and told me to put my face near it. Depending on the sound, the pigment shook slightly. That's when, without realising it, it sunk into my conscious mind. At that moment, listening to it equalled touching and seeing sound at the same time. Like a flickering lamp, the sound and colour repeatedly crossed the surface of my senses. Seeing sounds, hearing colours. After experiencing his works, we aren't apt to forget that colour is also vibration.'

I witnessed a similar realisation at Sonic Boom at the Hayward Gallery. A work by Max Eastley, *Phantom Drawings of a Procession of Ghosts*, was placed in a difficult part of the gallery, close to far louder works. The piece consisted of long steel wires, suspended from motors attached to the ceiling. Each wire divided into two near its foot and a strip of white paper lay across a platform below the wires. As each wire was turned by its motor, the two feet would drag slowly over the paper or freeze in stasis until sufficient force accumulated to set them free. The sound was hardly a sound at all, closer to the faint powder of graphite clinging to paper surface after the stroke of a pencil than an audible trace. A number of people warned me that the piece would communicate nothing in a setting vulnerable to disturbance, though as curator I wanted to test these preconceptions. Walking through the exhibition one morning I turned the corner to find a line of visitors, their heads all close to the paper, listening intently to the sound. They had been drawn in by the mysterious action of the wire, then discovered the pale scratch that traced invisible drawings into whiteness.

Julius is telling me stories about the perception of silence. 'Near Okayama,' he says, 'there is this garden which goes diagonally into the nature, so there is an artificial thing that goes visually into the nature mountains which are behind. I was there and I was enjoying. If you have seen many Japanese gardens then you can become blasé,' he admits. 'So I was not so concentrated, realising how beautiful it is or how quiet it is. And then, in the distance I heard a very big noise. This stopped suddenly, and after this big noise I realised the beauty of the garden. But later I learned it was a concept of 500 years ago. They had a cage and there were cranes and they know cranes, I don't know, every hour or so they get crazy and make a big noise. They kept maybe 10 or 20 and they all got crazy. Later I asked people and they said, oh, you found out. I like this situation. The brain was again ready for listening and for looking. For both.'

Julius was born in 1939 in Wilhelmshaven. During the war he would go to the countryside to stay with his uncle, who was a farmer. 'I remember all the animal sounds, the cows and the pigs,' he says, 'and now it's coming back, how you cut wheat, these old machines, k-k-k-k. They were fascinating, very soft, I remember. The things I remember listening to the most were the hens and the geese. Therefore I'm very happy when I think about these. When I listened to the geese sound, I was a little bit scared but I liked the sound. It was like early music. It was like Stan Kenton.'

Julius studied visual art, making drawings and very minimal photographs. Undecided about how to select and exhibit the many hundreds of photographs he had taken, he tried using sound in 1979 as a way to show a small number of them – a series called *Dike Line* – but bring them to life. Influenced by the music of Morton Feldman and the experimental music he had heard on Radio Bremen in the early 1970s, he made a tape recording from two pieces of metal: one click sound for one loudspeaker, then the same click recorded with lesser fidelity on the other side. 'Then I listened to that,' he says, 'and then something happened. Because of this klick klack, all of a sudden the lines started to dance a bit. It was not fantasy. We checked it, double checked it with other people. So I think that is fine. If you have art, if you have sound, you get one more, so you can have three things. Then it started.'

Much of his work since that time has played with these small illusions, or mysteries. An imagined piece from 1982 described two steel guitar strings, E and B, stretched 150 centimetres from each other in an empty white room. Hidden loudspeakers would play a tape composition by Julius, suggesting that the strings were somehow miraculously making these sounds. His work also interposes ambiguity into the relationship between what has been made and what already exists. 'I like natural sound,' he says, 'because when you hear sounds from a distance you hear sounds which are interfering, you hear atmosphere, something like that.' He looks pained as he tries to explain phenomena that are fugitive, perhaps inexplicable. 'Maybe my brain starts to work. When I talk about natural sound I'm interested not actually in sounds themselves but in the quality of having the distance. Something coming from a distance I like very much. Also, personally I like distance. When people sit together very close I like to make some distance. Also visually. And with sounds, I like sounds coming from a corner. But that means I like the air in between. And sometimes the air in between is not thick enough so you can add some other sounds. Then you can organise the atmosphere, which is material, but in a more abstract way.'

He shows me a photograph, taken in Finland last summer: water, reflected sky, some stones, a small loudspeaker. 'Actually I know this area for a long time, for more than four years,' he says. 'The weather conditions, there was no wind at all. It was warm. It was the first time there were some clouds because the colours change. What I wanted to do, I made fake sound installations. I put this stone into this water and this stone was already in there so I put a speaker on top of it, just to make a photo, not to make a photo but to do a kind of sculpture work. But I didn't connect the speaker to sounds. That was just kind of fake. It was not fake. For me it was to put sounds ... I just wanted to say it was just absolutely nothing, just quiet. I was using a symbol for not being quiet, but a loudspeaker says, loud. I just was using it to create a piece which says, oh, it's very, very quiet, so I'm using the opposite to create stillness or quiet.'

4 Sampling the world

pussy would sing soprano

During the 1950s, the work of pioneering Danish wildlife sound recordist Carl Weismann was plagued by dogs. The dogs of Denmark were so devoted to their life's calling as man's best friend that their vocal enthusiasm allowed no silence in which other species could sing in peace. Weismann's recordings of birdsong were repeatedly ruined by the barking of these dogs. Many tapes had to be salvaged by skilful editing with a razor blade. Weismann then had two categories of tape in his studio: the desirable birds and the discarded dogs. Perhaps the thrifty strain common to many adults in this postwar period compelled him to put the dogs to work. As an experiment he chose one of the simplest melodies ever written, searched for the appropriate and approximate pitches among his dog bark out-takes, then edited these together into 'Jingle Bells'. Originally intended for a children's radio show, this canine Christmas novelty was pressed up onto a four-track disc in 1955 and released by RCA Records in America. There it sold 500,000 copies. In November of the same year, the tune reached number 13 in the British charts. Then in 1971, as is usually the case in these stories of revived 45s, a radio DJ played the song on his show and sparked a second moment of madness. This time, the record sold more than a million in the U.S. Long players, as they were called in those days, followed. The back cover of *Singing Dogs* shows a photograph of the late sound recordist (whose more serious wildlife recordings are now archived at the National Sound Archive in London) surrounded by stacked reels of ¼-inch tape. His assistant, a human, is cataloguing the barks of a terrier named Pearl. According to the sleeve notes, Pearl and the poodle Dolly would sing in-between notes, Pussy, a Doberman, would sing soprano and two German shepherds, Caesar and King, would sing the bass.

news from nowhere

Weismann's method for realising this crazy project was a form of what we now call sound sampling. Histories of sampling tend to concentrate on precedents referenced from the avant-garde: the dadaist collages of Kurt Schwitters, Man Ray's assemblages, Pierre Schaeffer's *musique concrète*, John Cage's early tape pieces, the phonographic experiments of Edgard Varèse, Luc Ferrari's *Hétérozygote* and *Presque Rien No. 1*, and so on. Marcel Duchamp, of course, must be in there with his moustachioed *Mona Lisa*, his shovel in advance of a broken arm, the ball of string *With Hidden Noise*, and his urinal; Erik Satie with his paraphrasing of cakewalks and rags; Andy Warhol with his soup cans and 'wanted men' posters, and Robert Rauschenberg's Angora goat encircled by a car tyre; we should also insert Brassai's photographs of street graffiti and the paintings of Antoni Tàpies into this history. The list is familiar and can expand seemingly in every direction as sound sampling becomes an increasingly diverse and complex practice.

Such histories may also move closer to the present by including the real-time turntable exploits of hip-hop DJs such as Grandmaster Flash, Grand Wizard Theodore, Jazzy Jay and Afrika Bambaataa, the versioning of previously recorded tracks by reggae toasters and dub masters like King Tubby and Lee Perry, the jump-cut mixes made in disco and hip-hop by studio auteurs such as Double D & Steinski, or the ultrapaste density of the Bomb Squad productions for Public Enemy, then finally alight on contemporary sampling composers and turntablists such as John Oswald, John Wall, Philip Jeck, Janek Schaefer, DJ Spooky, Christian Marclay, Otomo Yoshihide, Tom Recchion, DJ Olive, Rob Swift, Terre Thaemlitz, Vicki Bennett, David Shea, Kid 606, Kid Koala, DJ Disk, The Tape Beatles, Negativland, Akira Rabelais, Matmos, and so on in a very long and winding list.

But an important contribution to the concept and technical development of sampling has come from the novelty and comedy sector. Records by The Singing Dogs, Spike Jones, Dean Elliott and his Big Band, Jack Fascinato, Buchanan and Goodman, and the BBC Radiophonic Workshop took everyday sounds, copyright material and sound effects and shoehorned them into absurd yet recognisable melodies. In a collaboration with *Tom &*

Jerry cartoon sound effects creator Phil Kaye, Dean Elliot's 1963 album, *Zounds! What Sounds!*, featured cement mixer, air compressor, boxing punch bag, hand saw, bowling pins, a clock factory and (anticipating Beach Boy Brian Wilson's vegetable chomping sessions for *Smile*) celery stalks. None of these records depend upon connections with experimental music of any kind, though Fascinato, producer of *Music From a Surplus Store*, was influenced by Bartók and Schoenberg. Their creators realised certain possibilities of ambient sounds, the recording studio and magnetic tape, just as clearly as Luc Ferarri, Richard Maxfield or Bernard Parmegiani, and found ways to shape them into an anarchic, surreal and formally adventurous style of humour.

Also, as entertainers, they were aware of a remarkable if inconsistent public adjustment to schizophonia, the continual disruptions and dislocations of temporal and spatial context piped into the home via radio and television. Montage, voices laid over music, sound effects, news and weather breaking into sequences of music, live audience reactions, chaotic rolling news, split screens, scrolling banners and multiple audio 'viewpoints' are now so commonplace in radio and television that they pass almost unnoticed. Experiments in mass delusion that once highlighted the propaganda potential of mass communications seem unlikely to provoke panic reactions in contemporary audiences more prone to conspiracy theories, cynicism or passivity.

Buchanan and Goodman's 'The Flying Saucer', released in 1956, was based on the notorious Orson Welles radio play *War of the Worlds*, broadcast in 1938. Welles had demonstrated how powerful the effects of simulation could be. By breaking into dance music with an announcement that a 'huge flaming object' had landed in New Jersey, then describing the emergence of aliens from a Martian spacecraft, the play spread panic in America. People fled for the hills or hid in cellars, even wrapped wet towels around their heads as a protection against Martian 'weapons of mass destruction'.

Bill Buchanan and Dickie Goodman realised the satirical possibilities of the audio break-in in a pluralistic world increasingly subject to the seductive influence and fragmenting effects of advertising and mass media. 'The Flying Saucer' used a linear technique of editing lines from popular songs, then linking the fragments with dialogue and effects. Two struggling New York songwriters, Buchanan and Goodman had the idea of basing a song on 'The Great Pretender', by The Platters, a record whose romantic story of truth and pretence implied the wider issues of reality and simulation raised by Welles. Using *War of the Worlds* as their template, they broke into a Nappy Brown track to announce the presence of a flying saucer hovering over the city. In a hectic 4' 18" of jump cuts, Buchanan played an Alan Freed-style disc jockey who can't get the names of the artists or their song titles straight and Goodman played the reporter covering the invasion story. Lines from songs by Little Richard, Fats Domino, Elvis Presley, Smiley Lewis, The Platters, Chuck Berry and Carl Perkins cut in and out of the drama, though the names of the original artists are changed to Skinny Dynamo, The Clatters, Huckleberry and Pa Gerkins.

After the break-up of his partnership with Bill Buchanan, Dickie Goodman continued to switch the names of popular recording artists, television shows and films, either to make satirical comments on the media or political situations of the moment. As Dickie Goodman and Dr I. M. Ill, he made 'Ben Crazy' (derived from the hospital TV show *Ben Casey*); other targets were renamed as 'Schonanza', 'James Bomb', 'Touchables', 'Watergrate', 'Mr. Jaws' and 'Star Warts'. Anticipating the referential obsessions of Austin Powers, *Not Another Teen Movie* and the bastard pop bootleg mixes of the early 21st century, Dickie Goodman also successfully negotiated the copyright battles more recently encountered by samplers and MP3 websites. After interventions by the Music Publishers Protective Association, along with a number of record labels and artists, their tracks became subject to a deal whereby royalties were split between the publishing houses whose songs were sampled on the record.

Although the technique was linear, it broke the taboo of racial segregation by allowing a multiplicity of voices to speak within a single drama. The record may have been a comedy novelty, but in 1956, the implications were political. The impact of a break-in depends on familiarity. An evolving narrative can be developed in which each point is underlined by the ingenuity of the source material. More self-consciously serious in its musical and political intent, though still descended from radio drama and the novelty break-in records, *Avant Slant (one PLUS I=II?): A Twelve-Tone Collage*, was an album released in 1968 by the John Benson Brooks Trio, and, as the psychedelic cover puts it, 'Assisted by inhabitants of the World-at-large and Assorted Vibrations Still in Orbit, catalyzed by Milt Gabler'. A friend of Gil Evans and George Russell, Brooks had worked for years as a pianist/arranger and songwriter, composing tunes like 'You Came a Long Way From St. Louis' before he studied with John Cage. His most critically successful recording was a hybrid of contemporary composition, jazz and folk themes entitled *Alabama Concerto*, released in 1958 and featuring Cannonball Adderley and Art Farmer. As for Gabler, he was a record producer, songwriter, founder of the Commodore label and the first person to run a specialist jazz record shop. His foresight into the future of the record business also contributed to the intellectual and economic origins of sound sampling. During the depression in the 1930s he was quicker than anybody in realising that profits could be made from a small capital outlay by leasing previously released recordings and reissuing them on his own labels. To recycle music as a commodity in this way was a conceptual breakthrough that affected the creative and historical implications of mechanical reproduction as well as its economic structure.

Avant Slant was a disrupted, haphazard narrative based around a live recording of the John Benson Brooks Trio. Captured at Howard University in 1962 during the trio's only public concert, the intense angularity of the live playing, heavily influenced by Ornette Coleman, is intercut with recordings of comedy routines, poetry, piano solos and songs performed by singers such as Judy Scott, Lightnin' Hopkins, The Tarriers and Corrine. The subject matter is a scattershot spray of late 60s themes – spaceflight, sexual liberation, the Vietnam war, racism and civil rights, identity and personal freedom – punctuated by speeches and poems that range from Herman Goering's 'guns and butter' speech justifying Nazi Germany's rearmament policy in 1936 to a brief excerpt from *Black Dada Nihilismus*, Amiri Baraka's violent verbal assault on white imperialist civilisation, originally recited and entwined with the music of Roswell Rudd, John Tchicai, Lewis Worrell and Milford Graves, still unpalatable to American conservatives forty years later.

The idea for *Avant Slant* began when Brooks made a tape, described in John Clellon Holmes's sleeve notes as 'a curious melange of air-shots, record-excerpts, sound effects and one-liners that Brooks had put together, more or less experimentally, under the generic title, *D.J.-ology*'. Perhaps the title should be called prophetic, rather than generic. The influence of mass media was affecting all innovative artists in this period, and comparisons could be made with the assemblages, prints, sculptures, films and paintings of Robert Rauschenberg, Jasper Johns, Richard Hamilton, Jeff Keen and Eduardo Paolozzi, or film maker Kenneth Anger's strategic use of pop songs in *Scorpio Rising*. Since the advent of radio, music could always be heard in contiguous sequences, interspersed with the chatter – inane, informative or inspired – of the disc jockey, so the accepted presence and mediation of this voice adds a specific history to audio cut-ups and break-ins.

towards a poor music

> 'They were encouraging me to record. For the year I've had the machine, I've tended to give it the cold shoulder. The needle to watch out for, the record to watch out for, the record to change after three minutes, the needle to watch out for again, the groove to watch while you play, to think it's a *piece* when it so happens you don't like pieces, but repetitions, long boring passages, just going my way, but there is no way, to return, to return to the same thing, to be a litany, a litany like life, to take a long time before the ending, not to decide really to make human music and especially not composer's music, and especially not Western music rather make sparrow music, of a rather indecisive sparrow, perched on a branch, a sparrow who could be trying to call out to a man ...'
>
> Henri Michaux, from *First Impressions*, 1949

In 1918, Man Ray created a readymade called *Homme*, a mechanical whisk with erectile handle pointed upwards and concluded in the south by two testicular circles (globular, by illusion at least, when the whisk was turning). What did the whisk sound like? To Man Ray that was hardly the point but for musicians exploring the way in which contact microphones could amplify and animate the sound of surface and friction, a stuttering engagement of cogs and the passage of thin metal blades through viscous fluids, or air, could sound very interesting indeed.

Having worked as an assistant to Karlheinz Stockhausen in the 1960s, Hugh Davies participated in performances of works such as Stockhausen's *Mikrophonie I*, a piece composed in 1964 in which a large suspended tam-tam is activated by groups of performers, one group using various materials to draw sounds from the metal, another group passing microphones over the surface and a third group using electronic filters and potentiometers to transform these sounds and simultaneously relay them to loudspeakers. For Stockhausen, this broke down the dualism between traditional instruments or other acoustic events and electronic music. 'The title *Mikrophonie*,' he wrote, 'also points to the fact that vibrations that are normally inaudible (in this case those of a tam-tam) can be made audible by means of an active process of auscultation with microphones (in much the same way as a doctor uses a stethoscope); in contrast to its previous passive function as an extremely faithful recorder of sounds, the microphone is used actively, as a musical instrument.'

'Stockhausen also used contact microphones to amplify metal percussion instruments in *Mixtur*, which I also performed in,' writes Hugh Davies in answer to my question about his early influences. 'The technician at the WDR studio, Jaap Spek, was the expert on all these things, and gave me advice. Contact mics [sic] were also used, as far as I remember, by Johannes Fritsch (in Stockhausen's group) on his viola, and in pieces by a couple of students on Stockhausen's composition course. In autumn 1965 Max Neuhaus played a solo concert in Cologne, with a programme similar to his solo LP, including contact mics on percussion and use of acoustic feedback. I also knew some of Mauricio Kagel's recent work, such as *Match* and *Tremens*, which could be described as instrumental theatre, one strand of which led to his first invented instruments being included in compositions in 1968, so I can't have been influenced by these; but I'm pretty sure that it was near the end of 1966 that I visited his storeroom, which included a wide range of unconventional and non-Western instruments, perhaps even some devised by him (like his "keyboard" of large castanets).'

After two years in Cologne, Davies returned home to England in 1966, armed with a small array of electronic equipment and plans to develop his own electronic projects. 'Living at my parents' home for a few months in the summer of 1967, before I moved to London,' he writes, 'I finally started. There was a radio set in their bedroom with an extension loudspeaker, so I wired up a connection from my room so that I could plug my mixer into the radio and work in my room using the extension loudspeaker with the door closed. In that period I was still thinking primarily of making tape music, and produced a few small pieces using a considerable amount of splicing, including a short piece based on modified musical extracts taped off the radio that would now be described as plunderphonic.

'Wanting to extend my sound sources, I ordered a sine/square wave generator from Heathkit in kit form, which I assembled (excellent practice for my soldering, and it worked first time!), and I started putting contact mics on found objects – including a quartet of combs mounted in holders, and an upturned tea-tin with several small springs stretched across a wooden "bridge". After I moved to London I discovered that colleagues like Anna (now Annea) Lockwood were amplifying egg slicers with a contact mic. Around that time I also discovered magnetic pickups (from old telephones), and with these I produced what I felt were more interesting sounds from egg slicers.'

With the live electronics group Gentle Fire, the improvising quartet Music Improvisation Company, and in solo performances, Hugh Davies turned away from conventional technologies and introduced a new informality to the challenges of creating electronic music in real time. Beginning by building homemade ring modulators and a stereo preamplifier, in 1968 Davies began to incorporate any ordinary found object with sonic possibilities. He called a collection of these objects a 'shozyg'. Some of the collections were housed inside the empty covers of an encyclopaedia as a representation of direct experience given primacy over text-based learning and classification, so the name was derived from SHO to ZYG, the alphabetical alpha and omega of subject matter printed on an encyclopaedia spine. The objects included a 3-D photograph, sounded by amplifying fingernails running across the grooves at different speeds, amplified springs of various lengths, some of them pitch-adjusted by means of key rings, a plucked or blown egg slicer, and a cardboard accordion file interleaved with doll squeakers of varying pitch.

Although strongly influenced in the 1960s by techniques pioneered by Stockhausen, Cage, David Tudor and Gordon Mumma, Davies stood out as an idiosyncratic inventor of singular originality. His unique vision of an accessible, humorous approach to live electronics – a way of making music too often hidden behind the technocratic alienation of mysterious processes, expensive standardised equipment and an atmosphere of remote science – has threatened to marginalise him from the electro-acoustic mainstream. Yet over the 40 years in which he has been active, his influence on younger generations has grown noticeably. In London, the Bohman Brothers, for example, have continued his explorations into found objects, using homemade string instruments, spoken narratives and the amplified detritus of consumer society to journey further into the subsurface of a world in which matter is a web of dynamic energy patterns rather than a comfortingly solid, static, three-dimensional thing occupying only physical space.

For the instrumentation of his 1997 CD, *Last Orders*, Adam Bohman lists prepared violin and balalaika alongside wine glasses, wire brush on tiles, springs, toy telephone, while his brother, Jonathan, plays wine glasses and tins. A strong scent of the comic pervades this focus on materials that are risible, trashy, unimportant (because they belong to the world of children) or so functional that they have become almost invisible. In his use of toy pianos, wind-up and battery-operated toys, toy record player, toy electric guitar, lo-fi electronics and other small devices, pianist and multi-instrumentalist Steve Beresford is acutely aware of the connections between bathos, humour and melancholy. The more sophisticated, expensive and impressive our tools, the more grand we seem. In the end, this is all hubris; comedy exists as a brutal reminder of our foolishness and inadequacy, the small impact of our passing moment.

After studying music at York University, Beresford found that venues in London in the early 1970s rarely had pianos. The small sounds made by the Spontaneous Music Ensemble, the sight of People Band drummer Terry Day playing Coke cans on a sofa, and John Cage's *Suite for Toy Piano*, all encouraged him to develop a way of improvising that combined a pianistic enfolding of many musical references – memories from childhood, the piano as an instrument of pomposity and exaggerated gesture, the ease of genre cliché – with the sounds of more humble and garish noisemakers. 'At the time,' he writes (pencil on paper, for a change, rather than e-mail), 'composers of repetitive music were talking about "people processes" which seemed to me to characterise people as inefficient machines. I preferred the idea of machines as inefficient people; for instance a small plastic pipe organ I found which played tunes from little discs, notably a slightly wonky "Happy Birthday".'

'Make for yourself a world you can believe in,' wrote Jonathan Safran Foer, editor of *A Convergence of Birds: Original Fiction and Poetry Inspired by the Work of Joseph Cornell*. Toys, like the Singing Dogs, are an imitation of life. Used in a serious musical context, they obstruct the possibility of virtuosity, with all the flashy emptiness that implies. In his notes, Beresford writes about Joseph Cornell 'turning prosaic things into magical ones'. Of course, Cornell has never been valued as highly in the 20th-century American art pantheon as Pollock, Rothko or Warhol. His work eludes the group reinforcement of trends, genres and movements: too private, too humble, too singular, too self-contained. In compensation, his boxes and their internal contents reinforce the strangeness and significance of personal symbolism within a society that reduces the individual to feelings of powerlessness and perplexity.

private music

Some of the vaudevillian spirit of the Hollywood samplers, albeit from a less garish, more melancholic English source, can be heard in the early music of Gavin Bryars. Steve Beresford cites *Marvellous Aphorisms Are Scattered Richly Through These Pages* – as an inspirational example of a piece that connects the private to the public, the secret to the open and evident. Essentially a coat that opened to reveal small, quiet sound-making devices, this piece could be performed as part of a broader work called *Private Music*, a set of instructions that specified private sources such as earphones, headphones, scents, food and drink, even telepathy and spiritualism. 'Simply keep your privacy private,' wrote Bryars, 'depriving others of the possibility of your privacy.'

Composed between 1970 and 1974, *Jesus' Blood Never Failed Me Yet* is a composition for pre-recorded voice and chamber orchestra. The song, so frail that a fall into some terrible abyss seems imminent yet also full of hope and wonder, was sung by an elderly tramp. The recording was made in 1970 by a friend of Bryars', Alan Power, who was making a film about homeless people in London. Affected by the performance, Bryars found it was roughly in tune with itself and with the piano and so looped a section which was transferred onto a full reel of tape.

The original version of the piece Bryars composed around this sample was orchestrated for a small ensemble that gradually adds to the voice, then recorded in 1971 as the soundtrack to an independent film by Steve Dwoskin. Subsequent recordings included a release on Brian Eno's Obscure label in 1975 and a more recent version with added vocals by Tom Waits. The poignant simplicity of the Obscure version can't be beaten, however, and it was for sleeve notes for the CD issue of this record in 1998 that I interviewed Bryars.

Compositionally, the work can be traced back to Erik Satie's *Vexations*, performed in the 1970s in all of its 840 repetitions by Bryars and Christopher Hobbs, or with the marching band juxtapositions and vocal multilayering of Charles Ives. In *Experimental Music*, Michael Nyman tells a story of Charles Ives' father, George Ives, which echoes the decision of Bryars to promote the old tramp's religious singing to featured soloist in a concert piece. 'When someone asked him [George Ives] could he stand hearing old John Bell (who was the best stonemason in town) bellow off-key at camp meetings, he answered: "Old John is a supreme musician. Look into his face and hear the music of the ages. Don't pay too much attention to the sounds. If you do, you may miss the music."'

Imagined as a kind of pop art, *Jesus' Blood Never Failed Me Yet* could be linked with the work of Robert Rauschenberg, Claus Oldenberg and Ed Keinholz. Their methodology was, as Bryars says, 'the idea of assemblage, and taking iconic things and recycling them'. He had first heard the recording of the tramp on a tape recorder abandoned by bassist David Holland, who had left London for America to play with Miles Davis. Bryars had hoped that the song would be suitable for a composition idea inspired by a patriotic American war film called *The Sands of Iwo Jima*. 'As the credits come up at the end,' Bryars recalled, 'you have the distant sound of the Mormon Tabernacle Choir singing, "John Brown's Body Lies A-Moldering In the Grave", very quietly coming towards the microphone, and in the sky behind the credits you see the projection of all these heroes who have died in the battle, fading up and down. It was so incredibly over the top that I thought I'd like to write a piece that did that. It builds and builds until it becomes almost too much.' In fact, the dignity of the piece and its emotional force demanded an approach that was more subtle, less intellectually distanced from its source. Like a strange music hall act, a Little Tich who has lost his way in the world yet found redemption at the last, the old man is caught now in a pocket of frozen time, encircling the same landmark of faith with undiminished ardour and doughty persistence. Perhaps for this reason, the impact of the piece has grown as steadily over time as the arc of the work itself.

bird of paradise

Thanks to the efforts of Gary Todd and his Organ of Corti label in California, a hidden side of composer Terry Riley has emerged in recent years. Most people who know Riley's music will associate it with the American minimalists of the 1960s, the group of composers that included La Monte Young, Philip Glass, Steve Reich, Charlemagne Palestine, Terry Jennings and Tony Conrad. But the Riley records that almost became pop hits for the psychedelic generation – *In C* and *Rainbow In Curved Air* – were preceded by less easily defined experiments in sound sampling.

For *Bird of Paradise*, for example, he extracted small fragments from re-recordings of the Junior Walker and the All Stars Motown hit of 1965, 'Shotgun'. These were edited into tape loops, then accumulative feedback and distortion were added. All recognisable elements were fused into dark, grainy smudges of noise, simply by feeding the tape from one tape recorder to another, then feeding the signal from the second back to the first. A staunch fan of Terry Riley once described the Junior Walker track to me as a 'trashy pop thing'. Ironically, this kind of snobbish, high art/low art attitude was exactly what Riley was undermining with his all-night semi-improvised performances and electrified sound, his hippie image and the packaging of his records as rock albums. All the evidence suggests that Riley was well aware that the original track was rich with potential, as avant-garde in its own way as anything he was attempting. Walker's blazing tenor saxophone (considerably more accomplished than Riley's soprano playing) was directly descended from the R&B honking of 50s players like Rufus Gore and Big Jay McNeely, yet the song moves with an unfamiliar, disjointed feel, both in its brash aggression and strange lyrics. In his study of the Motown sound, *Where Did Our Love Go?*, Nelson George professes to be baffled by the lyric. 'All we can ascertain,' he writes, 'is that it relates to shooting something, then to putting on a red dress and high-heeled shoes, then to picking tomatoes and then to something Walker called "Twine Time".' Perhaps George is being disingenuous here, but what seems pretty clear is that Walker is singing about a night out with his girlfriend. With a randomised set of verbal cues similar to those used by James Brown and Rufus Thomas in records of the mid-1960s, Walker jump cuts from the name of one dance craze to another without too much anxiety about narrative logic. As for 'Twine Time', that was the name of a record released earlier the same year by Alvin Cash and the Crawlers, a group that specialised in dance-craze discs, so Walker is already sampling, to some extent, by referencing other episodes in the quick evolution of contemporary trends.

Through the intimate interplay between external source material and host composition, sound sampling can be a dissection, subversion and reconstruction of such historical associations. To erase the starting point of the process reasserts an obsolescent cultural hierarchy, as well as ignoring the complex symbiotic nature of the relationship between sampled, sampler and listener. The American cross-dressing composer Terre Thaemlitz talks specifically about this issue in the notes written for his 1998 recording 'Resistance To Change', a Billy Joel deconstruction released on the *Means From An End* album. '"I Love You Just the Way You Are", by Billy Joel, was chosen for its general ability to evoke a pleasant sense of nostalgia,' he writes, 'as well as for its historical lack of appeal as an "anti-Feminist" anthem against concepts of change. A resistance to social change may be fuelled more by a fear of unfamiliarity than any conspiratorial malice or cultural consensus that things are "fine as they are".' Transformations moving towards social change may need to engage in nostalgia, he claims, since radical breaks with the past repress powerful desires that threaten to erupt as conservative backlashes. 'The difficulty,' he concludes, 'lies in adapting deconstructive discourses which evoke a sense of nostalgia sufficient to establish familiarity without overwhelming the resultant scenario with a desire for the past.' In stages, the Billy Joel original emerges through spoken textual theory and electronic processing, to reveal itself through those saxophone and keyboard hooks and key lyrics strong enough to survive the most extreme masking.

The result is familiar from the atmosphere of dreams in which a song can be heard in blurred fragments, too elusive to be fully enjoyed but sufficiently clear to signal some communication between unconscious and repressed desires. In 1967, Terry Riley performed one of his all-night concerts for soprano saxophone and tape loop time-lag accumulator at the Philadelphia Art School, calling himself Poppy Nogood. Among the audience was the owner of a local disco. Impressed by the performance, he commissioned Riley to compose a 'theme' for his nightclub. For his source material, Riley deconstructed an obscure Philadelphia soul 45, a gritty, mid-tempo male–female 'argument' duet with a dismissive chorus: 'You're no good, I have to cut you loose, what's the use.'

Playing a Moog synthesiser that belonged to La Monte Young, Terry Riley opened 'You're Nogood' with a continuous tone in the right channel, a harsh pulse in the left. The drone gradually rises in pitch while the pulse stays steady. Two minutes and 39 seconds in, just when it's starting to get unbearable, the Moog cuts out and the R&B track cuts in. Riley lets it run for a while, perhaps mindful that he's supposed to be recording a theme here. Then as the chorus starts to repeat, he extends it into a loop: 'You're no good' from the female voices, 'You're no good' coming back from the male voice, a classic call-and-response routine in the mould of Ike and Tina Turner or Inez and Charlie Foxx. Riley moves this disputatious exchange around the stereo picture, then overlays other parts of the song on top until it generates the momentum of a vocal vortex.

Just as you're getting used to the unsynchronised layers, he throws in rhythmic pulses of piercing Moog tones, adding echo and delay to the voices, running the track backwards, until the whole piece is a ball of confusion. To administer the knockout he finishes up with a high speed reversed loop and another Moog tone that climbs unsteadily up towards infinity. Created on primitive equipment, the 20-minute piece feels too long and crudely pasted together. On the other hand, the nagging, obsessive incoherence is a heady antidote to the finicky microsurgery that characterises so much contemporary music. For Riley, these experiments were a prelude to composing works of repetitious cycles that could be played in real time by ensembles or soloists. Unreleased for nearly four decades and regarded as merely transitional by Riley himself, they remained underground until their blueprint for the future had already been turned into reality.

the spinvolver myth

Very early one morning in January 2003 I bump into John Oswald and Susanna Hood in the departure lounge of Heathrow Terminal One. They are in transit from Toronto and all of us are on our way to the Transmediale Festival in Berlin. The conversation drifts in that odd way of fatigued and unexpected encounters. John is explaining to me the strategy he has dreamed up for this festival. Instead of making an appearance himself, he will be represented on stage by Susanna. A dancer and performance artist, she will tell the audience she is there to discuss and explain Spinvolver, an invented technology or technique that is sure to appear entirely plausible for an audience hungry for new inventions, breaking news, unknown technical stuff. As they begin to throw questions or abuse, Oswald will feed her with responses from the wings via an earpiece. At breakfast in the hotel the next morning, Susanna tells me that the performance will certainly be awkward. There will be pauses. Nobody will understand what is happening.

The idea is founded on John's reluctance to appear as a performer of his plunderphonics recordings. These recordings are dense, sometimes inconceivably dense overlays of recordings made by other artists, edited and transformed in a variety of ways both intellectually and technically by Oswald in his Toronto-based Mystery Lab. There is absolutely no possibility of recreating this work in real-time performance and so every request for a 'performance' creates a dilemma. He tells me about a performance he gave in Switzerland, an untidy and difficult affair that provoked some members of the audience into heckling. There was a saxophone on stage, he said, and from time to time he would ask the audience if he should play it. The response was negative every time. Nobody wants me to play my saxophone any more, he complained with a smile.

Some ideas have a very difficult and protracted passage into the wider world. Back in 1969, Oswald began editing and reconstructing recordings made by other artists. Preceded by privately circulated cassette tapes such as 'Kissing Jesus In The Dark' and 'Dab', Oswald's first 'official' release of his experiments in plunderphonia began with the 4-track vinyl record *Plunderphonics* distributed free in 1988. A year later, he released the notorious *Plunderphonic* CD, again a free distribution to friends, critics, DJs, libraries and those musicians who had been plundered (the living ones, anyway). The dramatic consequences of this are fairly well known but worth rehashing. Thanks to a bit of gutter journalism, the *Plunderphonic* album came to the attention of Brian Robertson, president of the Canadian Recording Industry Association. Robertson held the opinion that Oswald's reconfigurations of recordings made by other artists constituted a form of theft and since that was their primary purpose (a judgement made without any reference to a considerable body of evidence to the contrary) they should be curtailed. In particular, this assertion of piracy focussed on Oswald's reconstruction of Michael Jackson's 'Bad', and by Christmas of that year the CRIA had demanded that Oswald give up all his remaining CDs, plus the master tapes, in order for them to be crushed.

Thirteen years later, a licensed and legal box set was advertised. Contained within would be remastered, often remade material from both previous releases, along with tracks from the *Elektrax* CDEP released as an Elektra Records commission in 1990, *Plexure* from 1990, a snippet from *Grayfolded*, the Grateful Dead reconstruction of 1994, and a few other things besides. This was a release that could barely be imagined as a legitimate possibility – in the absence of any acceptable or workable new model for the administration of intellectual copyright, the most powerful sectors of the record business were intractable on this issue of copyright. Although this was not Oswald's intention, his work had become a landmark statement to counter the inflexible and selective protectionism of organisations such as the CRIA. More important, this was a substantial, innovative body of music that had been withheld from its potential audience for far too long. Sure enough, things didn't go entirely to plan. After a delay, the CDs ended up being released through another outlet, the record company owned by another act notorious for sampling copyright work, Negativland.

Oswald's deeper reasons for subjecting familiar material to a variety of technical processes that reflect complex relationships to the original artists, to the chosen track and to wider issues relating to recording, music making, authorship, celebrity, the psychology of perception and the construction of multiple meanings are variable. Sometimes he has a strongly sympathetic feeling for the artist he chooses, or when he doesn't, as in the case of The Grateful Dead, he finds a quality in the piece of music he is transforming and then develops it to an extreme that can enhance the artist for an unconverted listener. He is a Beatles fan, for example, and the rich mythology of The Beatles adds countless layers of suggestion to his reconstruction of their songs. His choice of George Harrison's 'Blue Jay Way' is revealing, since the song experiments with studio effects, stylistic borrowing and repetition yet never quite rises to its initial promise. In this case, Oswald does what many pop fans dream of doing at those times when their heroes fail to deliver. He takes out the bad parts and emphasises the good.

This is a little bit like the Japanese noise artist Merzbow building an entire career on the moments when The Who or Jimi Hendrix Experience unleashed a chaos of destruction and feedback, though Oswald also rebuilds the artists from the ruins he engenders, as well as offering surprisingly new twists on their potential. Without Oswald, maybe we would have no Ricky Martin or Shania Twain, since these corporate composites of our synthetic times are prefigured by the plunderphonic vortex of androgyny embodied in such monsters as Bing Stingspreen, Jello Bellafonte, the male Dolly Parton or the country/jack-swing hybrid of Garth Brooks and Bobby Brown that adorned *Plexure*.

But Oswald also delights in the intellectual application of radically transformative processes to the fruitful redundancy of familiar music. So he will make edits using only the beginning of each bar of music, separate a song into tiny segments and reverse them all or condense a long sprawling piece into an incredibly condensed miniature. Oswald has always acknowledged the influence of fellow Canadian artist Michael Snow and there are persuasive connections between their respective methods. Snow is a musician and film maker. A pivotal statement for structural film, his 1966 film *Wavelength* was a 45-minute continuous zoom from a wide shot within a room, eventually narrowing to a close-up of a photograph of the sea, pinned to the wall. The soundtrack was sync sound combined with a sine wave that rises gradually from 50 cycles per second to 12,000. This relentless application of process contrasts with Snow's commitment to free improvisation. A similar paradox applies to Oswald, the free improvising saxophonist, who abhors the notion of adding his own playing to his plunderphonic works, yet whose improviser's logic and love of pure sound informs every moment of these two CDs.

In 1987, Snow also created an entire album of fakes in a record called *The Last LP*. 'The title of this album refers to the disappearance of the 33⅓ microgroove vinyl/stylus format,' Snow wrote in the notes to the CD reissue. 'This recording was issued in the last days of the LP and was conceived of then as an investigation into the effects (both negative and positive) of "Western" recording technology on the world's few remaining, at the time of recording, ancient pre-industrial cultures. Technological forced obsolescence (in the case of sound recording: wax cylinders gave way to 78 rpm disks, to 33⅓ LPs to various magnetic tape systems, to the CD) interestingly resembles the effects of the technology-based societies on the ancient traditional cultures.' The music documented on the LP includes a performance of Raga Lalat by Palak Chawal, interrupted by a terrorist explosion in which Chawal and all the accompanying musicians were killed; a Cree people gargling ceremony; Buddhist monks from Tibet, exiled in Bhutan, performing the welcome of Amitahba, and the Roiakuriluo dawn ceremony of the Sabane people of the north-eastern Brazilian rainforest. Of course, these recordings are all fakes made in Toronto by Snow and his friends, most of them fairly unconvincing, and the copious ethnomusicological notes to each track are erudite nonsense.

There is a strong element of fakery in Oswald's plunderphonics in the sense that he is manufacturing ambiguous new identities, though he never claims the music is anything other than its old and new self, and each track contains many clues to its original sources. What the copyright protectors could not understand was the importance of familiarity in Oswald's electroquote methodology. We need to recognise the source material, if only by the thinnest trace memory, for plunderphonics to work. As music insinuates itself into our deepest inner life, so a part of its creation passes over from author to perceiver. The financial transaction that rewards authorship and ownership can only be a partial representation of this subtle, uneven relationship. Little stabs of happiness, Oswald's painstakingly fanatical surgeries suggest new myths that truly justify our love.

death and the groove
a drawing is a record   a record is a drawing

> 'There was a racket fit to wake the dead. The gramophones tried
> to drown each other out.'
>
> From *Dan Yack*, by Blaise Cendrars, 1919

Mike Hammer, Mickey Spillane's tough guy private eye, suffered few scruples. There is a scene in Robert Aldrich's 1955 film of *Kiss Me Deadly* in which Hammer prises information from an old man. He holds back from physical force, though he's quite capable of that. He needs a lead, knows the old man has it, knows he won't give it up without a struggle. 'I know nothing,' says the old man, 'Nothing!' Hammer knows he's dealing with a passionate opera lover, so he starts on the old guy's record collection. 'Quite a stack a records you got here,' he says. 'Hey! Caruso's *Pagliacci*. That's a collector's item.' Snap it goes, broken in half. The old man crumbles. 'Please, what you wanta to know?' All the information Hammer needs pours out, lanced like an abscess.

A violent scene in a violent film, but something about the ruthlessness touches a sensitive nerve. Unlike CDs and other digital playback formats, the record is an object that perfectly symbolises and embodies its morbid role in the preservation and transmission of sonic culture. A spiral scratch, its gleaming dark circle is the black hole into which memories are poured, only to emerge again as ghost voices, life preserved beyond death. Frozen in time within the grooves, a voice, an instrument, a sound, becomes the living dead and is worshipped in the way that a loved one, deceased, may be adored for years by the bereaved.

From the earliest days in his working life, Christian Marclay has played with, and upon, such elements of sound, its visual manifestations, its metaphorical and symbolic significance, its central place in the documentation and fabrication of memory. 'Marclay's work with found photographs and found sound often explores the themes of absence and loss that always haunt the recorded object,' wrote Christophe Cox in his catalogue essay for *Audible Imagery: Sound and Photography*, shown in 2001 at the Museum of Contemporary Photography, Columbia College, Chicago.

Marclay's *Record Without A Cover*, first released in 1985, was a perfect illustration of this. On a 12-inch vinyl record, all the information relevant to the work was embossed in a spiral on the side without grooves. This included the title of the work; the instruction: 'Do not store in a protective package'; the technical nature of the content: 'Manipulated records on multiple turntables'; along with the usual details of where, when, how and who with. In one sense, the work was a mechanically reproduced artefact conforming to all the standardised procedures of the entertainment industry, yet the instruction to leave the record unprotected broke the first rule of record collecting.

Over time, the record gathers dust and dirt, scratches and perhaps more serious damage. In other words, it has a life that extends beyond the usual point of closure that occurs as soon as a recording enters the manufacturing and marketing stage of its existence. The sound, itself an aetherial, faintly nostalgic montage of previously existing recordings that includes a lot of surface noise, transforms over time according to the level of abuse the artefact receives at the hands of its owner. I've had mine since the mid-80s. Some years ago I used to lay it on a pile of 12-inch singles by the window. Soaking up the rays as the sun moved over the house in the mornings, it made an attractively warm bullseye on which our cat would sit and gaze out of the window at birds in the cherry tree. A lot of unmentionable stuff got embedded in the grooves through that particular example of functionality and when she was out trying to catch those birds, sunshine warped the disc into a picturesque wave. And then there's the dust, collecting on the record, as a testimony to my ambivalent attitude to order.

Throughout the history of recorded music, we have been encouraged to take care of our records, to protect them from dust, dirt and grease. Marclay's wit surfaces here, since he is acutely aware of the strictures of serious collecting (whether for obsessive or financial motives), but also an amused witness, surely, to the way in which male collectors of vinyl would implore their wives, girlfriends or children to replace a record in its correct sleeve, not leave it on the turntable or on the coffee table as a convenient resting place for cigarette butts, coffee cups and half-eaten bananas. This is Grandmaster Flash, speaking in *Yes Yes Y'all: Oral History of Hip-Hop's First Decade*: 'From what my big sisters tell me, I must have been in my single digits, and I got interested in this object called a record. My father had his prize collection of records. He knew I loved whenever the stereo was turned on – when I was a little baby I used to get in the centre of the room, and I used to start dancing. But he would say to me, "Listen, don't ever touch my records."

'I used to watch where he put these prized records – it was a closet near the front door. So when my father went to work, I would go grab a chair out of the kitchen, against my mother's instruction and my bigger sisters saying, "Don't go in there touching Daddy's records," and I used to drag this chair to this closet, just high enough for me to turn the knob, and then get down, go in there, get a record. And I would crawl over to the stereo, and I would just put any record on, and I would start dancing.

'So early on my father used to say, "If I catch you in there, I'm going to give you a beating, give you a spanking." My mother was able to protect me, up to a point ... So after a while, the yelling started turning into serious beatings. Like beatings, beatings, beatings, to the point where I was like almost unconscious. My pop used to really bust my behind, and that used to cause a lot of problems between my mother and my father. In some reverse sort of way, I learned the value of a record because he used to bust my behind for me so much.'

Along with this mirror image of Mike Hammer's brutality, *Record Without A Cover* may also remind its owner of times as a student or drop-out, drugged or drunk beyond the point of caring and piling one unclothed record onto another in search of the perfect nocturnal soundtrack.

In a broader context, the release of *Record Without A Cover* coincided with a gradual switch from the supposed imperfections of vinyl to the equally doubtful perfection of digital compact disc, in which the process of sound reproduction is invisible and the extraneous noise floor associated with vinyl recordings – hum, hiss, crackle and scratches – is largely eradicated. Marclay's framed photograph of Simon & Garfunkel's 7-inch single, 'The Sounds of Silence' alludes to the paradox of recording: the capture of a phenomenon no longer in existence, only activated through conscious agency; the silent image of this 'music' that precedes and follows any act of audition; the drive to perfect the so-called signal to noise ratio, implying an end point of perfectly recorded, perfectly reproduced, silence.

Records are like birds that carry the spirits of the dead. Among a host of complex reasons for accumulating them as objects, sometimes divorced from the sounds they carry, they become precious for their capacity to mediate between corporeality and aether. In simple terms, they are a passage to emotional fulfilment. To break one is to commit a sin, though records are made to be broken, as they say in sport. In the early 1960s the Czechoslovakian artist Milan Knizak began breaking records. He called this Broken Music, or Destroyed Music. A photograph shows one of these records sitting on a little portable record player, the black surface scored, scratched and pitted, the course of its grooves impeded by two strips of masking tape. To play this record would probably destroy the record player needle, which was Knizak's intention, yet the photograph is an invitation to hear what this music might sound like, assuming the needle survived, in which case these acts of destruction were a beginning, rather than an ending.

Records transmigrate: the sound of jukeboxes in bars, the sounds of radios on which the signals would fade, swell, decay and merge; later, the way records were mixed by the first disco DJs, fusing into each other, losing their identity, approaching a state of anonymity, a state of flux. The composer begins to vanish. Based in Liverpool, Philip Jeck collects old record players, the Dansette type with an automatic arm and a stacking device that allowed more or less continuous play, at least for the sequence of up to 10 45rpm singles sandwiched together on the central spindle. His speciality is to create a literal wall of sound from these record players, homage to Phil Spector of course, but more specifically a simultaneity of discarded records collected from charity shops and car boot sales, an oceanic wash of recorded fragments caught in a Groundhog Day of mechanical loops. Jeck makes the loops with small strips of tape and similar rudimentary techniques. These force the stylus or arm back to the starting point, though why these multiple layers of random fragments and surface noise from old records should sound so mournful, as if neglected memories collecting in the air had suddenly erupted into cloudy nostalgia, is a mystery.

'More Encores', released by Christian Marclay in 1989, was a collection of tracks named after the artists whose music was used to create each respective track. 'John Cage' was produced by cutting slices from several John Cage records, then gluing them back together into one disc. Simultaneously, Cage's dedication to chance is honoured and the tendency of recorded music to become a library of fragments, mixing, overlapping and perhaps becoming confused in the mind of the listener overwhelmed by so much sonic history, is made material.

Memory is the most potent element of the recording age. Performance itself began to change quickly once recording artists realised that mistakes captured and embedded in shellac would be heard over and over again by listeners. In his book, *A Century of Recorded Music*, Timothy Day quotes the French composer, Francis Poulenc: 'We are all,' he wrote in 1938, 'victims of the treachery of "the wax".' The memory of a single recorded work accumulates in inverse proportion to the fading memory of the original act. 'Footsteps', released on vinyl in 1989, was both document and artwork in itself. Marclay had covered the floor of one of the Shedhalle galleries in Zurich with 3500 copies of 'Footsteps', a 12-inch vinyl record of previously recorded footsteps mixed with the sound of Keiko Uenishi's tapdancing. Dedicated to Fred Astaire, the silent records acted as a border, almost a minefield, which had to be crossed either to 'view' Marclay's exhibition or to look at exhibits in the other galleries. At the end of the exhibition, these records were collected up, boxed and sold, complete with the damage and visible footprints of the 1500 visitors who passed over this inert audio floor.

What Walter Benjamin called the aura of art is despoiled by art believers who come to worship at its altar. Like the early Catholics in Japan who were forced to step onto images of Christ, they are compelled to break their faith, their footsteps on identical records the proof of Benjamin's proposition: 'that which withers in the age of mechanical reproduction is the aura of the work of art.' Walking on this exhibit broke one of the fundamental rules of art gallery attendance – that the works on display should not be harmed – yet the contradiction of the piece lies in the fact that this destructive physical contact only becomes audible when the objects are fetishised as a limited edition, boxed recording, some signed and numbered and available for sale to record collectors. This invited tension between destructive impulses versus art fetishisation or the commercialisation of music products is inherent in much of Marclay's work. Born in California in 1955, Marclay was raised in Switzerland, where he attended the Ecole Supérieure d'Art Visuel, before moving to Boston, then New York. In some respects his work explores impulses similar to those prominent in the work of the Swiss artist Jean Tinguely. Focussed obsessively on the machine age, Tinguely's work revealed the inherent self-destructiveness of mechanisation and modernism. His machines, many of them colossal, either threatened to drive themselves to oblivion or Tinguely would hasten the process. 'Life is play, movement, continual change,' Tinguely told Calvin Tomkins at the beginning of the 1960s. 'Only the fear of death makes us want to stop life, to "fix" it impossibly forever. The moment life is fixed, it is no longer true; it is dead, and therefore uninteresting.'

Assigned by a newspaper in the early 1990s to cover the story of Chris Blackwell's sale of Island Records to the corporate umbrella of Polygram, I wrote notes as a record executive took his opportunity to boost the CD format as a logical successor to vinyl. I cannot believe, he said, that formats involving the friction of tape passing over playback heads or a needle in a groove can be superior to a CD. Perhaps if he had experienced a vision of the future at that moment, a vision of digital media such as MP3s grinding huge holes in the profits of record companies, he might not have been so confident.

Record player design encapsulates the idea of self-destruction in perpetuity. The needle ploughs through the spiralled groove, wearing away both itself and the message it transmits. At the end of Carol Reed's 1947 film of Graham Greene's *Brighton Rock*, the young, violent gangster at the centre of the story, 'Pinkie' Brown, makes a record in a recording booth. These record-your-own voice booths were once set up in public places such as railway stations. 'The booths closely resembled photo booths,' wrote Steve Beresford in *Leonardo Music Journal*, 'and one could record around 2 minutes of music. I think there was a clock which counted down the time. Maybe the machine played it back before dispensing it. I don't remember which year Gavin Bryars devised his version of Alvin Lucier's *I Am Sitting In A Room*, involving recording something in a booth and then recording it over and over. I think that my main attraction to the machine was that it produced an artificially aged artefact, like a Joseph Cornell, although I doubt I knew that name in 1974.'

Pinkie marries a waitress called Rose, though he has no feelings for her other than contempt and fear that she could send him to prison. Shortly before he dies he records this message: 'God damn you, you little bitch, why can't you go home for ever and let me be?' In the book, she walks home to hear this record, believing it will be a last message of love and devotion. Pressured by censors and his own misgivings, Greene decided this ending would be too strong for the film's audience. In his script, he added a scratch to the record. The posthumous razor cut Pinkie aims at his doting wife is transformed into a slash in the record, a gouge into the circling blackness that entraps and neuters his viciousness, allowing Rose to continue loving him beyond the grave.

Decay follows death as an inscription on the body. 'A drawing is a recording of some sort,' Marclay has said, 'and a record is a kind of drawing; the groove is like an etching, but the difference is the extra dimension of sound, the sound transcends the object. The elusive vibrations of that spiral drawing need to be decoded by a turntable. This type of drawing needs a machine to make it vibrate into life. Or if it's a score, it needs a performer to interpret it. But when you watch somebody drawing or playing music, you can still identify with their physical presence.'

Christian Marclay's *Guitar Drag*, a video piece created in 2000 for Sonic Boom, the sound art exhibition I curated for the Hayward Gallery in London, pushes these themes of death, destruction, iconography, implicit (or explicit) silence and explicit (or implicit) noise to an extreme. A Fender Stratocaster guitar is tied by its neck and roped to the back of a pick-up truck. On the back of the truck is an amplifier and the guitar is plugged into the amp. The video shows these preparations, then shows the truck driving off through a dusty landscape, dragging the guitar behind it. A bellowing, crashing roar of pain and rage maps the aural progress of this strange rite as the amplified guitar bumps over stones, crashes into obstacles. Immediately, many images spring to mind. Some of them relate to artists briefly associated with the Destruction In Art movement of the 1960s: Tinguely, Gustav Metzger, John Latham. But the iconography is more specific: the guitarist and the gunslinger; a racist killing in Texas, 1998, in which a black man – James Byrd Jr. – was tied to the back of a truck by drunken whites, who drove away at speed (the victim's head and other body parts were later found on the road they travelled); Billie Holiday's southern trees bearing 'Strange Fruit', blood on the leaves and blood at the root; Jimi Hendrix, bouncing his Fender Stratocaster off the stage at the Monterey Pop Festival, then setting it on fire; the pre-climactic scene in Sam Peckinpah's film, *The Wild Bunch*, in which the Mexican revolutionary, Angel, is dragged behind the car of the dictator, Mapache; Jayne Mansfield beheaded in a car crash near New Orleans. The confused mythos of the electric guitar intersects with the persistent mythos of the old American West and its lonesome roads.

As an improvising performer on turntables, working over the years with musicians including John Zorn, Keiji Haino, Elliot Sharp, William Hooker and Otomo Yoshihide, Marclay once alluded to the slightly comical image of gunslinger guitarist by posing with a customised 'phonoguitar' turntable. Ironically, post-hip-hop turntablist dexterity, speed and flash has displaced guitar heroics as the central arena of gunslinger shoot-outs, confirming Marclay's original intuition that the record (somebody else's music) and its mechanical means of reproduction is one of the prime sites of 20th, now 21st-century music. But two other images come to my mind when I watch *Guitar Drag*: I think of Fluxus performance, Nam June Paik nonchalantly dragging a violin on a string behind him, bumping it over concrete, or a Fluxus group event, *Kicking Robin Page's guitar around the block*, performed at the Yam Festival in New York, May 1965. An acoustic guitar was kicked past the Museum of Modern Art and the Whitney, around the block and so on, until only the back of the guitar survived. Snap the record in half, why not? The collector may be wounded but musical life can begin again.

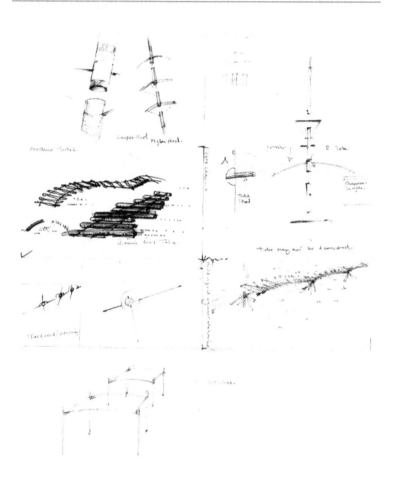

Max Eastley
Nagoya notebook

5 Growth and complexity

> 'Music is a hidden exercise in mathematics by minds unconscious of dealing with numbers.'
>
> Gottfried Wihelm Leibnitz

In the early 90s I interviewed Salif Keita, the remarkable singer from Mali. I was asking him about the relationship between the music he made in France, using a lot of synthesised sounds, and the music he made earlier in his career. 'Whatever the branch is, the tree takes its roots from the same place anyway,' he replied. For some time, this answer bothered me. Clearly, he was speaking personally, about a strongly centred approach to music that could survive all kinds of migration, cultural influence, political oppression and technological evolution, yet this was also a central philosophy of so-called world music, in itself a confused mix of folk forms, pop hybrids, religious rituals and rock stars. In fact, world music also falls under the rubric of roots music – not even a diasporic outgrowth but improbably, still fixed deeply into the soil as a point of origin despite the passing of years and the invasive ubiquity of mass media and consumerism.

Giving his own amusing analysis of this subject, musician and vocalist Robert Wyatt has said that vegetables have roots, so are stuck in the ground, whereas humans have legs, so enjoy the freedom to move around and change themselves and their environment. An alternative to the tree metaphor and its 'arborescent rootedness' was proposed by the French philosophers Gilles Deleuze and Félix Guattari in their book *A Thousand Plateaus: Capitalism and Schizophrenia*, first published in English translation in 1987. Rhizomes, the underground stems of plants such as grasses and bamboo, grow laterally in lines, have no central, governing point or hierarchical organisation. 'They defy categorisation as individuated entities,' writes Sadie Plant in *Zeroes + Ones*. 'These plants are populations, multiplicities, rather than unified upright things.' Observing the rhizomatic growth of plants in my garden I can note their creeping progress over time, discovering new shoots appearing far from the original plant, sometimes like delicate islands, sometimes (in the case of bamboo) like aggressive spears invading forbidden territory. In Japan, certain species of aggressively invasive bamboo are notorious for spreading under tarmac roads and bursting through the surface.

The model of deterritorialised alliances, transverse movement, networks and non-hierarchical structuring that attaches itself to this natural phenomenon has become a central tenet of digital music theory and the geo-communities of the Internet. Artists working in this field often 'compose' through exchanges of sound files, sample and resample and resample again in a continual diffusion of material always embedded with the genetic code of an original, process existing samples, incorporate the accidents of digital glitching, collaborate in shifting networks. Although the theory clarifies digital sound work, it also applies to earlier musical strategies that have contributed to this work: the non-hierarchical growth within dub mixes and disco remixes, for example, or the continually shifting networks of improvisation, non-hierarchical in its structure and always oriented towards lateral movement rather than static, centralised rootedness.

Few sound artists are actually gardeners but Carsten Nicolai is an exception. Born in the industrial town of Karl-Marx-Stadt, East Germany, in 1965, he studied landscape design from 1985 to 1990. Under the name of Alva Noto he works with vibration, light and the physiological effect of intense sound waves heard in empty space. His *empty garden (inside. out)* was created in 1999 as an installation for the Watari-um Museum of contemporary art in Tokyo. The sound – crystalline, sparse yet powerful clicks, pops and brief high tones placed precisely in a three-dimensional field – led people along a designated route. The effect is analogous to a Japanese dry garden, albeit starkly contemporary. In her description of a contemporary dry stone garden created by designer Yoshiji Takehara on the slopes of Hieizan, a sacred mountain near Kyoto, Michiko Rico Nosé explains the Japanese term *tachidomaru*. 'This word is a combination of "stand" and "stop" and means "to pause, stop, and look back",' she writes. 'One feature found in temples' – and Takehara draws attention in particular to the Daitoku temple in Kyoto – 'is that the route that has to be taken to reach one part or another is always circuitous, with twists and turns, so that progress towards the destination always contains the unexpected.'

In Nicolai's installation work, this feeling of a hidden element is an important aspect of the impact of the pieces. In Tokyo, at the Sound Art – Sound As Media exhibition at ICC in 2000, he exhibited a huge glass flask containing water. Low frequency sine tones were directed at the water through long tubes. Although the sounds were barely audible, the wave forms they created on the water surface were made visible through light shining on the water, then reflected onto a wall. I asked him if his training as a landscape designer overlapped onto his sound work. 'Landscape architecture and gardening,' he replied, 'is still about space and the complexity of thinking.'

decomposition   deterioration   decay

In 1986, Jae-eun Choi, a Korean artist and film maker, initiated a series of experiments that she calls the World Underground Project. She buried sheets of Japanese paper in the soil of eleven locations around the world. The first pieces were excavated from the site in Kyong-Ju, Korea, after four years. Others, including those buried at sites in Kenya, France and Italy, were still underground in 1998. Japanese paper begins with a strong character, before a single mark is made on, or into its surface. The absorbency and texture encourages accident and generates unpredictability. Those sheets that were excavated had been transformed by the years of their interment into gorgeous maps of organic growth.

'According to Chinese myth,' wrote Akira Asada in a commentary on the World Underground Project, 'in an attempt literally to give the featureless face of Chaos eyes and a nose, a new hole was dug into his face each day, until finally, when its features were completed, Chaos died. In order to capture Chaos, human beings cannot inscribe order into it. Not to represent it ourselves, but to let it represent itself naturally. In this way, Jae-eun Choi is attempting to capture living Chaos.'

Now think about Japanese paper in relation to compact discs. Unless the silver disc malfunctions or aborts, the promise of this carrier is to remain true to an original state throughout its so-called life. False optimism, no doubt, but aside from the occasions when they go drastically wrong, CDs don't exhibit the slight variations in playback sound and gradual deteriorations and fluctuations that characterise vinyl and tape. A CD is more or less a dead thing, or seems that way until it really dies.

At the polar opposite of that inertia is Christian Marclay's *Record Without A Cover*. Just from a simple instruction embossed on the surface of the vinyl – 'Do not store in a protective package' – a supposedly 'final' artefact is transformed into an ongoing musical piece that the initiator cannot control. Like an awful lot of music enthusiasts, in my own house I'm vanishing into a vast housing estate of miniature tower blocks built from CDs. The more oppressive this static, one-sided arrangement seems to become, the more I'm interested in the idea of a music that can generate itself over time, giving itself up to the user in the way that Jae-eun Choi's Japanese paper surrenders to a colony of micro-organisms under the earth.

The notion of music that can be generated by an instruction or set of rules is not particular to our time. Within their description of Vox Populi, an interactive evolutionary system for algorithmic music composition, four Brazilian researchers give the example of Guido d'Arezzo, an Italian monk who, in 1026, 'resorted to using a number of simple rules to map liturgical texts in Gregorian chants due to the overwhelming number of orders he received for his compositions'. Guido d'Arezzo believed that his method of finding what he called an 'unknown melody' was given to him by God, so forestalling any impulse to own, copyright and police the system. Instead, he offered his 11th-century shareware in a spirit of generosity, with apologies for his unavoidable absence, but adding the caveat that his monochord based method could help beginners but was no substitute for proper music study.

dust breeding   glitch

In 1920, Marcel Duchamp moved to a new apartment in Manhattan. The Large Glass on which he was working was laid flat. 'For three months he let dust accumulate on the lower panel,' wrote Calvin Tomkins in *Duchamp: A Biography*, 'so that he could glue it down (with varnish) over the funnel-like sieves, thus giving them a colour arrived at by chance and by time.' May Ray, then seeing Duchamp nearly every day, had recently discovered a talent for photography. 'He came over one day,' wrote Tomkins, 'with his big view camera and, using only the light from a single hanging bulb, took a time exposure of the *Glass*'s lower panel, which had been lying flat on workhorses collecting dust. The resulting image was like a lunar landscape, with hills, valleys, and mysterious marking in low relief.' Duchamp gave this joint work the name *Elevage de Poussière* (*Dust Breeding*), then fixed the dust with varnish in preparation for the next phase of the work.

In 1995, Markus Popp, Sebastian Oschatz and Franz Metzger of Oval released an album on the Mille Plateaux label. The title was, or seemed to be, *94diskont*. The melancholy, circular sound of the CD, like a complex music box drowning in its own sadness, was created by Berlin resident Markus Popp, who believed that music was finished. The era of synthesisers, drum machines and other forms of electronic equipment was history. Electronic music had become so abstracted, so distant from what it once seemed to be, that it made far better sense to call it audio.

Diskont was created by Popp from CDs. He had noticed the tendency of CDs to skip at random across the entire programme on an album, or to get stuck in one spot, then stutter at a furious rate until the user could be bothered to move it on or press eject. This fairly common fault revealed the random nature of digital information. When a vinyl record sticks, we can see exactly what is happening. The needle is trying to move forward through the spiral groove but something like a scratch across the record or a lump of fluff accumulated in the groove stands in the way. The record stick-stick-sticks and we see the cartridge go bump-bump-bump, straining helplessly to continue on its way. The first LP I ever bought, *Chuck Berry Live On Stage*, used to stick at the beginning. I solved this problem by loading coins onto the arm until the needle gouged its way through the obstruction. Naturally, the groove was very swiftly worn down, transforming 'Sweet Little Sixteen' into a blurred, low frequency noise, though this seemed quite compatible with the record as fake documentary, since each track was a studio recording overdubbed with audience applause and released while Berry was in jail.

Audio CDs don't allow this interactivity. Their workings and faults are invisible and inaccessible, and the sticking is either non-sequential, jumping from track 5 to 3 to 7 in random bursts, or a repeating glitch that no longer bears any relation to the original sound of the music. Popp discovered that this effect can be generated and manipulated by damaging the silvered surface of a CD. A similar discovery had been made independently by the Japanese sound artist Yasunao Tone, who released his *Solo for Wounded CD* on Tzadik in 1997. An artist associated with the 1960s Fluxus movement, Tone questioned the separation between music and the visual arts. In the 1950s he had applied the automatism of Jackson Pollock's drip painting to music by forming an improvisation group with Takehisa Kosugi and Shuko Mizuno. Marcel Duchamp's readymades also suggested a way out of the impasse in which music foundered, still trying to detach itself from 19th-century romanticism and the iron embrace of the concert hall. 'I was not satisfied with recording,' he told Alan Licht in *The Wire*, 'because it presupposes to repeat the same sound over and over.'

Tone had studied the error correcting program in CD players, then experimented with sticking Scotch tape perforated with pinpricks onto the playing surface of CDs. As well as misreading and changing the information into bursts of sound, this technique also altered pitch, timbre, speed and directionality of the disc. 'The results are uncontrollable, unrepeatable and unpredictable,' wrote Licht.

'What I wanted to provide was to suggest some additional criteria so music has to be discussed in terms of user interface design, interactivity or on-screen editing,' Popp told me in 2001, discussing his new software that allowed people to make their own Oval music, 'and not so much discussed in terms of frequency or music as we know it. It's not interesting at all for me to discuss music in terms of frequency. I see it as my obligation to provide mildly innovative multimedia authoring.' In response to a query sent to Richard Ross, programmer for Markus Popp's *Oval Process*, my attempt to discover if this software could be described as a generative work, Ross e-mails me back his own question: 'I was wondering what constituted generative music and were computers necessary?' he writes from California. 'I came to the conclusion that if you dispensed with computers as a component of it then things like wind chimes and Aeolian harps might arguably fall into that camp. Other possibilities might be Cage's *Imaginary Landscape No. 4* as a live performance. If generative music is music created on the fly, by some kind of rule based system, then these things follow very loose sorts of rules, but rules none the less.'

In issue 5 of *Musics* magazine, published in 1976, Max Eastley wrote a short history of Aeolian harps, including the story of St. Dunstan, who narrowly avoided incineration at the stake in the Middle Ages for the suspiciously demonic crime of making a harp that played by itself. Eastley also related the interesting case of Ichabod Angus Mackenzie, a sculptor and musician who produced 53 wind sound sculptures in 1934. 'During an interview he was asked if it disturbed him to leave his instruments performing alone without a human audience,' Eastley wrote. 'He replied, "That's up to humans. They're never without an audience."'

This raises some of the core issues challenged by 20th-century music, and 20th-century thought in general: the relationship of the composer to the audience, for example, or the use of chance and accident in the creation of music; the construction of feedback systems or self-generating and adaptive mechanisms that shape sound; the exertion or abdication of control of a musical result; the modelling of music based on eco-systems and similar complex environments and the setting in motion of events that question the definition of music as a cultural production distinguished from noise or sound unorganised by human agency and intentionality.

In the 21st century, such ideas have been expanded dramatically by the evolution of the Internet, in itself a self-propagating web lacking any central command or control. *Sound Drifting* was a large-scale generative sound installation curated by Colin Fallows and Heidi Grundmann for Ars Electronica 99. A web of sub-projects, sourced from six different countries, could be heard simultaneously and continuously, either onsite in Linz, online as a virtual installation or on air via Austrian National Radio. The sub-projects included Seppo Gründler's *Dunes and Redundancy*, a room in which sand was blown by ventilators and vibrated by loudspeakers; Tim Cole's *Intermorphic Koan^Oasis*, composed in real time by his generative SSEYO Koan system; and the orchestrated sounds of the air supply, the extraction system and the chilled water circulation pumps of the plant room in the Liverpool Institute For Performing Arts, recorded on microphones set up by Colin Fallows in an arrangement that replicated the recording method used by the sound engineer with the Liverpool Philharmonic.

'More recently,' the introduction to *Sound Drifting* explained, 'there has been a growing interest in generative systems by artists working with the internet, especially using sound, but increasingly with the appropriation of games software, search engines and so forth. Some of this work is highly critical of the ubiquity and unseemly power of generative systems in modern decision making. But the most conspicuous cultural use of generative systems has been in the field of music – which means that the word "generative", when used in relation to sound, usually causes people to think of music. However, although some music drifted in, *Sound Drifting* was not about "music" – nor was it conceived as a concert hall, showcase or gallery space for the works of individual artists. *Sound Drifting* was about networking, communication and collaboration; about control-sharing between artists, users and machines; about letting go of one's own art and making ecological use of existing things; about listening to the world without adding to it; about the different concepts of duration and evolving processes at work in the material and immaterial realities of which we are part; about the aesthetics of different but connectable sounds, images, texts appearing on line – on air – on site as fugitive interfaces to a complex, invisible and not yet properly understood system of data processing.'

In March 2001, Brian Eno gave a lecture at the ICA in London, linking his ideas on generative music with the model of John Conway's *Game Of Life*. Conway, a Cambridge mathematician, invented *Life* as a cellular automaton, a game regulated by three logical rules: I. Every counter with 2 or 3 neighbouring counters survives to the next generation (i.e. the next move). 2. Every counter with 0 to I neighbours 'dies' (of loneliness) and every counter with 4 or more neighbours dies (of overcrowding). 3. Every empty cell with exactly 3 neighbouring occupied cells gives birth to a new counter. 'With these simple rules of birth, survival and death,' Paul Davies wrote in *God and The New Physics*, 'Conway and his colleagues have discovered the most astonishing richness and variety in the evolution of certain counter configurations.' In other words, out of a set of very basic conditions, or limitations, surprising events will emerge by themselves.

A week after his lecture, sitting in a patch of sunlight outside his studio, speaking on his mobile phone, Brian Eno talks about connections between that proposition, developed from ideas investigated by mathematicians such as John von Neumann and Stanislas Ulam, and the compositions that first sparked his own interest in generative music. 'I think the Steve Reich pieces and Terry Riley's *In C*,' he says. 'I would call those the predecessors of this. I would say anything where the composer doesn't specify a thing from the top down. What I think is different about generative music is that instead of giving a set of detailed instructions about how to make something, what you do instead is give a set of conditions by which something will come into existence.'

The Steve Reich pieces he refers to are the early voice works for tape – *It's Gonna Rain* and *Come Out* – both of which explore the strange accretion of phenomena that occurs when two identical tape loops play in sync but then run progressively out of phase due to slight variations in motor speed in the tape machines. 'I thought the economy of them was so stunning,' says Eno. 'There's so little there. The complexity of the piece appears from nowhere. You think, my God, it's so elegant to make something like that. Of course, I was hearing this at the time when 24-track recording had appeared and people were making huge, vast, heavy, soggy pieces of music with no economy whatsoever. Suddenly to hear this Reich piece, which I thought was the most beautiful listening experience, and to realise that it was made from just a few molecules of sound – that really impressed me.'

As a member of the Scratch Orchestra, he was also impressed by Paragraph Seven of Cornelius Cardew's composition, *The Great Learning*. Written in 1969, this piece has been described by Michael Nyman in *Experimental Music* as an example, alongside Christian Wolff's *Burdocks*, Frederic Rzewski's *Spacecraft* and Alvin Lucier's *Vespers*, of 'Contextual processes [which] are concerned with actions dependent on unpredictable conditions and on variables which arise from within the musical continuity.' Using a Confucian text, Cardew gave a few rules for an ensemble of any number of untrained voices. Each singer chooses his or her own note, then sings the phrases or individual words from the text for the length of a breath. 'For each subsequent line choose a note that you can hear being sung by a colleague,' Cardew instructed. 'It may be necessary to move to within earshot of certain notes.' There are a few other rules, but that, in essence, is the piece.

In 'Generating and Organising Variety In the Arts', an article written for *Studio International* in 1976, the art & experimental music issue guest edited by Michael Nyman, Brian Eno wrote an analysis of the way in which the 'variety reducing' clauses in the score suggest that the piece might thin out to a small stock of random notes, yet in practice, variety is encouraged by a set of 'accidents'. These include the 'unreliability' of a group of singers of mixed ability, transposition of notes, the occurrence of beat frequencies, and the resonant frequency of the room in which the performance takes place. 'The composer, instead of ignoring or subduing the variety generated in performance,' he wrote, 'has constructed the piece so that this variety is really the substance of the music.' One example of how Cardew's contextual process could result in quite breathtakingly beautiful music can be heard on either of the two reissues of *The Great Learning*.

A day after our first chat about this subject (though in retrospect, all our conversations over the years seem to have been about this subject), Brian comes back to me with an aphorism: 'Generative music is like trying to create a seed, as opposed to classical composition which is like trying to engineer a tree.' Gardening and engineering are key metaphors. 'I think one of the changes of our consciousness of how things come into being, of how things are made and how they work,' he says, 'is the change from an engineering paradigm, which is to say a design paradigm, to a biological paradigm, which is an evolutionary one. In lots and lots of areas now, people say, how do you create the conditions at the bottom to allow the growth of the things you want to happen? So a lot of the generative music thing is much more like gardening. When you make a garden, of course you choose some of the things you put in, and of course you have some degree of control over what the thing will be like, but you never know precisely. That's the wonderful thing about gardening. It responds to conditions during its growth and it changes and it's different every year.'

Even professional gardeners are on to generative music. An article in *The Guardian* newspaper exhorted amateurs to throw out their wind chimes and water features and plant sound-rich ornamental grasses such as *Arundo donax*, evening primrose, which opens its blooms with an audible pop, or common broom, with its exploding seed pods. Just as Cornelius Cardew's method for *The Great Learning* produced an implicit social model, this approach to constructing a sound environment connects music to ecology and, perhaps unwittingly, connects gardening to the chance methods and theories of John Cage (who was in turn so impressed by the Zen garden created by the painter and gardener Soami at Ryoanji Temple, Kyoto that he wrote two compositions based on its structure of 15 stones).

In the late 1960s and early 1970s, collaborative group music was one of the most powerful available tools for experimenting with new models of society, forms through which individual expression might thrive within collective organisations of inclinations ranging from hippie anarchism to Maoism, along with new ideas about the importance of ecology in the relationship between humans and the environment. In the early 2000s, the equivalent of this seemed to be events like *Sound Drifting*, the New York-based *Unity Gain*, described by organiser David Linton as 'a systematic JAM of "systems"', or the California-based network computer music group known as the Hub. At roughly the same time that Brian Eno was experiencing the Scratch Orchestra at first hand, I was taking part in performances of Eddie Prévost's *Spirals*, a composition for large ensemble that attempted to apply some of the psychological characteristics of small group improvisation to very large groupings, as well as attending the weekly workshops held by John Stevens.

During the period in the late 1960s when he shifted his group, the Spontaneous Music Ensemble, away from the compositional models of Ornette Coleman, Eric Dolphy and George Russell into uncharted territory, John began to formulate pieces that could help musicians who were new to this way of playing (and that included just about everybody at that time). *Click Piece*, for example, was a simple instruction to play the shortest sound possible on your instrument. The difficulty of this varied from instrument to instrument, player to player, and quite a considerable amount of concentration was needed to pare each sound down to its smallest event and keep it there. As a player, you became aware of the way in which a group sound was emerging only after some time had elapsed. The paradox lay in the way that a complex group interaction, quite ravishing to listen to on occasions, could emerge from individual self-absorption. The piece seemed to develop with a mind of its own and, almost as a by-product, the basic lessons of improvisation – how to listen and how to respond – could be learned through a careful enactment of the instructions.

Improvising saxophonist Evan Parker remembers the way in which his duo with John Stevens pushed this atomistic way of playing to a limit. 'The moments of interaction got shorter and shorter,' he says. 'You couldn't go any further than that.' So a method that stimulated considerable variety in a large group comprising players of mixed ability and experience, quickly became an unproductive limitation for a duo of two well-matched, skilful and confident musicians.

I put it to Evan that Brian Eno's gardening analogy might be applied to his solo playing for soprano saxophone, along with many of the theories of webs, swarms and emergent phenomena found in books such as Kevin Kelly's *Out Of Control: The New Biology of Machines*. 'We are all delighted if we can find some way of talking about something that is very difficult to talk about,' he admits. 'Fractal maths and chaos theory are very useful for talking about the solo playing, though of course the number of calculations involved to arrive at a fractal diagram or drawing is probably a magnitude of millions different from the number of calculations involved in me playing a solo. But in the sense that the whole design is built up from one calculation, the output of which becomes the input for the next calculation, there is in some way a connection with the way I work in the solo thing. I set up loops of stuff and then observe the loop and listen closely to the loop and say, ah, now I'll emphasise that note, or now I'll bring out that difference tone, or I'll try and put something underneath it in relation to that or on top. Gradually the centre of attention in the loop shifts somewhere else. The loop suddenly is a different loop. It's something that's still bearing fruit for me. I'm not saying that's exclusively the method I'm using in solo playing but it's the core method.'

This sets up a complex feedback system between the saxophone and independently functioning regions of his own distributed consciousness, enabled by Parker's circular breathing and his knowledge of the overtones available through advanced fingering techniques. 'Absolutely,' he agrees. 'It's the key notion of the 20th century. I'm not an expert on cybernetics but bringing an ability to generalise about feedback is a 20th-century phenomenon. Before that there were specific applications but I don't think there was a general awareness of how many control systems can be analysed in terms of the feedback between inputs and outputs. It's certainly high on my list of analytical tools.'

Parker was drawn to sonic overtones through what he describes as two crucial, formative experiences. 'One was, in the very early 60s,' he says, 'going to the Daphne wine festival, near Athens, when I was a student on holiday there, and hearing Greek clarinet and lyra music. I didn't know enough then to be sure but one thing that was sure was that it was a very overtone-rich music. I had the sensation of insects or buzzing. Hearing that layer in the music, not in an absolutely analytical way, but suddenly thinking, ah, this is very important, what's happening up there, on top of the line.'

The second occasion was a sitar concert at which he felt sure that two concerts were happening simultaneously: one in the fundamental tones and one in the overtones. 'Then I thought about the conscious control of all of that,' he says. 'There are thousands of places where you hear a careful use of overtone control to enhance the musical message or impact. I've gradually become more aware that's a place where your consciousness can be, and can be occupied. In fact, sometimes, in the solo playing especially, I can put certain patterns, things I've described as loops earlier in the conversation, I can set up a loop in the finger section of the instrument, have that on hold and then really focus my attention on the overtones.'

As Parker described these experiences, I thought of the cumulative overtones proliferating like swarms of bees in the music of guitarist Rafael Toral and composer Charlemagne Palestine. I also thought of my friend Werner Durand in Berlin, the large PVC clarinets he makes, fitted with buzzing resonators, and the glowing orange, cellular image shown in the artwork of his CD, *The Art of Buzzing*. Since this was a record of drones, containing explicit references to bees, I assumed the cover image was honeycomb, shot inside a beehive, then thought of Claude Lévi-Strauss and his structuralist theory of myth: oppositions in search of resolution; the raw and the cooked, from honey to ashes. I was wrong, or half-wrong, on both counts: 'That was Michaela Kölmel's image, a photograph of copper pipes which I used for installation work which we did together,' says Werner. 'I was not using buzzing instruments when we did that but I was tuning my instruments to the resonant frequencies of her pipes. It was an analogue idea of the light filtering through from these pipes and the sound filtering through pipes. When I was looking for a cover I wanted something thematic and the buzzing thing was very strong so I thought, why not use this image of a beehive?' As for Lévi-Strauss, 'I never read anything of his,' said Werner, though the idea of pure glutinous sound from a resonant tube as raw food, and its rich overtones as the beginning of cooking, is quite appetising.

wave forms

During a cold February we were staying in St. Ives, Cornwall, in a sparsely furnished apartment whose picture window looked out at the Atlantic Ocean crashing onto Porthmeor Beach, just under our balcony. 'Again, far away, she heard the dull sound, as if nocturnal women were beating great carpets,' wrote Virginia Woolf in *Jacob's Room*. In the evening we watched an episode of Steven Spielberg's *Taken*. At the end of the programme, I wondered about this continuing obsession with alien abductions, despite the lack of plausible supportive evidence. At 11.20 that night, I stood on the balcony to experience the sea at low tide. The wide sands of Porthmeor looked supernatural in the moonlight, a haze of bleached blue luminescent mist that appeared to float and merge with the distant surf. From the breaking waves I could feel a phased sound, white noise and a very low frequency drone, rolling across the horizon; not really sound, more a pulsating pressure. No need for aliens, given this strangeness.

frogs   clocks

Tape delay systems were means of creating unpredictable variety in music. Terry Riley's system, the time lag accumulator, was a technological equivalent of the feedback system later developed by Evan Parker and one of the inspirations behind Brian Eno's use of tape loops. For Eno, the system that allowed him to create *Discrete Music* was fine, except it was limited to the length of a vinyl LP. 'All of those phase systems,' he says, 'they're theoretically endless, generating new stuff as they go, new combinations. I always wanted that kind of music – not only *Discrete Music* but the things that followed it like *Music For Airports* – to be endless pieces. I saw them more like paintings – just things that stayed in place – than compositions, things that had a structure to them. I was always looking for creating, not a recording of the results of the generative process, but creating a generating machine itself.' This led to his use of Tim Cole's Koan software, a program he had hunted for in research centres in Stanford and Palo Alto but failed to find.

The desire to make a music that exists in a state of being, theoretically without beginning or end, is paralleled by Evan Parker's interest in relatively long forms and their relationship to improvising. 'What happens when you work with the longest elements?' asks Parker. 'Maybe you're not improvising any more. You're just remembering.' That dialectic, at the core of his music, contributes to the subjective impression in the listener that something is alive and growing, like a time-lapse photograph of plant growth, one of the creatures grown in the 'garden of unearthly delights' by William Latham's computational breeding program or the volatile communities generated by Conway's *Game of Life*.

The observation of nature, either through bioacoustic study, environmental sound recording or ecology, has led some musicians to the creation of emergent systems based on non-human source material. Mamoru Fujieda, for example, wired up plants using a Plantron interface devised by botanist Yuji Dogane. The data collected by electrodes recording changes to the surface electric potential of the plant leaves was converted to MIDI and then transformed into melodic patterns using MAX, the graphical music programming environment developed by Miller Puckette and other authors at IRCAM in 1986.

In 1966 and 1967, Pauline Oliveros produced two tape pieces – *Alien Bog* and *Beautiful Soop* – using Don Buchla's Buchla Box 100-series synthesiser and her own tape delay system. Working at The Tape Music Centre at Mills College in Oakland, she had been influenced by the sounds of frogs living in the pond outside her window at Mills. At a different time, in a different place, Felix Hess also found inspiration in the complex interactivity of this hypnotic sound.

Born in Den Haag in 1941, Hess studied physics in Groningen from 1959 until 1967. Captivated from childhood by the idea of boomerangs, he decided to use his knowledge of physics to study how they work. Having completed his doctor's thesis on the aerodynamics of boomerangs in 1975, he took up a job in applied mathematics at the University of Adelaide. Learning about the properties of air, he also heard tree frog sounds every night from the creek at the edge of his garden. 'Later, as I travelled in the outback and camped in very quiet spots,' he has written, 'the beauty of the nights was overwhelming, the richness of small sounds unending, and frogs became my teachers before I was even aware.'

'It is very, very three-dimensional, this phenomenon of a flying boomerang and the sounds in Australia,' he has said, in conversation with Bernard Schulz. 'What I was interested in is the space aspects of the sounds, not the way the sound is going in time, but mostly how it goes in space, the very three-dimensionality.' Hess enjoyed the frogs so much that he made recordings to take back to Holland, though the loss of this spatial element was frustrating. Something else was missing. In the sleeve note for *Frogs 4*, a vinyl LP he released in 1985, he defined this absence: 'A recording has a definite beginning and end, whereas a real chorus continues indefinitely, with a diurnal and even an annual rhythm. And there is a lack of something utterly fundamental. The essence of the moment of listening, *this* moment in time, is absent in any recordings: the "past" and the "future" have been arranged already along the tape.'

In answer to this lack, he began to build a group of small electronic machines that could communicate together by listening to each other, and to the sounds of a room, then make sounds in response to the conditions of the moment. From here, he progressed to other machines, some sensitive to air pressure fluctuations, others sensitive to light. Through these experiments, he became fascinated with air pressure fluctuations that lie below our hearing threshold. With a pair of infrasound microphones, a computer and software that he developed with his son, he found a way to make recordings of these sounds. Using a time compression factor of 360, one hour of audible sound on a CD represents 15 days and nights of recorded infrasound, originally in the range between 0.03 Hz and 56 Hz. The sensation of hearing this CD is deeply strange, like being buffeted by a high wind and at the same time hearing the extreme high frequency activity of neural processing. 'One hears high-pitched whistles, beeps and insect-like buzzes,' Hess writes, 'which come from the deep rumblings of factories, trains, and trucks and other motor cars, or even nearby washing machines. The opening and closing of doors gives rise to countless tiny clicks, which may add up to form a sound like soft rain on autumn leaves ... Finally, an extraordinary presence: a rich, deep drone, originally at 0.2 Hz, audible like a multi-engined heavy airplane in the distance. This deep droning sound, at times all but inaudible, is formed by oscillations in the atmosphere – microbaroms – caused by standing waves on the Atlantic Ocean, far away. The space is very wide ...'

Felix Hess's work, or pieces like *Chaos & the Emergent Mind of the Pond*, created by sound recordist and composer David Dunn in 1990, are illustrations of the way in which 'shaped' soundscapes can become a category of found art that links to generative work of all kinds. In his book, *Why Do Whales and Children Sing?*, Dunn quotes the anthropologist and musician Steven Feld, whose research and recording among the Kaluli people of Papua New Guinea and the rainforest in which they live has drawn new maps of the relationship between favoured sound patterns, aesthetic preferences and social relations. 'Steven Feld describes the New Guinea rainforest as a world of coordinated alarm clocks,' writes Dunn, 'an intersection of millions of simultaneous cycles all refusing to ever start or stop at the same point.' In books such as *Music Grooves*, co-authored with Charles Keil, and *Sound and Sentiment*, Feld has written extensively about valued sonic qualities among the Kaluli, including 'interaction of patterned and random sounds; playful accelerations, lengthenings and shortenings; and the fission and fusion of sound shapes and phrases into what electroacoustic composer Edgard Varèse called the "shingling" of sound layers across pitch space.'

Feld's observation of simultaneous cycles working out of phase, or the Kaluli love of 'in-sync, out-of-phase patterning', recalls Brian Eno's enthusiasm for *In C*, *It's Gonna Rain* and Paragraph Seven of *The Great*

Learning. One of the most enthralling examples of this phenomenon can be heard when large groups of frogs are calling, each frog responding to another, calls sometimes falling in perfect synchronisation, moving in and out of phase, then falling suddenly silent for reasons a human can't divine. David Dunn has extrapolated from his recordings of this emergent mind to develop a series of real-time, multi-channel electro-acoustic performances and installations for live computers.

'They explore the global behaviour of hyperchaotic analogue circuits modelled in the digital domain,' he tells me, via e-mail from New Mexico. 'These circuits exhibit an immense range of sonic behaviour, all generated from the equivalent of three sine-wave oscillators linked together in a feedback path that exhibits two of the essential traits of a chaotic system: non-linearity and high sensitivity to initial conditions. The emergent complexity results from the dynamical attributes of cross-coupled chaotic states interacting in a multidimensional phase space. My role as composer/ performer of this "chaos" instrument is to explore various regions of these behaviours in a manner analogous to the exploration of a physical terrain. While I can influence the complex sonic behaviours, I cannot control them beyond a certain level of mere perturbation, the amount of which is constantly changing. The experience is often tantamount to surfing the edge of a tide of sound that has its own intrinsic momentum.

'The compositions are to be regarded as improvisatory in structure but based upon a prescribed set of zones where particular chaotic behaviours reside. The opening and closing of virtual switches determines various combinations of structural coupling between distinct chaotic circuits, allowing different self-organising behaviours to arise. The composition is a charting of transitions between these different zones of behaviour that arise from a fundamental generative structure and its behavioural diversity, much like a genetic code.

'My fascination for these sounds has less to do with the underlying mathematics, or the current fashion for applying complexity science to music, than with the similarity these sounds have to natural sound environments where the same dynamical properties might be operating. These sounds excite me because they are so physically reminiscent of the global sound behaviours that emerge from natural habitats such as swamps, forests and oceans.'

'My main question on generative music is: can we trust machines to create for us?' asks David Rothenberg, musician and author of *Hand's End:*

Technology and The Limits of Nature. The life's work of John Cage could be interpreted as that question almost in reverse: can we trust humans to create music? Through the influence of books as much as anything else – the oracular hexagrams of the *I Ching*, James Joyce's *Finnegan's Wake* and the writings of Gertrude Stein – Cage arrived at *The Music of Changes* in 1951, a composition he described in *Musicage*, his conversations with Joan Retallack, as 'where the process of composing was changed from making choices to asking questions'.

Although Cage's ghost is present almost anywhere we care to look, his philosophy of non-intentionality has become a resource, rather than a way of life, for many musicians currently working with electronic media. Certain pieces suddenly seem to find their moment in the zeitgeist. *ASLSP*, for example, was a commission given to Cage in 1984 for the University of Maryland Piano Festival. The title abbreviates the instruction, 'as slow and as soft as possible', but also alludes to an exclamation in the last paragraph of *Finnegan's Wake*: 'Soft Morning, city! Lsp!' A later version was composed for organ. Although the score is vague, Cage felt that if the piece was being played as slowly as the musician could manage at that point in time, then that was slow enough. In Halberstadt, Germany, Dr Michael Betzle decided to push the vagueness of the instruction to the limit, so on 5 September 2001, playing began on a performance of *ASLSP* intended to last for 639 years. The work begins with a pause, so no sound was heard for 18 months, then the first three notes on the organ were played on 5 February 2003.

As a member of the think tank (also including architect Paul Shepheard, landscape architect Georgina Livingston, digital sound artist Joel Ryan and Brian Eno) that offered guidance to Jem Finer in his development of the *Longplayer* project, I remember a phase during which Finer considered using a segment of John Cage's prepared-piano music as the source material to feed through SuperCollider, the real-time audio synthesis environment developed by James McCartney. Finer's concept for *Longplayer* was to generate a piece of music that would last for 1000 years. Industrial strength mechanical devices were considered as a way of realising this idea, though his experiments centred on SuperCollider's capacity to loop small segments of music and gradually move the start point of the loop, with each new loop applying the same process to itself to create a nest of loops, all working within the differing boundaries of its parent loop to create constant evolution. Fascinating, but, though informed by Cage, perhaps not a particularly Cageian way to compose.

Eventually, *Longplayer* began its long life on I January 2000, sited in Trinity Buoy Wharf on the River Thames and also (erratically) available for audition via live stream at www.longplayer.org. Initially, the sound has been generated by a computer playing 6 loops from a pre-recorded 20' 20" composition for Tibetan singing bowls, though the form of the player will develop over time. Finer's background in computer science and his long experience of working with musicians such as Shane MacGowan (in The Pogues), Joe Strummer and Kirsty MacColl seems ideal for the kind of utopian vision and technical ingenuity uniquely represented in *Longplayer*.

I asked him if using SuperCollider and thinking in 1000-year trajectories had affected any aspect of his thinking or playing. 'Having spent 15 years playing banjo and assorted other instruments I started to use the computer more and more to make music,' he answered. 'Working on *Longplayer* meant abandoning even the input of data with keyboard as I was working more and more with emergent systems. By the time *Longplayer* started I was having a problem finishing anything. The nature of working with *Longplayer* was so much based in long durational processes that my whole approach to "composing" had changed beyond all recognition.

'I wanted to find some way of using these new strategies to actually perform music live – something I'd started to miss. I spent a bit of time working out a framework in SuperCollider so that I could have on call a library of "instruments" which I could call up and run in parallel with control over both their parameters, via individual edit windows, and their relative volumes, via a global mixer. This worked in a modular manner so that as I wrote new "instruments" I could simply add them into the library. Their functions ranged from simple effects – delays, filters etc – to various emergent systems. For example, there's an instrument that's based directly on *Longplayer* – except it takes between 10 and 60 minutes to play itself out.

'I played a bit using this system with samples and then mixed this approach with sampling other people and using that input as material. I felt though that something was missing. I realised that somewhere along the line I'd managed to reduce my physical participation in making music to one hand on a mouse – or a finger on a track pad – and my brain, eyeball and ears. I may as well have been some sci-fi freak with a robo arm wired to a pulsating brain floating in solution.'

The solution, rather than the solution, was to play guitar. In SuperCollider he wrote a simple 'instrument' that could read the pitch of the guitar, which then set the playback rate of a sample. If this was the guitar note itself, then the resulting feedback loop could be hard to control but the results were 'live' and exciting. Error made a contribution. 'My buggy programming added to the unpredictability of the computer's response,' Finer says. 'A lot of the instruments I wrote didn't work exactly as planned. Things would start to happen and I had no idea where they came from. So I got (some of) my body back and then found a way to perform music based on emergent processes. The outstanding problem of computer crashes found a resolution in accepting that these were decisions of the computer, my collaborator, to call a halt. So a crash meant that that was the end of the piece.'

hypernatural
Yoshio Machida is a musician and visual artist living in Tokyo. His 1999 album, *Hypernatural*, was supplemented by the release of two floppy disks that remixed the CD tracks with SSEYO's Koan program. 'I like to enjoy "texture" and I was looking for some generator that makes the texture of soundscape,' Machida writes as an explanation of how he came to use Koan. 'I like to see changing view of landscape through a window of a train or an airplane. Especially, the view from airplane is wonderful. At first I was using ALPS. This is a Japanese Mac-based software. It's very simple but this can generate some phrases by itself. Then I knew Koan through some info about Eno. I thought, oh, that's what I want! These softwares generate some not-perfect things by themselves.

'These textures are unique for me. I want to get some dynamics with not only my own power but also the other power, and I want to keep balance of instinct and thought. That's my way. *Hypernatural* sounds aren't always perfect in chaos. It's an amorphous thing, not a crystallised thing. I think what is important is the thing between sound and listener, not only sound. So this software helps me to make "amorphous things". For me, this is similar to field recording sounds and some analogue sounds. John Cage said he can enjoy listening to all sounds, except the sound with someone's intention. I feel so, too.'

Issues of intentionality, linearity and the model of active composer and passive listener are being challenged by software and software users yet held in place by the dominant carrier of music, the compact disc. 'Our minds have become nodes in the expanding space of the Internet, connecting freely with other nodes in a rhizomatic manner,' wrote

Californian electronic musician and sound designer Kim Cascone for the liner notes to *Selected Random Works*, released on Ritornell. 'Comparing this fluidic, smooth space with the linear space of the audio compact disc, we find that a linear model of time has been imposed onto an inherently non-linear medium.'

Live streaming, installations, MIDI files and the release of authored software, rather than finished product, offer ways around this contradiction, though the effect at the moment can feel and sound like the aimless exploration of a huge choice of possibilities, something like the experiments of the 1960s when the excitement of process and change could obscure the imperatives of making music that was worth a second listen. 'The limitation of the range of possible parameters changes focuses within the music, giving a distinct character,' says Olivier Alary, whose *Sketch Proposals* CD was released on the Rephlex label in 2000. 'The output of such a system can be familiar and different at the same time, but never repetitive. It could be compared to the weather or the movement of clouds in the sky.'

There is a significant difference between software programs such as Logic Audio or Cubase, basically digital emulations of the analogue recording studio, and more open applications such as MAX/MSP, SuperCollider, Cloud Generator developed by Curtis Roads and John Alexander, or interesting curiosities such as Akira Rabelais' Argeïphontes Lyre (elliptically explained to me by Rabelais by means of a lengthy chunk of Greek mythology). Composers who have devoted a lifetime to compositional methods that go beyond the customary means of committing sound to tape, its equivalents or emulations, are increasingly important in this shifting field: the late Iannis Xenakis, for example, for his theory of stochastic processes, derived from mathematician Jacques Bernouilli's 'law of large numbers', or the cybernetic and entropic compositions of Dutch composer Roland Kayn.

Inspired in 1956 by Max Bense, a pioneer of information theory, Kayn found his way slowly to a method of composing electronic music that was self-regulating, like any thermostatically controlled system, that avoided narrative elements, hierarchy, tension and release and emotional climaxes (all of which can be found to excess in much academic electro-acoustic music). *Tektra*, composed between 1980 and 82, radiates weird beauty, like a huge celestial choir with no more religious connotations than the weather, held in suspension with no compulsion towards release, no straining towards ecstasy. Enormous structural complexity is generated from within each section of the piece, yet nothing external disturbs their equilibrium. From this point of view, they fulfil Gregory Bateson's concept of the plateau, described in *Steps to An Ecology of Mind* as a key to Balinese character and culture. Later developed into a central principle of Deleuze and Guattari's *A Thousand Plateaus: Capitalism and Schizophrenia*, the continuing plateau of intensity was described by Bateson in 1949 as a substitution for climax which applies as a generalisation to music, trance, quarrelling and other forms of art and ethos. As Bateson says, Balinese gamelan is a working out of formal relations. Modifications of intensity are determined by that process, rather than by 'the sort of rising intensity and climax structure characteristic of modern Occidental music.' Ironically, modern Occidental music was not far behind Bateson in the exploration of plateaus. 'To make things possible, the limitations and hindrances must disappear,' Kayn wrote. 'The music becomes autonomous once the composer has no control over the direction it takes once he has set it in motion. Music is sound which is sufficient in itself.'

These experiments with the potential autonomy of machines can raise questions of both authority and authorship. From 1967 until his death in 2002, the Italian composer Pietro Grossi experimented with digital media: presenting computer music software at the Venice Bienniale in 1970; in the same year organising one of the first experiments in telematic performance through a telephone line between Rimini and Pisa, then by invitation of Xenakis, producing another telematic concert between Pisa and Paris in 1974. Born in Venice in 1917, Grossi was opposed to entrenched ideas of musical virtuosity, copyright ownership and artisanship. Writing in 1969, he envisaged a dramatically utopian future for computer music, imagining 'complete disposal of the "sonic whole"; liberation from the "well tempered system"; disappearance of the performer/interpreter; the "middle-man" between the composer and the listener; and the possibility of going beyond the limits of human performing skills.' Developing software that produced open, unfinished musical compositions or graphic works, Grossi then distributed these around the world 'to be used for various compositional purposes'. As soundscape artist Albert Mayr writes in his sleevenotes to the CD release of Grossi's computer composition *Battimenti*: 'Obviously his intentions were misunderstood and ridiculed (the golden age of plunderphonics was still far away).'

Grossi's *Collage*, from 1968, is a dense, hectic piece of complex textures that explores the computer's capacity to produce endless variations of source material. Anticipating the file sharing, remixing and anonymity now familiar within the electronics scene, Grossi felt that anybody should feel free to develop these materials as they wished, and they were presented as creations of The Studio, rather than under his own name. *Unicum*, composed in 1985, is more typical of Grossi's minimalist aesthetic of pure sinusoidal tones, organised in endless permutations by means of mathematical calculations. In 1969 he had designed one of the first interactive computer systems, the DCMP, and as a later development created *Unicum* on the TAU 2, a polyphonic, polytimbral audio terminal controlled by an IBM mainframe computer. Grossi was clearly more interested in the process of programming non-repeating automatic music than in any metaphorical or sonic elaboration. Nevertheless, there is a weird hypnotic beauty to this work, a fascination that grows with immersion in the brief bursts of energy, frequency swoops and beat frequencies that wriggle and twist within its very limited range. Listening to its unfolding makes me think of fireflies dancing against an opaque night sky.

The recent emergence of composers such as Grossi and Kayn out of relative obscurity reflects the currency of their prophetic ideas within 21st-century electronic music. Notorious for their cryptic titles, Autechre – Sean Booth and Rob Brown – met in Manchester and released their first record in 1992. For them, electronic music is an environment for creativity; digital music offers greater possibilities for making their music sound exactly the way they want it. 'You probably know already that sound design using digital gear takes more maths than using analogue gear,' they write. 'You have to put the right numbers in to get the numbers you need out. Computers just speed up the process for us. They make the maths easier. They also paradoxically provide more opportunity to claim responsibility for the resulting music, as the user has to define so much in order to get personally satisfying results (depending how much they like to get their hands dirty). This can be applied to sequencing and sound design, though thanks to clever high level developing environments the boundaries between the two stages are disappearing. The way computers can help make things easier and faster sometimes means we're pursuing ideas that maybe would have been abandoned previously. Keeping the vibe has always been important and rather than sitting with a calculator working out when exactly two beats are going to re-align we can get on with being inspired. Also, being limited is more interesting when you've set the limits yourselves – or for each other.'

For Markus Popp of Oval, one of the most important factors in his recent trajectory is the presentation of his *Oval Process* software, developed with Richard Ross, as an interactive installation object. 'That is this tangible interface,' he says, speaking from his studio in Berlin, 'declaring the interface public domain and just handing it over to the audience or whoever is present at the given time of the exhibition or wherever the unit is on display. This is one aspect of it, and the other aspect, which might even be considered the stronger statement is, of course, the available audio content which is on my CD, which is a quite vigorous statement against the typical productivity work flow in music.'

He describes CDs such as *ovalprocess* and *Commers* as the tangible front end of an attempt to introduce an alternative rhetoric to the production of electronic music. At the same time, *Oval Process* is a statement to encourage non-expert audiences. He compares the interface to a Game Boy running *Tetris*, though when I ask him if he plays, thinking of my personal episodes of addiction, he throws up a denial. 'It is immediately visible for the user whether it's cool or crap,' he says. 'I never considered this would be groundbreaking in the sense that it would hand over the interface,' he continues. 'It's just a simple gesture. It's just the defining principle of something like an info terminal at the airport. You hand over the interface, otherwise the info terminal wouldn't be usable. A very simple question: how would Oval be like an info terminal? I would happily take the risk of making *Oval Process* just this box.'

Popp interprets the current situation in music as a moment for making statements that jump out of established historical frameworks. When people are confronted by music designed to grow and evolve beyond the composer's intentions or even understanding, the old science fiction anxieties of humans enslaved by their machines still recur. 'I understand that people are easily led when all they see is this designed object which provides the tangible means of approaching this type of Oval music in this very strict and impersonal way,' he says, 'just being a sound installation that doesn't require any assistance and is completely interactive. So, of course, people are easily led to assume that this is the Kraftwerk approach driven to the extreme, just placing this object somewhere which would eventually replace myself as the protagonist in Oval music, which has never been intended. It's very simple,' he concludes. 'I just want to create a contemporary statement.' Like Japanese paper buried underground, the final organisation of the music is relinquished by its maker, though the elements remain intact as a beginning, etched in memory.

6 To play

'Chance favours only the prepared mind.'

Louis Pasteur

Two of the most influential artist-potters of the 20th century, Shoji Hamada and Bernard Leach, searched for a similar kind of simplicity in their work and in the objects they collected. Hamada talked about the time he resolved the dilemma of body and mind in the course of this pursuit of simplicity. 'I already know how to work with my body, but not so much with my mind,' he said, in *Hamada: Potter*, written by his friend Leach. 'So I again posed the question of intellect and intuition. What I did this morning is an example of what I mean by body. I had a round pot in front of me for salt glaze. The next thing I found myself doing was dipping my brush in wax and I just went bom, bom, bom, all over the pot... It was not from my mind it came from but from my whole body; it emerged out of my middle, my lower abdomen. I have such a good feeling about having done this pot, though I have not yet seen the fired result. But I know, I can feel it, it feels good.'

This question, of the relation between intellect, intuition and body, arises in music a lot. In the utopian emergence of computer music technology and the Internet during the mid-90s, Zen was frequently invoked as a way of expressing the unusual feeling of weightlessness or disembodiment associated with these new ways of working and communicating. This quality of aether that is so much a part of sound in any circumstance was emphasised by a gradual displacement of the human body in the actual making of music. With the computer, music could be pure mind, or spirit.

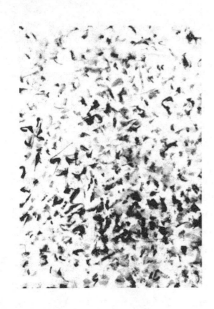

John Stevens
Untitled

Making music, or watching somebody make music, using computer software to manipulate and transform source material such as WAV sound files, encourages this fantasy: that the man–machine fusion happens not as a merging of old-fashioned mechanics and equally old-fashioned flesh, but as the kind of consciousness download envisaged by artificial intelligence fanatic Hans Moravec.

Some years ago, maybe 1993, I was having serious difficulties with playing music, or finding what music it was that I wanted to play. I had been writing about music too much and was disengaged from the practice of it. Walking down the Portobello Road in London, I bumped into John Stevens. Although it was a long time since I had attended his music improvisation workshops, the lessons learned had been applicable to many other ways of making music and many other aspects of life. What I didn't know, when I bumped into him, was that within another year John would die, suddenly and unexpectedly. He asked me, 'Are you playing?' and I felt slightly ashamed. 'I'm having problems with it,' I said. 'I think you've got to start with your instrument,' he said.

That feels like Hamada's story: bom, bom, bom. From the physical relationship to an instrument come the answers to seemingly deeper questions. Of course, a laptop computer is a legitimate instrument already, yet its narrowing of focus down to the contact between fingertips and a small surface area of the computer seems problematic to me. 'I have always started by looking at the body, since that's the essential thing,' fashion designer Issey Miyake said in the catalogue to his *Making Things* exhibition of 1998. 'The body is thrilling. My greatest desire is to make clothes that are as thrilling as the body.' Somehow it seems that the effort to move beyond a Cartesian split of mind and body has precipitated strange confusions – obsessed with sex yet living in virtuality, for example – that blind us to this kind of revelatory simplicity.

The simplicity, or apparent simplicity, of Issey Miyake's aims, highlights another problem: choice. My initial relationship with an instrument was developed with a few, fairly simple tools. Now I have maybe six different computer software programs for making and editing music, all with a multitude of choices accessible through digital plug-in effects, plus racks of analogue equipment, all with their own array of choices, and a large number of sound-making devices. The choices of what I can do and how I do it are only limited by my own imagination (or so the Microsoft propaganda tells me).

But that's not so different from gardening. A program pushed too far will crash; a plant grown in the wrong soil or conditions will die. There are infinite choices of how to make a garden. Omission is a virtue. Without limitations there is only confusion, vulgarity, the loss of meaning. I can't truly live by it but I bear it in mind: who feels the need to have so many things?

face to face

In 1969 I was working at the Roundhouse in north London, bringing drinks up from the cellar to the bar and serving in the café on Sundays, during weekly rock gigs that featured bands such as Love and Quintessence. For Christmas of that year the Roundhouse staged an ice show. A band somehow formed itself out of random connections and rehearsed all night by the ice. Drummer Paul Burwell and I met on that occasion and after many permutations of the original line-up, we ended up as an improvising duo.

We called ourselves Rain In The Face but had no gigs and little idea of how to get any. Paul gave up his job to pursue this life; I gave up a place on the painting course at Hornsey College of Art. To replace the job, Paul managed to wangle himself a place at Ealing College, to study fine art. He befriended pianist Christopher Small, now renowned as a music theorist but then a teacher on the Ealing music course. The connections are all a little vague at this remove but Chris invited John Stevens to hold improvisation workshops in a classroom at the college. Paul and I attended most of these workshops and John invited us to play as part of the large ensemble – Stan Tracey, Paul Rutherford, Jeff Clyne, Lol Coxhill, Lou Gare and many others – that performed *Encompass* on BBC Radio 3 in 1972.

He also offered us a gig, our first, at the Little Theatre Club. A jewel of a venue, the Theatre Club was set in the crow's nest of a building in Garrick Yard, a gloomy courtyard barely visible to the tourists and theatregoers who choked St Martin's Lane and Monmouth Street. All drummers, double bass players and electric guitarists hated the climb up those stairs, particularly since drum kits were expanding at that time to include huge amounts of exotic gongs, scrap metal, giant bass drums and scaffolding frames. Right by the entrance was a bar the size of a cupboard, curtained off from a few rows of raked seats that focussed on the floor area that served as the stage.

It was quite possible to find yourself playing in a theatre set of flimsy doors and opaque windows, a room within a room. None of those disadvantages mattered because the acoustics and velvet atmosphere of the space were wonderful for intimate music. Paul and I were feeling our way into something unknown, improvisation with elements of loose structuring that mixed intensity with reflective playing, loud electrics with quiet acoustics. The Theatre Club was an ideal context for those tentative early explorations. The audience might be just a few people – usually lovers, friends and other musicians. People Band drummer Terry Day came up to us once, after we had played opposite his OMU trio, and said the music was sweet, man, the way Terry talks. AMM drummer Eddie Prévost was equally positive, but in a slightly different language, and so you learned who was openly supportive and who kept their own counsel.

The minimalist SME duo of John and saxophonist Trevor Watts recorded their duo album, *Face To Face*, during a live session in 1973 and performed there frequently, often opposite Derek Bailey playing solo electric guitar. From time to time, extraordinary free jazz sessions would erupt like bushfire racing over parched land. One night during a 'free jazz' festival organised by Martin Davidson, now the proprietor of the Emanem Records label, virtually everybody in the club ended up playing at top volume. The seats were full of trumpeters and saxophonists, all howling at the moon. At one point a policeman appeared in the doorway. He had heard the commotion from the street and climbed the stairs to investigate. Astounded by this hellish scene, he pointed his walkie-talkie towards the music, hopeful of giving his colleagues back at the station a full measure of the night's delirium.

The most regular fixture at the Little Theatre Club was the Spontaneous Music Ensemble in its various incarnations, though always led by John. At its heart, the club was a workshop space in which very new ideas could be explored without the pressures of a jazz audience, nightclub drinkers, flock wallpaper or menacing landlords. On the 18 January 1972, during a 12-day free jazz festival that featured the Evan Parker/Paul Lytton duo, AMM, Iskra 1903, the Lol Coxhill/David Bedford duo, alto saxophonist Mike Osborne, SME and a Derek Bailey group, I played as part of a large SME workshop band. Lou Gare, Lol Coxhill and Mike Osborne all played on that night and perhaps they also contributed to the large group. Lou certainly did. I remember seeing him to my left and being slightly awestruck by the close proximity of somebody who had contributed so dramatically to my musical path through his work with AMM. I taped the group that night on a cheap mono cassette recorder and through extreme low fidelity can hear the endless interplay of call and response that characterised the John Stevens method.

Martin Davidson wrote a review for the *Melody Maker* of a Theatre Club performance by the SME duo of Stevens and Watts. The exact date is unknown to me but a small ad on the reverse side of the clipping – 'Coloured group requires versatile amateur or semi-pro organist' – helps in locating the era. 'For what these two are doing,' Davidson wrote, 'is running along a rhythmic cliff edge together, pushing each other forward knowing that if either one makes one false move they will fall off. So all of their effort is put into moving ahead leaving no time to play anything extraneous. Meanwhile, the audience on the edge of their seats is witnessing one of the closest musical relationships that has ever been achieved.' At the foot of his review, he devoted a few lines to the support band, Rain In The Face: 'Their youngness precludes any advanced togetherness, and there is no cliff edge in sight; but they could well work towards that.' I'm not sure we ever reached the cliff edge but our progress in the general direction of danger was helped immeasurably by the sympathetic environment of the Little Theatre Club and its inventor, John Stevens.

According to Derek Bailey, Stevens is still underrated for his greater invention, that of a group music. In fact, it's difficult to define what this invention was: a way of playing; a way of listening; a group music; a group sound; a sound imagined by John and then projected on to all his acolytes? The quintessential record of this early period is *Karyobin*. The full title is *Karyobin are the imaginary birds said to live in paradise*, which gives a better idea of the content. Recorded by Eddie Kramer, Jimi Hendrix's engineer, at Olympic Sound Studios in 1968, the record is a six-part improvisation played by Stevens, Bailey, Evan Parker on soprano saxophone, Kenny Wheeler on trumpet and flugelhorn and Dave Holland on bass. From such a faraway time, the music sounds more like jazz than it once did, almost segmented in its first minutes, as if the musicians were still detaching themselves from the conditioning ruler of eight and sixteen bar lines. Then a propulsion takes over; not the ecstatic ascension of free jazz but a wriggling complexity of lines moving outwards and over increasingly ambitious durations, like a Mark Tobey painting that fills the volume of a room. Physical touch – the delicate if emphatic manner in which Stevens voices a drum sound or a cymbal, light rhythms that stop and start, taps, choked sounds – is a light that guides everybody in the group. There are no themes or head arrangements, no front and back, no engine room or cavalry, since this interplay, this equality, is absorbing enough without reintroducing memories of structure, or other formalised relationships based on models of authority or containment. The character of the music comes as much from the physical nature of each instrument and its relatedness or difference, as from the character of each player. Anton Webern is present, as is Ornette Coleman, but to listen closely to this deep listening is the equivalent of sitting in a relaxed, open state, watching the fugitive drawings made by birds flying with busy yet mysterious intent through a clear sky. The music is elegant, intricate, perfectly poised, yet at the time, the assault on hierarchical organisation was shocking, as much a political statement about social stagnation and repression as an aesthetic breakthrough.

a chair creaks   playing fools

A debate on the subject of John Stevens comes about during a conversation with Derek Bailey in February 2003. We are sitting in his kitchen and the kitchen lies in close proximity to Clapton Pond, which is a less picturesque feature of east London than you might imagine and has nothing to do with another guitarist whose financially rewarded fame outstrips that of Bailey by a considerable distance.

Towards the end of the conversation I tell Derek an anecdote, since this is one of the ways in which our exchange progresses. In January I had been a guest on a radio show broadcast on Resonance FM, the tiny but thoroughly surprising station run by the London Musicians Collective. At one point, the host, Richard Sanderson, had wanted me to talk about the Little Theatre Club and so played a track from *Playing*, a duo album by John Stevens and Derek Bailey, recorded in 1992 by John's son, Richie, and released on Derek's label, Incus, in 1993. Others occupying the radio studio are visual artist Rob Flint, who shares the hosting duties with Sanderson, plus a magazine journalist keen to write a feature on the station and a young man who is caretaking for that afternoon. The track plays; we listen; we enjoy. Then, as the piece is about to end, a strange atmosphere collects in the room. Time seems to decelerate. My impression is that everybody present is focussed on a similar point and this has achieved a temporary communality of feeling. When the feeling has passed, there is a strong compulsion to laugh, as if something faintly embarrassing had popped up in our midst.

The track is called 'Reflecters', a word that anybody is entitled to spell incorrectly. Beautifully recorded with far more low end than is usual in records of improvisation, the music can be heard in intimate detail yet with an overarching sense of the warm, close environmental acoustic. On record, Bailey's playing often communicates as dry shortness contrasted by ringing expansions. Here we can appreciate fine intermediate sounds, a dragged dry brush loaded with paint that only gradually gives way to liquidity. Plectrum scrapes. Soft entries and sudden exits. The interplay is hectic, excitable and exciting, and the complexity of this reflection is difficult to describe, since it moves in many different directions, with multiple inferences and quickly abbreviated invitations. Never audible, the pulse carries on its shoulders a forward rush of movement with both players in front of each other and inside each other's actions. Each sound is quick, pepper sharp, but unvoiced sounds shape tension and volition within the overall form. That left unsaid is a window thrown open, brief gusts of air rapidly breathed in then shut out. After a particularly heated passage of snare drum rolls, watery cymbals, violent harmonics and blunt scrabbling, Bailey extrudes shifting chords from his electric guitar and amplifier using a volume pedal to suppress the attack of each envelope. Stevens reflects with deep resonance from a small drum, and repeats this in unison with a cymbal, as if marking a ritual. Sliding sounds wipe across the frame. A chair creaks. There are human beings in this room.

This rare phenomenon, composed of fragile moments when feelings of intense focus possess a space and the air seems to thicken, mystifies me, even though it has happened to me as a player on a few occasions. What I think takes place, a guess at best, is that patterns coalesce, or instruments resonate in some unexpected way, then this unexpected meeting point is recognised by the musicians almost simultaneously, who then communicate their concentration through the music to the listeners. I have asked musicians about it on a number of occasions. They all recognise what I am talking about yet have no words to explain it. I asked David Gilmour, of Pink Floyd, for example. 'I don't know what it is but I wish you could bottle it,' he answered. I asked David Harrington, of the Kronos Quartet, who acknowledged the importance of such fleeting moments but was similarly at a loss. As for Bailey, he makes it sound like forbidden fruit. 'I'm not sure whether I would want to understand it more,' he says, 'but if it meant that I could be involved in those situations then I would like to understand it more.'

This underlines the general belief among musicians that excessive knowledge of the process of playing is detrimental to the business of playing. In conversation, Bailey and I are trying to talk about playing. Not music or issues associated with music, but playing. 'See, nobody discusses playing, do they?' he says. 'What they discuss is what they play. The nearest I think people get to it is when they talk about improvisation and then you get a little bit of a sighting. This is a regular lick of mine, but those old jazz players, when they were asked what they do, they'd say, I just play, man. I think that's a philosophical statement. If you talk about what you play it's a bit like asking somebody to describe driving, and then describing a journey. I don't know anybody who's got into that. Very difficult, talking about playing.'

Of course, the sound of music is another subject rarely discussed, which leaves a substantial hole in a central place. And so we worry at the subject, like two Samuel Beckett characters encased in funerary urns, clinging on to our central conceit whenever an anecdote threatens to entertain us. One of the most stimulating players alive, Derek is also amusing, acerbic and incisive in conversation. Fools are not suffered gladly; pretentious flowerings are cut off at the root. On the other hand, his appetite for new initiatives, both in playing and discourse, seems undiminished.

Born in Sheffield, in 1930, his trajectory of work is surprising, yet makes such perfect sense that you wonder why there aren't more like him. As anybody who has read his book – *Improvisation: Its Nature And Practice In Music* – will know, he began to devise and explore a language of musical improvisation in a trio named after the so-called Cockney Wagner, composer Joseph Holbrooke. Working together above a pub called The Grapes in Sheffield, this group of Bailey, jazz drummer Tony Oxley and bass player, now composer, Gavin Bryars, made a transition from conventional jazz to total improvisation between 1963 and 1965.

Bailey had been working, and continued to work, in the kinds of jobs that existed for a professional musician during that period. There's a novelty value in the light entertainment anecdotes which Bailey is more inclined to downplay than exploit, but they have a usefulness, nonetheless. His ideas on music have not been gleaned from books or records alone; neither do they rest on a shaky foundation of ideological zeal or religious wish fulfilment. They come from experience.

He won't thank me for repeating some of his stories, but it seems important to know that a man who can hold his own with Anthony Braxton, Cecil Taylor, Tony Williams, Keiji Haino, Lee Konitz, The Ruins, Tristan Honsinger, John Zorn, Han Bennink, Pat Metheny, Min Xiao-Fen, Richard Teiltelbaum, tap dancer Will Gaines, Butoh dancer Min Tanaka – a seemingly endless list of demanding musicians and non-musicians that includes the youngest as well as the most reputable – has also worked in cabaret with comedian Bob Monkhouse, accompanied religious radio broadcasts, performed with The Supremes in a London gambling club and played on BBC TV's *Six-Five Special* at the birth of British rock 'n' roll. From the 1970s to the 1990s he convened groupings of musicians in concerts that he called Company. Since the line-up changed almost every time, many of these musicians would be unfamiliar with each other's work, even be unfamiliar with improvising without predetermined guidelines, yet in Company they would (hopefully) discover extensions of their own language that could be shared.

During a conversation in 1994, we strolled into the subject of audiences. 'Usually, I avoid talking about audiences,' he said, 'because I came to the conclusion that I know nothing about 'em at all. I've played the most appalling shit in front of huge audiences and they're really enthusiastic.' I assumed he was referring to the European avant-festival circus but he corrected me: 'No, I'm talking about when I worked with Shirley Bassey. Those people are masters at dealing with an audience. I worked with Russ Conway [a notorious and highly successful pianist of the late 50s/early 60s, famous for his sparkling teeth and dinner suited appearance]. Now he was a master both of playing rubbish and dealing with an audience. This guy was a virtuoso audience manipulator. A big chunk of his act would be just talking to the audience. He was a kind of lesson. Even now, I don't want to believe that the worse it is, the better they like it, but there's an awful lot of evidence pointing that way.'

In the present, we return to playing, and to the musicians who say, I just play, man. 'It was a whole philosophy in a nutshell,' he says, 'especially for the very early jazz players, like the New Orleans guys. I don't know to what degree drugs were involved, but some guys, they used to call them playing fools when they couldn't stop them playing. Mind you, they used to be expected to play for hours on end anyway, but some guy would take off on the clarinet or something and eventually they'd all have to jump on him to get him to shut up. That kind of thing is where the playing takes over but then you would have the stimulus of other people, which is where you're likely to discover the stimulus.'

So to play in this way is a kind of madness, I suggest, socialised by the music, its circumstances and responsibilities?

'I have to say, in the dim and distant,' he says, 'when I used to work in the musical trenches, as I sometimes describe it, you would meet people like that. I might even have been one. I used to play, as near as possible, 24 hours a day, like maybe 13-14 hours a day. Work in the afternoon, in a dancehall, work at night, in a dancehall, after that in a jazz club, and then, either do a morning gig, because in that period you could always do a morning gig. If anybody wanted music, they had to have musicians. So I played at, like, the opening of furniture stores, things like that. If there wasn't a morning thing, then practise, and practise in between sets. I wasn't alone in being obsessed with playing like that, and it was all playing. It wasn't practising reading or something.'

This compulsive relationship to an instrument is partly physical, tactile, a prosthetic embodiment of the extended self that can speak a foreign language and articulate feelings from another world, but also a motion in itself, a motion to carry along the business of living that makes living meaningful. The centrality of the activity is often valued above most, if not all, of the rest of life. Tax returns, bills, health, relationships, marriages, domestic duties, offspring, personal hygiene and etiquette are all known sufferers at the altar of playing. At the extremes of this devotion, musicians can be children, in fact, and either descend into the chaos of children lacking sure guidance or be cosseted like children as a benefit of financial success.

This centrality of doing may explain why critics and fans so often experience, and express, bitter disappointment at the hands of their heroes. Errant decisions, indecisions, inconsistencies, lapses, low points and follies all conspire to wreck the trajectory of critically perfect careers. 'We work,' film composer John Barry (another pragmatic but idealistic Yorkshireman) once told me. The projects may be mediocre and inspiration may not always fire at 600 rounds per minute but the act of working is what maintains momentum, equilibrium, even salvation.

Derek tells me about a guitar he has bought, an Epiphone Regent Emperor, an extremely large acoustic instrument that has tempted him for 50 years. When he finally found one, the price was too high but he bought it anyway. Through the persuasion of John Zorn he recorded an album called *Ballads*, an entirely unexpected move that fooled some people into thinking that Derek was now available for cosy recitals of standard tunes such as 'Laura', 'Body and Soul' and 'You Go To My Head'. In fact, there was no possibility of this. The Epiphone was not the best choice of guitar for this recording, which added an extra layer of interest to an already fascinating project, a scratchy edge that could leave splinters in the fingers of anybody hoping for nostalgia with a twist.

Now he was working on a solo CD called, nakedly, *This Guitar*. He laughs. 'I thought the guitar has done me so many favours I'll try and do the guitar a favour. It's about the characteristics of the guitar and that's that. The sleeve note says, 'This guitar is a 1951 Epiphone Regent Emperor.' At this point, I tell him of my interest in the work and writing of the potters Leach and Hamada, how their focus on materials was a way of approaching the act of making a plate or a tea bowl.

'An instrument has a presence, doesn't it?' he says. 'I've got about five guitars and they're totally different. Their presence is completely different. The character's different. Nobody might notice it but I would play differently on each of them. Karen's [Bailey's partner and the designer of all Incus covers] father was a cabinet maker. For instance, towards the end of his life he made this amazing Welsh dresser. He made this table, actually.' He bangs the table. 'Karen and her brother always took the piss out of him because of his obsession with wood.'

The thought of Hamada, with a brush, working from the body, bom bom bom, came to mind again. I also thought of the Los Angeles sound artist, painter, sculptor and film maker Steve Roden. Recording under the name of in be tween noise (the music tends to be called lower case and the titles lean in the same direction), his 1997 CD, *splint (the soul of wood)*, is created from sounds generated from a 1943 moulded plywood leg splint designed by Charles Eames and manufactured by the Evans Products Company. Connected to contact microphones, plucked, bowed, rubbed and scratched, the wood is then recorded directly or manipulated and processed electronically. Of course, without being informed of the fact, you would never know that the three compositions collected on this little 3" CD had emerged from plywood caresses, tappings and reedy friction, let alone Charles Eames plywood, but there is no question that their hollow resonances and plaintive wind tones teleport characteristics of the material into the digital domain.

From the very first solo recordings made by Bailey, recorded in 1966 and '67 and released in 2002 by John Zorn's Tzadik label as *Pieces For Guitar*, a strong internal logic has carried each improvisation from its opening to its ending with clarity, certainty, a complex unfolding of internal relationships and what guitarist Tal Farlow once called 'snap'. A sign painter as well as a virtuoso jazz guitarist, Farlow borrowed this term from the sign painting side of his life to describe a kind of freshness, a sure hand that is full of life and capable of accuracy. Timing and tuning are also part of it, not so much in relation to any rules of music, but to the suitability of the materials used and the honed, quick reflexes of playing. If a guitar or a drum is properly tuned, then its capacity to resonate will be maximised. As for timing, this is like discussing the subtleties of flirtation or the dynamics of an evening in the pub. 'We look to other fields to try to understand what's going on here,' wrote Steve Beresford in his sleeve notes for *Playing*. 'John Zorn invoked Jack Benny, maybe because we can talk about TIMING in stand-up comedy without having to refer to PULSE.'

For Bailey, internal logic appears to have grown organically from many acts of playing, as opposed to an intellectual approach to composition, though thoughts about music and a thorough knowledge of music are also busily at work. I ask Derek about thinking. 'I think it gets in the fucking way,' he answers. 'The worst thing you can do is thinking. I find that people who talk about thinking, think about what they're going to play. I find I have to avoid thinking. It doesn't do me any good at all. If I think about the music that I might play, or the possibilities, then I prefer to do that when I'm not playing and maybe some of that percolates through, I don't know. The most stimulating thing me for me before playing, strange as it sounds, is sleep. It's not easy always to do that. Now, in old age, I find it's much easier. People understand, they say, "Ooh, you'll want a rest, won't you?" I say, can I go and lie down in there? They say, "Yes, of course. Do you want a hand?" Otherwise you see someone you haven't seen for a long time and you're rabbiting away in the bar. Hopeless. I prefer blank.'

hydrotherapy with tin tacks

Both Bailey and I agree that the most enduring version of the Spontaneous Music Ensemble – John Stevens on drums, cornet and voice, Nigel Coombes playing violin, cellist Colin Wood and guitarist Roger Smith, then a trio of Stevens, Smith and Coombes, minus Wood – fulfilled every expectation of improvised music. The quality of their listening was intense, their attention to detail was microscopic, their responses were endlessly varied and engaging, their instrumental skills were given over to the creation of an unfolding group relationship rather than a showcase of parallel virtuosity. All of which may explain why not a huge number of people liked them.

Personally, I loved them. Bailey laughs, remembering Stevens telling him in all seriousness that the other members were eccentrics, as if he were absolutely normal. I miss the sight of this group, the singularity of their sound, the richness and unintentional comedy of their collective behaviour in front of an audience: John scattering clicks and rustles from his mini-drum kit like a demented dolphin, head thrown back to let out ghostly moans and ululations; Roger Smith apparently suffering a medically obscure cross-ankled, splayed-finger aphasia in the quest to pinpoint the smallest of notes concealed in his already quiet instrument; Nigel Coombes, ploughing through trace memories of Paganini, larks ascending, *Psycho* and Chic, still wearing velvet in the fallout days of punk; Colin Wood, Apollonian and upright as a hat stand, seemingly perched above the nervous ferocity of this near-inaudible scrapping and scraping yet deep within it.

During one of the few recordings released by this group, *Low Profile*, released on Davidson's Emanem label, there is a moment, 16 minutes into the very long 'The Only Geezer An American Soldier Shot Was Anton Webern', when Stevens drops a fantastic cornet bleat into the insectivorous scurrying. Like a platoon of industrious midges paralysed by the incoming fart of a predatory superbug, the others throw up a wall of silence in self-defence. The recovery is beautiful to hear, the process of improvisation laid bare, as in a painting of medical students surveying a dissected corpse. Less than 10 minutes later in the same piece, recorded in Derby in 1977, Stevens does it again, this time unleashing his famous West London Buddhist chant. Again, Coombes, Wood and Smith play musical statues. It takes them a little while to make the decision but when they clam up, they do so as one, momentarily abandoning Stevens, the implausible Tibetan monk, to a harsh spotlight of their spontaneous construction.

Lasting for only a few years before Wood disappeared to India, this was a group that relished such glorious incidents of embarrassment and hiatus. The mutual incomprehension tended to be addressed with a hurricane of hilarity and beer in the pub afterwards. In his workshops and groups, Stevens always passed on a vital lesson by example – be serious without being po-faced – and this created a robust context for music that was delicate yet far from fragile.

The last two tracks are recordings of the trio, made in London in 1984 and 1988. Listening to the quartet I hear a music of implication. Individual events are too fleeting, too fugitive, to be fully absorbed. This was music that refused to hang about or to make the obvious moves, a febrile cluster of flurries, stop-motion rhythms, blunted and truncated snaps, drones that lost the will to drone, pitches too brittle or transient to accommodate melody, larks that promised ascent then dropped dead out of the sky.

The trio was slightly different: more a 3-dimensional geometry of fluid colour lines, points of light and odd surface protuberances. 'Kitless With Elbow', so-called because Stevens had been advised not to play because of an elbow problem, highlights the difference between the three players. Playing mini-trumpet, Stevens brings some of his love for free jazz into a group that was essentially chamber. This was reckless music that somehow expressed sensitivity through insensitivity and if Stevens wanted to blast it, then the others weren't about to damp his ardour.

So, if this music was so outrageously good, why did audiences accept virtually anything else in preference? Why was it so low profile? The group should have been filmed. More of their gigs should have been recorded. On the other hand, perhaps there's just about enough. A hint of melancholy is pervasive, not in the tenor of the music but in the restless pursuit of an ideal that slips away when the pursuer approaches this closely. To listen closely to their music can be exhausting: like tuning in to the central nervous system of an ant colony; like hydrotherapy with tintacks. No rest, no comfort, no soft fluffy bottom. Just search and reflect, as John would say. To play.

7 Machines and bodies

'While the notion that technologies are prostheses, expanding existing organs and fulfilling desires, continues to legitimise vast swathes of technical development, the digital machines of the late twentieth century are not add-on parts which serve to augment an existing form. Quite beyond their own perceptions and control, bodies are continually engineered by the processes in which they are engaged.'

Sadie Plant, *Zeroes + Ones*

March 2003. A pain in my left knee, apparently of neuropathic origin, is being treated by intramuscular stimulation. Developed by a Canadian doctor, Chan Gunn, this involves very low intensity laser treatment and deep acupuncture into so-called supersensitive muscle. At the end of the treatment, my English doctor runs a Pointer Plus over the region on my back where he has been working. This device registers levels of conductivity by responding with sound. Over unbroken skin it emits a low pitch but where the skin has been pierced by a needle the pitch rises in response to a changing level of electrical energy.

inside the mouth
In the early 1970s, the Poetry Society, then housed in a grand building in London's Earl's Court, was enjoying its passing moment of radicalism. Advocates of sound poetry, concrete poetry, mixed media performance, sound art and electronic transformations had seized a strategic patch of territory from humble versifiers. As a guitar and flute playing member of the

Bob Cobbing
Shakespeare-kaku

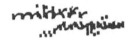

abAna trio with sound poet Bob Cobbing and percussionist Paul Burwell, I found myself involved in Poetry Society events at which the ghosts of T. S. Eliot and Sylvia Plath could only scratch their spectral heads and wonder.

Implicit in spoken poetry is a link that connects the listener back through history to rich traditions of storytelling, bardic oratory, the secret language of shamans, sacred incantations, the unfolding of oral sagas, praise songs and creation myths. Sound poets such as Cobbing consciously plugged into this ancient lineage, giving ritualistic, emphatically physical performances that exploded textual images into a dance of lexical fragments and oesophageal noise. Other sound poets were more interested in the new possibilities of electronic technology: once recorded, a voice could be transformed and expanded beyond recognition by editing the tape, reversing it, changing pitch and speed, applying filters, ring modulation, distortion and other effects. In live performance, Henri Chopin would rub a live microphone over his face, like a razor. Born in 1922, Chopin began using tape recorders in the 1950s, after seeing Isidore Isou's film *Traité de Bave et d'Eternité*. The film's soundtrack was recorded by François Dufrêne, using only noises made with his lips, throat and tongue. For Chopin, tape lifted the word off the page and from out of its private confines within books, giving him access to 'vocal micro-particles' and 'buccal instances' from within the mouth, the fine components of which he described as the 'infinitely mysterious oral'. 'For as long as can be remembered the major languages have presaged the grand designs of technical evolution,' Chopin wrote in 1995. 'They have sided with it, have known how to adapt to it and have been able to develop it further, thereby augmenting the number of languages itself. This has been the case with the poésie électronique, that almost never confined itself to pre-existing languages, and also with the Futurists and the Dada.'

After experimenting for some years with visual poetry made with Roneo and Gestetner duplicating machines and cracked Letraset type, Bob Cobbing created tape pieces in the early 1960s with film maker Jeff Keen, and with the BBC Radiophonic Workshop. '"Dotty and refreshing" was the verdict of another critic on Bob Cobbing's *ABC of Sound*, made at the Workshop as an experiment in concrete poetry,' wrote Desmond Briscoe in *The BBC Radiophonic Workshop: The First 25 Years*. 'The programme put to the test the first principles of radio: communication by means of sound. Cobbing read his alphabet – an extensive montage of carefully chosen words in various languages – which the workshop then speeded up, slowed down, dilated, distended, condensed and otherwise deformed. Dick Mills remembers it as "very much an inspired programme ... with a tartan background being woven by the Workshop while Cobbing recited all the Ms – Macpherson, MacFarlane, etc., to a treated vocal skirling of bagpipes and similarly heathery sounds."'

Cobbing's first experiments with tape were a revelation, first rectifying a physical weakness, then returning him to his own body as the richest source of sound. 'When I was at school I had a very feeble stuttering voice,' he told me in 2001, a year before his death. 'When I had my first tape recorder and started reading stuff into it I really was ashamed of it. It really was pitiful. I think the tape recorder helped – the fact that you can put a little sound in and amplify it and slow it down and get the vibrations going. I thought, if you can do it on tape, why can't you do it with your naked voice?'

Computers were beginning to be used for similar purposes and I vividly recall a demonstration given by the Swedish sound poet, Sten Hanson. Forced to wait in line for months for access to a mainframe computer, Hanson would have to spend many hours creating even the shortest sound poems. During those radical few years at the Poetry Society, a small number of us sat in rows one night, listening to the results of Hanson's computer generated works, either studying the floor, in the Rodin pose, or transfixed by a reel of tape as it threaded through the heads of a Revox tape recorder set up, somewhat honorifically, on a table in front of us.

Why has this experience stuck in my mind when the memory of so many other concerts has faded? Perhaps because of the extreme contrast between my own image of performed poetry – an intimate art form of small scale, completely independent of complicated technology – and the implications of alienation seeded by this configuration of spectators observing a tape recorder playing poetry generated (at least partially) by a computer. To an extent, this was the shock of the new, though disengagement from the body was real enough. The feeling was weird.

Visitors to the Ideal Home Exhibitions of the 1950s must have felt a similar pang as they gazed in covetous awe at demonstrations of labour-saving devices. Just as automation in the home implied a leisurely future of coffee mornings and afternoon cocktails, obsolete washing mangles and carpet sweepers consigned to the dustbin of history, so electronic music seemed to signal an end to the heavy industry of musical performance. The machines would surely have their day.

Thirty years later, the future just happened: not, of course, a laser beam of inevitability; more a crooked stick of hideous surprises with which we beat ourselves for our hubris. Live music still exists, as does housework and cooking, though all of these activities now take a certain amount of automation for granted. The computer controlled 'smart' house exists, at least in the pages of design magazines, and many musicians now sit on stage with nothing between them and their public but a compact, portable and unimaginably powerful laptop computer.

Histories of live electronic music tend to be written either as histories of the avant-garde or as rather less enthralling accounts of the industry devoted to developing electronic instruments. To some extent that is justified. Ideas and original inspirations flowed from composers such as Karlheinz Stockhausen and John Cage, and developers pushed forward the technological means by which the ideas could be realised (though those roles have been reversed often enough, particularly in recent times when the electronic toys can dictate both the sound and shape of entire careers).

For me, the acceptance of electronics in a live context has grown from a broader cultural spectrum. For somebody of my generation, teenage years coinciding with the 1960s, that might include going to the discotheque (as it was originally called) to dance to Motown and Stax records, or hearing Prince Buster 45s at The Flamingo Club; seeing Pink Floyd, in their Syd Barrett phase, at Enfield College of Technology, Jimi Hendrix at north London's Bluesville, or the UK debut of Frank Zappa and The Mothers Of Invention at the Royal Albert Hall; listening to the *Goon Show* on the radio; watching *Doctor Who* on the television; seeing Stanley Kubrick's *2001* or Hiroshi Teshigahara's *Woman of the Dunes* at the cinema and buying records by The Beach Boys, The Beatles, The Velvet Underground, the United States of America and Sun Ra. While electronic music inventors and composers such as Robert Moog, Don Buchla, Pierre Henry and Ilhan Mimaroglu were collaborating in various ways with rock or jazz musicians, some of the most prominent rock and soul celebrities of the period – Mick Jagger, Pete Townshend, Stevie Wonder and George Harrison, for example – were dabbling in experimental analogue synthesis. Although the content of these experiments was variable on both sides, electronic music acted as one of the agents that destabilised the hierarchical, class-based model of musical culture that prevailed until the 1960s.

The combined influence of all these examples has permanently transformed the way in which we listen. Although discotheques were an embodiment of 1960s modernity (the twist, urban soul, bouffants, fashion photography and Italian suits), there was no sense in their heyday of the real future that beckoned: the emergence of disco mixing and the hip-hop DJ in the 1970s, house and techno in the 1980s, ambient chill-out rooms and trip hop in the 1990s and ubiquitous, though largely uninspiring and conformist, club culture in the present.

Of course, to sit (these days more likely to stand) in an audience, only a studious face and a raised laptop lid to watch, can raise misgivings not too far from the disquiet I experienced at the Poetry Society three decades ago. Paying admission for the privilege of studying the Revox tape machine in action was a passing phase, the unsatisfactory front end of an electronic music revolution that seems to grow in relevance even as the tools used to create it join stone axes, sundials and steam engines in the museum of obsolete technology. Live electronic music has altered our idea of what live music can, and should be. At a deeper level, it also continues to pose questions about the relationship between humans, machines and the values associated with music in a period of rapid and disorientating transition.

Consciously experimental settings are not the only contexts in which such questions emerge. Writing for *The Face* magazine in the 1980s I reviewed a London concert by The O'Jays. Always a favourite band of mine, their Philadelphia International recordings such as 'Back Stabbers', 'Love Train' and 'For the Love Of Money' epitomised Seventies soul at its dynamic best: innovative, ambitious arrangements; lyrics built from stories – idealistic, realistic, compassionate and astute about changing values, politically sharp – sung with vocals that consistently hit inspiring levels of intensity and technique.

The support band on this occasion was Levert, led by Gerald Levert, the son of O'Jays lead singer Eddie. Promoting a dramatic ballad called '(Pop, Pop, Pop, Pop) Goes My Mind' at that time, Levert played with a machine precision that left me impressed but unmoved. Doubtless they would describe this precision as professionalism but I heard something underneath that: clear signs that inventions like MIDI (a protocol that allows drum machine, electronic keyboards and other sound and light sources to be cabled together and run in synchronisation), and sequencers (devices for programming all of these instruments with repeatable, error-free bass lines, drum parts and chord sequences), were changing the way in which musicians played in live situations. Under economic pressure and changing tastes, humans were learning how to be as accurate as machines.

After Levert, The O'Jays took the stage and the difference of two decades was apparent. Dressed in stage uniforms dating from their heyday and looking distinctly middle-aged, the band flowed organically around a collective pulse rather than marching to a metronome ticking in the head. Bands like this needed a musical director – arrangements to write or procure, charts to maintain, cues to conduct for new musicians, musical and social discipline to maintain – and the MD in this case threw himself into the task as if he were the only man on stage. At the front was Eddie Levert, the kind of undervalued singer who makes you wonder how somebody like Van Morrison ever got a job, let alone some showbiz hopeful propelled to fame by the votes of a reality TV show. Having worked with MIDI-linked keyboards and drum machines in recording studios since 1985, I could hear the contrast clearly. In all senses, this was the sound of two different generations divided by technology. Other people in the audience would be aware of this difference, but unless they were musicians I would guess that they heard it as a gap between old-fashioned and modern style, which of course is also true, though not the whole story.

One of the surest ways to make a fool of yourself is to predict the future of technology, or the future of anything. In 1982, Pete Townshend told *Rolling Stone*: 'The guitar will be gone within ten years – microchips!' Tell that to Oasis or The White Stripes. And in *The Wire* in 1994, Akin Fernandez wrote an anti-digital manifesto claiming that music recorded and reproduced in digital formats would deteriorate catastrophically after 10 years. 'Now, however, we face a situation where no remnants of whole bodies of our contemporary music are going to exist in 10 years,' he wrote, 'let alone 300 or 400.' As I write this, there is one year remaining before doomsday. No matter how appealing this silent spring might seem from within the tropical growth of back catalogue currently proliferating, the chance of 'no remnants of whole bodies' vanishing into the aether seems very remote.

excrescent fat   winter music

'Increasingly, technology conducts the business once performed by our bodies. A parade of labour-saving gizmos – the television remote control, the electric garage door opener, cordless phones, power steering, food processors – add up to an environment where fewer of us every year are expending the energy necessary to maintain a grip on our appetite.'

Ellen Ruppel Shell, *The Hungry Gene:*
The Science of Fat and the Future of Thin

Eighteen months ago, my daughter began learning to play the guitar. For years she had scraped away at a cello before deciding that the repertoire bore little relation to her own tastes in music. Seeing young women playing cello with Brazilian singer Vinicius Cantuaria or Pink Floyd guitarist David Gilmour, or hearing recordings of Pablo Casals and his wild flights through Bach, made little impression on this resolve. Now she strums along to Oasis or Avril Lavigne through her little Marshall amp and I can barely tell the difference between her playing and the music coming from the CD. This is one of the beauties of the electric guitar. The first part of learning is fairly easy, which means that higher levels of difficulty are more approachable. As for the instrument, it remains largely unchanged since the late 1950s. The way it works could be analysed in a few minutes by an extra-terrestrial with a basic knowledge of physics and a degree of common sense. The development curve of the electric guitar was remarkably steep and quick, levelling out at a point of perfection that balanced the necessity for smooth, in-tune playing, mechanical and electrical reliability, with unpredictable factors such as note bending, bottleneck playing, distortion, resonance, touch and so on. Many guitarists pay high prices to play vintage models, made by companies that were once small independents. Old can often be better.

What you can't do with a guitar is write a letter with it and then use the instrument to post that letter. You can't use the instrument itself to connect up with other guitarists unless you travel to meet them. From that point of view, the guitar has portability on its side. Have guitar will travel, as the saying goes, and the lonely parts of travelling can be brightened by another characteristic of the instrument. A guitar, like the considerably less portable piano, is a self-contained device for playing simultaneous melody and accompaniment.

A laptop computer is also portable, can also be used for recording, processing and composing music, downloading software and sample sounds, editing and mastering an album, burning a CD, designing the cover for the CD, launching a record company with an Internet website, making contact with distributors, shops and fans through e-mail, keeping track of the company accounts, then taking the computer on the road as a performance tool.

Many debates about contemporary performance in the world of electronic and improvised music begin and end with the laptop computer: live, there is nothing interesting to watch; the relationship between action and sound is hidden from the audience; if the musician died on stage, or fell asleep, the computer would simply keep on playing. During an interview with Björk in 2001, I asked her for her views on the use of computers and software such as the ProTools sound editing program. On her *Vespertine* album she collaborated with the San Francisco based electronic duo, Matmos, whose CD of the same year included sampled sounds of laser eye surgery, liposuction, audiological testing, acupuncture points, cauterised muscle tissue and the percussive noises of a human skull. Despite its alleged origins in the excrescent fat of California's surgical reinvention laboratories, *A Chance To Cut Is a Chance To Cure* is a lyrical, if viscous, exploration of the ways in which compositional narrative can be dissected and reconstructed into unpredictable sequences of barely related material through computer surgery. In the days of analogue tape, the scalpel blade shown on the front cover would once have served as the tool with which precise edits could be cut into magnetic audio tape. Now these edits are made with the computer cursor, often clicking on the visual representation of a pair of scissors; the scalpel returns to its original job of cutting into the human body, a (sharp) reminder of solid objects and penetrable surfaces in the increasingly virtual world of audio production.

Matmos is Drew Daniel and M. C. Schmidt, aided and abetted by musicians, devices and vocal interjections. Their fascination with the implications of object as thing in relation to object as sound source (what does it mean to take pleasure in listening to the sound of extracted human fat squirting juicily down a pipe?) found a name with their second CD, *Quasi-Objects*, released in 1998. Every sample noise lives in its own space, occupies its own history, carries its own symbolism and social meaning, though unlike a photograph, the recordings are ambiguous, their nature as visually and haptically perceivable objects or processes uncertain. An original function or purpose is buried somewhere deep within a track, jostling for attention and gaining new meanings alongside all the other quasi-objects. The claustrophobic world of the computer opens up into views of different rooms.

Quasi-Objects was the record that alerted Björk to their unusual methods. Of course, the idea of making music from the concrete sounds of surgical procedures could be considered disturbing, not to say ridiculous. Perhaps what she could hear was the Matmos expertise with structure and juxtaposition: a way of building a composition that holds together, evolves, engages, switches mood, almost (though definitely not) like a conventional song, yet mixes up contradictory emotional responses: turning away in disgust, voyeuristically looking just a little bit closer, appreciating the absurdity of the moment, experiencing some vague sense of regret, feeling charmed and amused yet somehow cast into the unknown.

For their remix of 'Alarm Call', from Björk's *Homogenic* album, Matmos recast her vocal as a multilingual outburst of gasps and phonetic fragments, a mouth confrontation delivered from within the kinetic stereo craziness of Esquivel updated into acid stutter electro-dub. I asked Björk if she feels there is a contradiction between the intimate, internal body technology of the voice and the assemblages of computer editing. 'You can't separate yourself from nature,' she replied. 'I think most technology, it's tools. What we do with them, whether it's cold or soulful, that's our choice. I also think there's a lot of guilt there that was put in me and my generation. I'm not going to blame all that on my mum. That's more of a generational thing. What are you going to do? Move to an island for the rest of your life and be barefoot? Why drive a car all your life and feel guilty about it? Do it or skip it. I think it's important to have a unison – the lives we're living and what we're doing, the music we're writing and the books we're reading and writing, that it all makes sense. We're not doing one thing and feeling it's ugly. Not going, "Well, if I could choose I'd actually be in a Fred Flintstone car." Get a life, you know? I think my generation was very interested in sorting that one out. In the 80s, having 50 TVs in a stack and learning to find it pretty. I definitely come from that school of thought, that you can be organic and pagan and have ProTools.'

This drive to unite the digital domain with corporeal and imaginative worlds contributed to some unusual choices of instrumentation for *Vespertine*. Harp, clavichord, celesta and music box are all percussive, brittle, melodic instruments with a limited frequency range. 'They are for me, like winter music, like frozen,' she says. 'On a musical level, I was obsessed with my laptop. I was really getting into it, the last three years, doing beats and recording my vocals straight on it, which was revolutionary for me. So I was really obsessed, obviously downloading stuff from the Net and e-mailing back and forth and getting occupied with that element of laptops. It's all a secret. There's no oxygen in that world. It operates like your mind. Your thought process is very similar.'

Her reaction to record companies and musicians who objected to file sharing and free MP3 downloading of copyright music practised through Internet sites such as Napster and Gnutella was to look for ways to adapt to these new conditions. 'We've been doing folk music or whatever you call it for 2000 years,' she says, 'and the instruments, the tools you use, if they're limited it means you have to be more imaginative and creative. 100 years ago, radio arrived and the first music that was going then sounded crap on the radio. Later on, humans became genius at writing and arranging and producing specifically for radio. Now we've got the Napster thing, the Internet and downloading and you write specifically for that. I use micro-beats, a lot of whispery vocals, which I think sound amazing when they're downloaded because of the secrecy of the medium. It's all about being in a little house, on your own. You're creating paradise with your laptop, or underneath your kitchen table where nobody knows about it. It's survival in that sense. I can't lie when I sing. With ProTools, it's not like you're lying but it's easier to focus on what you want things to be. For me, ProTools is more connected with a fantasy and my voice more with reality. With the tools I can have everything I want and think of ridiculous things that don't exist but with my voice I'm always gonna show what happened to me that day, that month, that year. I can't hide anything and I actually quite like that.'

pitcher plants welcoming flies

On a Tuesday afternoon in February, 1993, I'm sitting on a leather sofa in a BBC recording studio with guitarist Robert Hampson of Main. In front of us, on two television monitors, and to one side of us, through a glass window, obliquely, is a quartet assembled by American guitarist Jim O'Rourke, now a member of Sonic Youth but at that point still a free agent roving through many different approaches to playing.

Resonances open like pitcher plants welcoming flies. O'Rourke squeezes canine growl drones, rusted gongs and late night refrigerator hum through the interstices. The process is fascinating, because, O'Rourke, despite his other activities in far louder musics, is the quiet man in this subtle web of assured improvisation. 'Where do you get that hunted look from, Jim?' asks Derek Bailey during a lull. 'It could be very useful.'

So there is Bailey, snapping and brushing singing bells from his guitar with fierce economy and temporal precision; vocalist Vanessa Mackness, the contrary contralto whose fleshy lip trembles conjure lyrical Tuvans, loony toons, disembodied divas; and Eddie Prévost, rolling with the flow, tam-tamming and tom-tomming, abrading, striking and slicing his percussive devices with the quick delicacy of a sushi master. The last piece ends with a sliding pitch convergence of guitar and voice, just a fleeting moment left to evaporate in the studio air, but sufficient in its implicated beauty for somebody to rush off and build an entire career out of it.

'Auditory jerking off,' says the recording engineer, confident that only those of us in the control room can share his little joke. Perhaps he is right, in some sense. My conversation with Bailey on playing revealed an obsessive, private, solitary, physical need to play, a compulsion to return to a configuration that satisfies emotional hunger. At one point, Bailey had described solo playing as 'disgusting', an implication of playing with yourself or, as the saying goes, to be a bit of a wanker. Absent, however, both here at the BBC and in the 'playing fool' condition Bailey is describing, is any inevitable drive towards climax.

Six years after sitting in the BBC studio, I am standing in a large hall at the Sonar Festival in Barcelona. On stage is the trio of Christian Fennesz, Jim O'Rourke and Peter 'Pita' Rehberg. All three are playing laptop computers and the movements of their fingertips on trackpads are projected on screens. This assertion of human presence within the improvised evolution of their performance – a dense layering of musical samples and digital processing – adds to the disorientation of music created in the moment, with minimal physicality and a technology that conceals, rather than reveals. The discomfort of hearing it in a large hall, standing up, surrounded by a half-interested crowd that mills and chatters, leaves me stranded in a mood of ennui. The music sounds wonderful but this is not how I want to hear it.

endless summer

> 'I look at the machine and I think of a world where each
> memory could create its own legend.'
>
> From *Sans Soleil*, directed by Chris Marker

One of the busiest musicians in the electronica scene, Ryoji Ikeda, once sent me an e-mail to say that he was composing and recording new work on long-haul flights. I wondered about changing time zones, the extraordinary sights that can occasionally be seen from the window of an aircraft, constant engine drone and the bizarre suspension of ordinary life within this moving capsule. To some extent this busy-busy pragmatism is just an update of normal musical practice. In the 1960s, James Brown would stop off at local studios to record new tracks whilst on tour, and throughout history any number of composers, arrangers, conductors and musical directors must have pored over music charts on bus, train, ocean liner or stagecoach. To be able to record on the move adds another dimension, however, an extra level of imaginary space which interacts with the virtual communicative and informational spaces already established by computer networks.

Physical placement is becoming less important to a music's conviction of its own worth, a tendency that can be found in most forms of music, whether it's the musician from Ethiopia, constantly on tour throughout the world, playing to displaced persons from the homeland and to world music fans; the DJ whose record boxes double as flight cases and contain entire soundworlds; or the TV nurtured pop star whose career has avoided any of the traditional associations with a regional music scene, a local club or pub or a fan base built up through live touring. In this context, the imaginary dimensions of space can become more significant than its actual physical character. Computer music can pull sound out of 'nothing' (from the mathematical generation of sound, shaped by adjustment of numerical parameters), or can transform a recording of a place and past events, to establish a new mythic location, more closely located within the consciousness of the musician than in any locale we can directly experience as a haptic reality.

While writing this book, I e-mailed Christian Fennesz, who replied from the night train that runs from Paris to Vienna. He was unable to answer immediately, he wrote, because he was working on his laptop, trying to finish a collaborative track for David Sylvian's *Blemish* album. In 2001, Fennesz released a CD called *Endless Summer*. Born in 1962, he lives in Vienna, which places his personal history far from the beaches of California or Hawaii. One topic we don't hear too much about in songs from equatorial Africa, or the central Australian desert, is the endless summer. Endless summer is a peculiarly American West Coast invention, indelibly associated with the lost dreams of the 1960s, and subsequently borrowed by countries with a more variable climate and similar economic privilege. Impressionistic variations on this theme are explored with varying degrees of intelligence in surfing films such as Bruce Brown's *The Endless Summer*, a global pursuit of the perfect wave, and John Milius's *Big Wednesday*, or any Beach Boys song that wrestles with the melancholy burden of loss and transition.

As an example of this, the Brian Wilson and Mike Love composition, 'The Warmth Of The Sun', was written for the Beach Boys just hours after John F. Kennedy was assassinated, its lyric a dreamy, ecstatic exploration of natural cycles in nature and human love. It was Mike Love who followed Bruce Brown's lead by dreaming up the title, *Endless Summer*, for a 1974 compilation of past hits that rescued the Beach Boys from a sharp downward spiral, and this potent encapsulation of attenuated nostalgia was reprised many times in the group's long decline, whether 'Keeping The Summer Alive' or the tragically euphemistic *Endless* [dis]*Harmony*.

Such impossible, almost alchemical, yearnings have given deadly poignancy to a ruined fairy story that is central to popular music and its myths. Is there any connection between this odd history of seasonal wish-fulfilment and Fennesz, a leading exponent of Viennese digital transmutation? One of the answers to that question might be the Jesus and Mary Chain, similarly engaged in quite another era by the Sisyphean task of burying Brian Wilson's piano in the legendary sandpit without totally obscuring its radiance.

Fennesz was, and is, a guitarist, and just as the Jesus and Mary Chain explored an ambivalent relationship to pleasure, offering cyclical surf chords to a sacrificial Glasgwegian kiss of fuzz pedals and overdriven loudspeakers, so Fennesz sprays atmospheric distress all over the screen of his paradise longing. As formulas, or procedures, or processes, go, it's painfully effective for addressing the emotional (and cultural, and geographical, and ideological) distance that separates many of us from the music we truly love. No love is more poignant than that which is denied, lost, withdrawn, or otherwise unattainable.

No palm trees for 10 kilometres; that seemed to be the artwork message of *Fennesz Plays*, his 1998 release containing a 'cover' of the Brian Wilson, Tony Asher ballad from *Pet Sounds*, 'Don't Talk (Put Your Head On My Shoulder)'. This meditation on stillness and romance drowned itself rather beautifully in a confusion of emotions. Traces of its source were picked apart with fastidious care to leave a web of memories hanging in electrolysed air. That track, in particular, was a hard act to follow: ravishing sonic texture, vertiginous emotional implications, a pop-art instrumental apparently aware that this strategy of the pop-art instrumental, so central to 21st-century music on the broken edges of dance floor, jazz dive and conservatoire, was a move that Brian Wilson had more or less invented with tracks like 'Fall Breaks And Back To Winter' (the Woody Woodpecker Symphony that finally turned a few pages in the calendar).

Fennesz was one of the first musicians to realise the possibilities of the laptop computer as an instrument in its own right. I asked him if he felt a difference between playing the guitar and making music with a computer. 'Not for me,' he says. 'I was always more into sound, production and studio work. I just didn't have the possibilities to do it. Playing guitar in bands was perhaps more a result of having to compromise, as there was never enough money to rent a good studio where I could realise my ideas. I love to play the guitar. I still play it, but being able to have total control over my sounds and productions is absolutely fantastic. This was a revolution for me.'

Within the best of his music, the play on withheld sensuality, an ambiguity of intent and meaning, is deeply engaging. Familiarity is adding its reductive presence, along with a slight suspicion that the process of shadowing a direct emotional response with technological masks may be just a little too easy to copy, to copy, to copy. This fluctuation between two states, a music that seems in some way familiar and another layer decomposing from that source material, evokes a feeling of nostalgia. Perversely, a desire suggests itself, to holiday for eternity in this endless summer without a place. How to travel there? 'The beach itself has eroded over time, literally washing away,' wrote Lena Lencek and Gideon Bosker in their book, *The Beach: The History of Paradise on Earth*. This sense of the inexorable erosion of perfection, sweet dreams fading in the harsh light of mediated emotion, seems to me to be central to Fennesz, and when he arrests that dissipation, paradise momentarily out of focus as if video-paused, the feeling is bittersweet.

This is what I perceive. Is it an effect he intends? 'It is intended,' he says. 'For me it is important to have some kind of "history" within my music, something that makes people, and myself too, remember things that they normally wouldn't expect from this kind of music. it is of course a very subjective view upon history. I think my music is the opposite of "self generating music". I enjoy working with self-generating software, but when I use it, it sounds like sweet sadness again. To say it in a simple way: I like to hide things and like to distort simplicity. What I'm trying to perceive is this feeling I get when I discover something in a film that reminds me of a feeling and atmosphere I once had, some kind of déjà vu. Photos and paintings can do this as well – some hidden atmosphere that turns out to be very simple once you discover it.'

flat earth

With the exception of certain percussion instruments like cymbals and flat gongs, most musical instruments need a resonating chamber to shape and project their sound. This interior space, a dark secret place full of air, began to disappear at the beginning of the 20th century. The invention of the electronic theremin turned this principle inside out, since the metal rod of the instrument was surrounded by an invisible field in which the sound seemed to float. Electric Hawaiian guitars, then guitars, then bass guitars, pianos and organs, violins, saxophones and finally drums all spawned solid and more or less flat versions of themselves, their need for natural resonance partly or entirely displaced by electronics: instruments as surface rather than chamber.

In *Writings Through John Cage's Music, Poetry, + Art*, Alvin Curran, a member of the pioneering improvisation group Musica Elettronica Viva, talks about the early days of MEV in the mid-1960s: '... we found ourselves busily soldering cables, contact mikes, and talking about "circuitry" as if it were a new religion. By amplifying the sounds of glass, wood, metal, water, air, and fire, we were convinced that we had tapped into the sources of the natural musics of "everything." We were in fact making a spontaneous music which could be said to be coming from "nowhere" and made out of "nothing" – all somewhat a wonder and a collective epiphany.'

From the late 1960s onwards, many improvising musicians – George Lewis, Tony Oxley, Chris Cutler, Phillip Wachsmann, Jon Rose, Jin Hi Kim, Keith Rowe, Nicolas Collins, Toshinori Kondo, Fred Frith and others – have responded to this technological evolution by extending the range of their instruments through a wide variety of methods: contact microphones, processing devices such as delays, distortion, filters and ring modulators, multi-effects units or MIDI connections to external modules such as samplers, sound generators and computer programs.

Then in the late 90s, a steady trickle of players who had combined their conventional instrument with electronics began to abandon the instrument in favour of the laptop computer. Whereas the urge to extend an instrument's range was a logical development, evidence of talented players giving up their specialist instrument seemed more shocking. Phil Durrant, for example, had begun as an acoustic violinist in the UK improvisation scene of the 70s, then became involved in dance music after acid house. During the 90s he combined violin with electronic processing, or worked with other musicians such as saxophonist John Butcher, sampling and processing their improvisations in real-time. In Cork, in 2001, I saw him playing with a quartet called Ticklish. By this time, he was playing only the computer. Trying to play and process the sound simultaneously was difficult, he said during one of our conversations. Without the advantages of four hands and parallel brain processing, the playing suffered and the processing was clumsy.

Another violinist, Kaffe Matthews, had developed ways of amplifying and processing her instrument through analogue devices, then conducted research at Steim, the Dutch centre for research and development of electronic instruments and sound interfaces, where she began to use a real-time sampling and audio manipulation program for Macintosh called LiSa. At the Drift Festival in Glasgow I heard her play live, violin lying on its back to one side of the computer, sampled sound feeding in from the exterior and interior of the room, absorbed into a web without centre, beginning or end. Occasionally she would strike at the violin strings to add another input to the mix. Then the next time I heard her play, with Christian Fennesz in London, both were playing high volume digital music from laptops. The violin had vanished. More recently she has been using a small theremin and microphone feedback from both inside and outside the live space as her performance materials.

At the time I asked her about the live aspect of her work in relation to software, she had recently come back from a silent retreat. Part of her reason for undertaking this temporary vow of silence was to recover from the itinerant musician's life: the airport check-in, hotel checkout, packing and unpacking, highs and lows. In the summer, she was considering giving up live playing altogether, trying to work out a simpler sonic aesthetic which allowed more spontaneity, humour and transparency, but only having the time to iron out the details in front of live audiences. 'I guess the silence I searched for was not a silence in the space around me,' she said. 'I didn't need to get out of the city. Just for me to shut down. To shut up. To stop. To ground. To empty. Then to figure out what was going on.' Her mind fought back with elaborate techniques of seduction, making her realise how noisy she was inside. For the next month, she felt more alive and alert to sound, enjoying all kinds of music in an orgy of auditory pleasure.

'Having been through silence in my own communication,' she says, 'the world became vitally noisy again, from the tiniest hair to the most spectacular din. Nowadays, my current practice is working much more quietly and minimally, so having my perceptions retuned has been just the job. I'm now exploring making music with "silence" in it, no longer at the mercy of this desire to fill the air with continuous streams of sound. No, the bits in between and the nude revealing of simple sounds has become quite a focus. How they appear and disappear. Also, to work sometimes entirely with the tiniest sounds I can find within a room, live, and then to make something tiny with them, but in digital bits and patterns. Then the real room can occasionally breathe in between, or feed back in lilting waves.

'The live process seems as important as ever, which I think, simply, is all about communication. The audience witnesses this grappling with simple elements. Visibly, of course, there is very little to watch. I play in the near dark in the middle of the space with a laptop and small mixer and the audience all around me. The audience can switch off their eyes and go full-on aural, so that we are in the sonic G-spot if you like, all together. However, of course there is an illuminated face. A face, I am told, which reflects the hazards and pleasures of the process, and so a doorway into the work.'

to pass through the door

'After several years of bizarre playing in a sort of anti-jazz style that always ill-suited his supposed role of rhythm guitarist, Rowe now seems on the point of demonstrating that his individual approach to jazz guitar is fully vindicated.' That was in 1965, the opinion of a *Jazz Monthly* critic despatched to cover the Plymouth sound of Mike Westbrook's Jazz Band.

A full vindication leaves little room for manoeuvre, yet 35 years later Rowe was continuing to challenge that vindication with a style so anti-jazz that it makes one marvel that the Mike Westbrook Jazz Band could ever contain it. My first exposure to Keith Rowe's horizontal guitar-shaped amplified string, wood resonator and short wave radio improvisations came two years after *Jazz Monthly* with a string of AMM concerts and sessions held in venues as diverse as The Roundhouse, The Place, The Queen Elizabeth Hall and Ronnie Scott's Club. At the beginning of the 1970s, I would go once a week, or whenever I could afford the train fare, to a London dance studio and theatre called The Place. The quartet version of AMM – Rowe, Eddie Prévost, Lou Gare and Cornelius Cardew – or perhaps the quintet with Christopher Hobbs, would play there in the dark, Cardew padding around in his socks to make the least possible sound, Gare wandering slightly, since his tenor saxophone allowed him a certain freedom to roam. Light and shadows played across the only window in the room. There was no stage, no formal arrangement of players, instruments or audience. The experience still has an emotional clarity for me, despite the fact that more than 30 years have passed, and the question of a door, in the sense that Kaffe Matthews uses the word, is answered by an equally clear feeling that the space of the room itself was a door. The music immersed all those within that space in its structural complexity. Just to sit and absorb, without anxiety about looking or playing or instruments, was to have passed through the door.

In the *Sunday Times* of 13 June 1971, Felix Aprahamian's summary of the QEH performance was an amusingly pithy one-liner: 'Most of it consisted of endless microtonal inflections and percussive accretions to a held organ chord – B flat major, second inversion – a chord with which, as Sir Jack Westrup recently declared in similar circumstances, I am not unfamiliar.' Listening to *Harsh*, a solo album released by Rowe in 2001, happily reveals that little has changed. There is no organ and the tonal centre couldn't be pinned down to a B flat major of whatever inversion but the methodology – microtonal inflections and percussive accretions – remains consistent. It's a sound with which I, too, am not unfamiliar.

Rowe's cartoon drawings for the CD cover, somewhat in the style of early Patrick Caulfield, are abstractions of guitar strings under assault from saw blades, crocodile clips, mini-fans and springs. Familiar devices, as are the Cageian murmurings of short wave voices and North African musics that cavort at the periphery of audition, yet Keith brings a new sensibility to old methods. For Rowe, usually a player who soaks himself with preternatural skill into the environmental grain, the sound is *Harsh*, as advertised on the tin: out-of-register, brutal, calculatedly (perhaps only in retrospect) repellent and dominant. None of those seemingly negative descriptions deny the compelling force of this performance. In his brief sleeve notes, Rowe suggests some points of consideration: the technical means of producing his sounds have been in use for more than 35 years, the music resists the consumerism that infects our culture, the circumstances of recording were bleakly opposite to the comfortable conditions of AMM's recording for the ECM label, the harsh surface of the playing is a statement about the harshness of global poverty, political repression and cultural deprivation.

The apparent stasis in method should be considered in the light of what improvisation means, or the political movements with which improvised music has been associated through its now lengthening history. Paradoxically, a stubborn continuity of approach is apparent among improvisers who have relished collaboration with younger players using computers, software and other new versions of the live electronics pioneered by Rowe and others so long ago. Though consistent and identifiable, this method can prove itself to be highly adaptable, as Rowe proved with his *Weather Sky* CD with Toshimaru Nakamura, who plays only with high feedback tones created from within a small mixing desk, or in groups with Kaffe Matthews, Phil Durrant and many of the most interesting improvising musicians who emerged in the 90s: Kevin Drumm, Thomas Lehn, Oren Ambarchi, Rafael Toral, Marcus Schmickler, Peter Rehberg and others. Implicit in the *Jazz Monthly* review of 1965 was the idea that improvisation in Europe was detaching itself from the continuity of jazz as a predominantly African-American art form and turning its attention more directly to its immediate environment and historical context. American music and the English language, so dominant in jazz and popular music for so long, no longer exerted such a powerful influence.

In the 1950s, cold war politics, race politics and their portrayal through the global theatre of mass media tattooed indelible marks on the postwar generation. A strong undercurrent of resistance to technology (the weapons of total annihilation that stood ready), or access denied to all but the most successful of African-American jazz musicians, contributed to the overwhelmingly acoustic feel of so much early free jazz and free improvisation. Inside the studio, sound recording was beginning its experiment of physical and audio separation; beyond that, the sense of alienation in an increasingly mediated, commodified landscape was intensifying. 'To feel is perhaps the most terrifying thing in this society,' Cecil Taylor has said. 'This is one of the reasons I'm not too interested in electronic music: it divorces itself from human energy, it substitutes another kind of force as the determinant agent for its continuance.'

Sun Ra's use of electronic keyboards was prophetic, not just because he was almost alone among free jazz musicians in using the Moog, Clavioline, tape effects and so on, but because his use of these instruments and techniques was so utterly liberated in comparison with the highly structured and theorised (or mytheorised) trajectory of the rest of his work. If hearing Sun Ra's Arkestra was an audio hallucination of the ballrooms of Chicago transplanted into the midst of verdant rainforest on a lonely planet where chaos was beauty, the effect of hearing Albert and Donald Ayler for the first time was like hearing the drum and fife music of Napolean Strickland and Othar Turner, the gospel saxophone of Vernard Johnson, the slide guitar moans of Blind Willie Johnson, the R&B tenor shriek and roar of Big Jay McNeely, the androgynous whooping and screaming of Little Richard, the New Orleans marches of George Lewis and the Eureka Brass Band, all refracted through the turmoil of civil rights,

Malcolm X's assassination, the riots in Watts, the media futurism of the space race, the escalating war in Vietnam.

Just the titles of Albert Ayler's breakthrough albums – *Spirits*, *Spiritual Unity*, *Spirits Rejoice*, *Bells* – were clear signs of the elevated consciousness he brought to music. In 1964, Ayler had recorded a selection of gospel tunes with Call Cobbs, Henry Grimes and Sunny Murray. Gospel was the well-kept secret of African-American music at that time, the voices of Archie Brownlee, Julius Cheeks, Claude Jeter and Inez Andrews little known beyond the sanctified circuit, despite being the foundation of soul. These were voices that inhabited the body to a point beyond its corporeal limits, screaming to the spirit, rising through registers to a place beyond conventional existence. Ayler inhabited the saxophone in the same way, bursting through its mechanical and physical expression of equal temperament to otherness. It was as if all the individual acts of instrumental subversion in jazz – from Bubber Miley, Joe 'Tricky Sam' Nanton and Cootie Williams of the 1920s Ellington Orchestra onwards – had now found a form through which their true meaning was understood.

From the mid-century, explorations in 'freeform' or 'abstract' music, improvised without a predetermined structure, were touched upon, or implied, by a small but impressive collection of musicians: Lennie Tristano, Warne Marsh and Lee Konitz in 1949; Dick Twardzik's piano improvisations of the mid-1950s, Charles Mingus in 1954, The Chico Hamilton Quintet and Cecil Taylor and Steve Lacy in 1955, George Russell and Bill Evans in 1956, Ornette Coleman and Don Cherry in 1959, Eric Dolphy in 1960 and, in the UK, Joe Harriott and Phil Seaman in the same year. In 1954 and 55, Charles Mingus, for example, recorded strange sombre pieces such as 'Gregorian Chant' and 'Abstractions' with the Jazz Composers Workshop, a group that included reeds players John LaPorta and Teo Macero and pianist Mal Waldron. 'Since I don't believe that such music can be classified as "atonal" or "weird" music (as atonal is often classified),' Mingus wrote in his sleeve notes to *Jazz Composers Workshop No. 2*, 'I would identify it as "a little beyond the elementary." If and when these present constructions are accepted, I will venture to delve a little more into the so-called dissonance of free form improvisation.'

At the time, the idea was shocking and while some quickly abandoned what later seemed an interesting diversion, a moment of madness, others recognised a lifetime faith. Faith was a requirement. Capitol Records treated the Lennie Tristano tracks, 'Intuition' and 'Digression', as worker rebellion. The company refused to release one of the recordings and initially withheld payment for the recording date. From the mid-1960s onwards, European improvising groups such as AMM, Joseph Holbrooke, MEV, Nuova Consonanza, The People Band and the Spontaneous Music Ensemble faced indifference or abruptly terminated interest from established record labels. Perceived as a branch of the entertainment industry, improvised music survived within an environment that was economically harsh and intellectually impoverished.

One means of ingress to improvising without a map was to interact through neoclassical counterpoint. Drummer Chico Hamilton's 'Free Form', recorded in 1955 at a club in Long Beach, California, is described on the *Spectacular!* album as a 'mobile abstraction with interspersing excitement [that] appeals to listeners of the third ear'. Chico Hamilton's early groups were adventurous at the same time as being fashionable: versions of the band appeared in the 1957 movie, *Sweet Smell of Success* and the 1958 documentary *Jazz on a Summer's Day*. Because of this unusual position half way between pop success and free jazz, it's easy to imagine hipsters of the time hearing the interplay between Fred Katz's cello and Buddy Collette's flute and slotting it somewhere between Béla Bartók, Jackson Pollock and sculptor Alexander Calder. For the unprepared listener, this relatively free approach may have been given legitimacy by the historical precedent of J. S. Bach and the baroque, but the social movements and politics of the period were destined to move in two contrary directions – towards self-exploration on the one hand; collective action on the other – and this paradox finally shattered any need to legitimise art through bourgeois history or exercise self-restraint.

Some of the reasons why free improvisation was a logical development in musical history can be understood retrospectively through relatively recent scientific studies of complexity and emergence. Creating musical coherence, variety and beauty without the instructions of a director was possible through the skills of listening and response that many musicians already possessed. 'This is the secret of cell assembly,' wrote Steven Johnson in *Emergence*. 'Cell collectives emerge because each cell looks to its neighbours for cues about how to behave.'

At one level, improvisation can be compared with the ultimate otherness of an ant colony or hive of bees. Perhaps it was no coincidence that in the wake of John Stevens and the Spontaneous Music Ensemble, certain strands of English improvised music were known, half-disparagingly, as insect music. In its earliest days, all of this music was classified under freedom: free jazz, free improvisation, or simply free music. The jazz musician's concept of playing 'outside' – outside the changes or metre – had moved one more step into anarchy. Eventually, as with any experiment in collectivism, the limitations of freedom began to assert themselves. Collective relationships in which hidden dynamics are not exposed can be breeding grounds for covert tyranny. The best improvisers realised that their music demanded constant awareness. As the history of automatism shows, spontaneity attracts the inevitability of collapse into repetitious themes and behavioural tics, stasis and empty chatter.

'We're taught that music is something special,' said saxophonist Trevor Watts, interviewed by the *Melody Maker* in the early 1970s, 'We intellectualise about it; that's how we're taught to function, so therefore it is necessary for us to have methods to cope with our environment, and yet play natural music.' In a society increasingly dominated by a marketplace of synthetic materials, electronic communications and the inexorable spread of mass media, this struggle between pragmatic strategies and 'natural' music became desperate. By the mid-1970s, free jazz and free improvisation were being written off as outmoded 'genres' that had promised visions of a new kind of society yet failed to communicate to an audience or develop an aesthetic. The truth, however, was more complicated and more hopeful. The challenges of creating music that dispenses with any hand of authority would now be addressed as issues central to a long-term project, rather than an expression of unfettered spontaneity and the utopia of freedom. After an extended experiment with absolutism, a new process had begun.

Improvisation may be the wrong word to describe this way of playing, though a better one has yet to come along. Writing notes about his duo album with John Tilbury, *Duos For Doris*, Keith Rowe gives greater importance to atmosphere and what he calls 'the decisive moment'. 'I have become increasingly preoccupied with atmosphere,' he writes, 'in particular the kind of atmosphere that one finds surrounding a Mark Rothko painting. It seems to me that when one is in the presence of a Rothko work, but also when one has departed and on reflection, I'm struck not by "phew", what great brush strokes, what an incredible technique, what a painter, but derive more of a feeling of the surrounding atmosphere, its sensation. Somehow I wanted to move what I'm doing (intention) towards this notion of atmosphere, an activity where we are not aware of technique, of instrument, of playing, of music even, but as feeling/sensation suspended in space. Perhaps this is what Feldman meant by music as time, energising the air, making the silence (un-intention) audible.'

A dogged determination to persevere courts nostalgia; learning, social familiarity, established patterns within the brain, audience expectations, all conspire to defeat the possibility of beginning from the beginning each time, tabula rasa. Experienced players develop personal strategies for dealing with the prospect of being washed up on a sandbank of nostalgia and ingrained habit. Far from sounding stranded, Keith Rowe's duet with Evan Parker on *Dark Rags*, a live-concert CD released in the same year as *Harsh*, pushes forward into deep water and open sea. Like Rowe, Parker could be perceived to have been 'doing the same thing' with his saxophones, reeds, breath and finger dexterity for some decades. Humans tend to function in that way, moving towards inertia, growing less innovative, less physically mobile as they grow wiser and more individuated (as C. G. Jung would have said). Through its emphasis on the fluidity of settings, a fracturing of expectation and the endless possibilities of complexity generated by combining unpredictable materials, improvisation goes some way to addressing this otherwise miserable paradox of human existence.

Dark Rags is heartening for being so astonishingly rich in its formulations and psychic power, yet still true to the course set so distantly back in the 20th century. There are passing suggestions of Indian classical music ragas, both in the inventions of a soloist against a complex drone (which doesn't begin to describe the fluctuations of this musical relationship) and in the allusions of the album's title, but also in the depth of these explorations. Feverish and magical, Rowe fires coarse animal bellows, industrial engineering, death rattles, dream dialogues and sine moans, at the lashing, twisting anime plant monster that Parker unleashes. This is a mischievous dialogue too. Aware of Parker's natural tendency to build upon what he hears, Rowe feeds him 'Strangers In the Night' from short wave. When Rowe pulls back from an intense assault, leaving only a shivering metallic microdance in motion, Parker sidles out of hushed ruminations into the barest hint of 'Fascinating Rhythm'. These are tones that invade the skin. In the heat of hearing, their origin within any framework of technology, musical genre or historical evolution is of little interest.

smell of sound

March 2003: sitting in a restaurant in Istanbul with Ilpo Väisänen and Mika
Vainio, the two Finnish artists who are Pan Sonic, I am listening to Ilpo talk
about painting. As is so often the case, Mika is quiet. With painting, Ilpo
says, the work is connected intimately with the smell of the materials.
When he switched from oil paints to watercolour and gouache, the process
of painting changed completely. Sound, on the other hand, is not a material
in the same way, he says, except for the tools with which you make the
sounds. He mimes the twisting of knobs on some ancient analogue sound
generator. Later that night at a club called Babylon they play a visceral set,
simple Roland 808 drum machine rhythms rolling like a steam train,
analogue sound generators stacking up layers of noise in a relentless build-
up of pressure.

Live, their music can feel as physical as a weather system. This
enveloping escalation of physicality seems a kind of materialism, even
though there is nothing to see other than the projected image of beats
activating an oscilloscope: the rawness of sawtooth, the sumptuous melted
wax massage of pure sine, the error sounds of contact and broken contact.
Although they operate in similar areas to the austere Japanese school of
sound phenomena artists recording for the WrK label, Pan Sonic's work is
less conceptual, more organised, more musical (if we can use that word).
Inevitably, there is a temptation to listen for signs of refinement or
romanticism, simply because the music goes beyond process and
phenomenology, broadcasting a manifesto for the poetry of electricity.

Comparing the 1999 CD they called *A* with earlier albums – *Kulma*, from
1996, or *Vaiko*, from 1995 – there are differences of emphasis but these are
slight in relation to their continuity of vision. Despite, or perhaps because
of their nakedness as sound sculptures (without visible objects), tracks
suggests vivid images, scenes, moods, drama. I try to listen, listening and
seeing nothing, but this is body music that refuses to exclude retina, cinema
and dream. Sounds become flares, vapour trails, LEDs, neon tubes close to
death, heart murmurs, apertures opening and closing in cement walls, tiny
mechanised guillotines snipping the heads from tin soldiers, sheets of lead
unfurling in underground car parks. That's the closest I can come to
nothingness. The final track, 'Voima', is two and three layers of buzzing
drones, an extruded 'Last Post', bisected by beats that seem, despite their
relative quietness, to crash and boom with menace. There may be some

implicit link to the thunderous beats and raw scratches of Marley Marl's early hip-hop productions, though this moves with the odd gait of someone in snowshoes wading sightless through deep drifts. 'Lomittain' is the bare bones of a Roland 808 drum machine, sounding the way it sounds when you switch it on and press play, the simple beats moving in parallel with pulses that seem to shift but actually stay still: optical art, but sound. Some tracks fade away into lengthy silence, a dream fall onto icescape, abandoned to survive, senses truly alert.

The following year, their *Aaltopiiri* album still followed this original path of tonal clarity and rhythmic minimalism, though with an added electro-dub feel reminiscent of the aethereal, electronic German dub of Pole. Interweaving delays on the sharp high click of the offbeat, a ticking hi-hat and the soft pulsing kick blossom into restrained feedback over a modulating drone, almost back in the territory of Farley Funkin Keith's first house tracks or the Joey Gardner/'Little Louie' Vega remix of Information Society's 'Running' – a rough grain video taste of hanging on the corner, chewing a toothpick, sipping on an ice cold beer, eyeballing the creatures of the night. The components of these tracks may be reminiscent of the old Pan Sonic but they sound more like 1980s drum machines than oscillators and disconnecting plugs. Now they breathe air, ripple out into an imagined distance, evoke cinematic scenarios. A 'Trans-Europe Express' for the 21st century, 'Aanipaa' motors on the locked groove of a gigantic stylus, forever stuck in the splintering channel of its vinyl cul-de-sac, sucking traces of horns and sirens into the slipstream.

This focus on simplified contrasts of space, volume and temporal division makes me think of the dancing of Saburo Teshigawara, who uses the drama of small body gestures so effectively, expanding to fill the emptiness of a vast blue backdrop with absolute stillness or shivering with movements so quick they elude even the most concentrated gaze. The programming on 'Liuos', for example, could hardly be more straightforward, yet there is an impressive mastery of illusion in the way the searing offbeat and bass drum thump are located somewhere between and behind the loudspeakers, then the ears are gripped and held by a mid-frequency tone that pans continuously from side to side.

Although their minimalism is executed with elegance and precision, Pan Sonic nurture a rougher, clumsy side. These maligned qualities occupy an important place in electronic music, a field haunted through its history by the deathly consequences of unlimited order, reason and control. The non-academic influences of reggae, rockabilly and the legendary New York duo, Suicide, ensure the opposite. One of their inspirations is the extraordinary rockabilly eccentric Hasil Adkins, a one-man band from West Virginia. When Adkins first heard rockabilly 78s in the 1950s, he assumed that all the instruments were played by one person. Beginning with instruments fashioned from wash tubs, bottles, jugs and a bucket, he graduated to electric guitar, bass drum and hi-hat to make primitive home-made recordings like 'The Hunch', 'Chicken Walk' and 'She Said', all of them characterised by wild vocals delivered in the grip of driven hysteria. Often forgotten in histories of technology and music, rockabilly is more likely to be discussed in the context of racial segregation in America, as a poor white southern hybrid of influences from hillbilly boogie and black R&B that revolutionised popular music. In fact, the integration of new advances in amplification and recording studio technique was central to its excitement. The sound was new, even when the songs had been borrowed, as was the case when Elvis Presley sang Arthur Crudup's 'That's Alright Mama' and 'My Baby Left Me' or Johnny Burnette sang Big Joe Turner's 'Honey Hush' and Tiny Bradshaw's 'The Train Kept a-Rollin''. The distorted tone of guitarist Paul Burlison with the Johnny Burnette Trio was an accidental discovery, made when a valve was knocked half out of its socket in Burlison's amplifier; guitarist Merle Travis (playing a hillbilly boogie style that was a little too sedate to be true rockabilly) was one of the first musicians to speed up his solos by recording them at a slower speed, then playing them back at the normal speed. Pulsating with echo, as if crying from outer space, vocalists like Charlie Feathers, Billy Lee Riley, Mac Curtis and Wanda Jackson yelped, hiccupped and screamed from within a sonic rush of percussive slaps and clicks.

Early Pan Sonic materials (when they were known as Panasonic) were simultaneously an update of this percussive language and a reversion back to the electrical inventions of Nikola Tesla, the Serbian master of lightning. The clicks and pops of their first recordings have influenced almost every electronica album made since. After a name change enforced by the Japanese electronics company, they have moved progressively towards a less austere, more open vocabulary. Interspersed among the electro-dub tracks on *Aaltopiiri*, a number of short tone poems establishes scenes suggestive of radio spiritualism, approaching trains, amplifiers left unattended, New

Age mood music as heard by sharks in an aquarium after hours, machines of esoteric purpose vainly struggling to achieve autonomous operation in deserted factories, or those great moments of tension in old war films when the submarine is trying to evade detection by destroyers overhead. Vainio and Väisänen cultivate a precarious balance between the elegant formalism of their own constructions and the threatened proliferating chaos of feedback, sun stroke, odorous nausea that overpowers, then thins to the buzz of a thermionic valve on the threshold of filament purgatory.

8 Silent music, secret noise

'Do nothing, then rest.'
                                        Spanish proverb

I am talking to Derek Bailey about the balance, or ratio at least, of innovation to habit. How does an improvising player discover new material, or fresh approaches to old material, in the heat of the moment, from within routines that are hardwired into brain and reflex? Playing is a negotiation between fixity and fluidity. To play is to learn and unlearn, a state of refinement and a state of becoming that have the power to undo each other's work.

'What you're saying is right,' he answers, 'but for me personally, and I've seen this with other people, it's to do with impetus. So the fact that you're running – let's say running – on the edge, on the front edge of the music, not sitting at the back end, gives the impression to you that you don't know what's in front. Even if you're groping around for more clichés, you have the feeling you don't know what's in front, and sometimes you don't. Sometimes you can find things, but then it comes out of the impetus of playing. But then again, I've always been attracted by very slow playing and there's something about that, where it's kind of suspended, and you have to decide in some way which is nothing to do with deciding, nothing to do with thinking. You have to decide what you're gonna do when at some point the thing is hanging there. I don't know how that works.'

In 1971, Bailey recorded a Willem Breuker composition called 'Christiani Eddy'. A real person, Eddy Christiani, was the first musician to play electric guitar in Holland, perhaps in Europe. Born in 1918, he recorded swing, pop and novelty tunes such as 'Papa Danst de Mambo' and 'Wild Geese'. Bailey

Akio Suzuki
kikko kikiriki

sums him up: 'He was the Dutch Bert Weedon.' Commissioned by Bailey at a point when he was still feeling his way into a music of his own, Breuker's composition could be construed as cruel, though the experience of having to listen to records like 'Papa Danst de Mambo' on the radio when young and full of fire is a kind of cruelty in itself. In Bailey's recording we hear a clock ticking. Bailey listens to faint recordings of fast, fluent jazz runs, then in the persona of Eddy tries to duplicate them on unamplified guitar. His frustration mounts as the notes collapse about him in increasingly untidy heaps. He ends with emphatic, simple phrases, played with a poor grace that seems to say, 'Fuck jazz, this is what I can do.'

The Argentinean composer, Mauricio Kagel, coincidentally wrote a comparable piece at a similar point in time. *Atem für einen Bläser*, or *Breath*, for a wind musician, was composed in 1969/70 and based, to some extent on one of Kagel's neighbours. A retired wind musician, this man would spend his day cutting reeds for colleagues. To test them he would play the same short sequence of notes repeatedly. 'Year in, year out, this signal can be heard at certain times of the day,' wrote Kagel in his explanatory sleeve notes for the recording. From this authentic scenario, Kagel constructed a fictional image of a retired wind musician whose sole purpose in life is to preserve the shiny surfaces of his instruments: 'Again and again he moves over to the cupboard, opens the boxes, takes the instruments to pieces, puts them together again, lubricates the mechanisms, puffs into the blow-pipe, dries the saliva, warms the reeds and mouthpieces, practising mutely, and likes to talk to himself, while at the same time polishing his instruments. In fact, he rarely gets as far as playing properly.'

As described by Kagel, and as played by Edward B. Tarr on the 1970s recording of the piece, this anticipated an approach to playing that emerged in the mid-1990s. Records by the Austrian quartet Polwechsel, Burkhard Stangl's *Ereignislose Musik - Loose Music*, Taku Sugimoto's *Myshkin Musicu*, *Temporary Contemporary* by Toshimaru Nakamura and Jason Kahn, Sachiko M's *Sine Wave Solo*, *Dach* by Phil Durrant, Thomas Lehn and Radu Malfatti, *Particles and Smears* by Kevin Drumm and Martin Tétrault, *Filament 1* by Otomo Yoshihide and Sachiko M, *Lidingö* by Andrea Neumann and Burkhard Beins and *Trem* by Rhodri Davies, all seemed to be asserting, in their different ways and through lack of assertion, an aesthetic of arrested action, microscopic gesture, minimal changes, extreme pitches, lengthy pauses and low, often imperceptible volume. Sometimes the sound is a thin high acupuncture needle of a note, held for some time; sometimes, nothing happens at all, for more than some time.

Morton Feldman's composing was clearly a precedent, along with John Cage pieces like *4' 33"* and *Prelude For Meditation*, Anton Webern's chamber music, Erik Satie's piano pieces, the small music of Akio Suzuki, Rolf Julius and Felix Hess, the fragile complexities of Max Eastley's sound sculptures, though all of these examples worked within an aura that supported their reticence. The effect of the new playing, on the other hand, was more demanding, more perplexing, more like sitting on the edge of an intimate conversation between very old friends, so familiar with their collective purpose that they communicate with dislocated phonemes, paralinguistic sighs, grunts and coordinated sips of beer or by trailing the gist of a thought rather than its full realisation, then lapsing back into silent rumination. The observance of what social psychologists call floor-apportionment, the delicate (often not-so-delicate) synchronisation of speaking and listening between two or more people, is almost pathologically courteous, as if the robust interactions of earlier improvising eras were no more dignified than a scrap with Mike Tyson.

> And one day, I decided to try and reach silence directly and with more resignation, giving myself up to the fate that rules all deep struggle. The millions of violent scratches turned into millions of dust or sand particles. Just like in the story of one who passes through the looking-glass, a new landscape opened up before me, as if to show me the innermost heart of things.
>
> Antoni Tàpies, *Comunicación sobre el Muro*, 1969

'Some Danes appear to "nourish" a silence as one might appreciate a cosy fire,' wrote Karl Reisman in his 1972 paper, *Contrapuntal Conversations in an Antiguan Village*. The connections between improvised musics and communication styles within specific cultural settings have barely been explored, perhaps because the dangers are clear. Any essentialising tendency to suggest that characteristically voluble, tactile and physically extravagant speakers will inevitably make hectic and noisy music can be discredited in a moment. Certain individuals within any group will value moments of quiet reflection, just as they value exuberance. Within improvisation, other musicians have worked in this constrained way in the past: John Stevens and Trevor Watts in their *Face To Face* phase; acoustic guitarist Roger Smith, whose volume seemed to decrease in direct ratio to his agitation, and percussionist Terry Day, who might go on walkabout during a set, or aerate, fluff, tickle and feather dust the smallest objects with the lightest possible pressure.

While staying in a borrowed sod hut in northern Sweden, Karl Reisman discovered difficulties with the local conversational style. His neighbours would drop by to check if everything was all right. Coffee would be offered, then accepted after a pause of some minutes. A question would be asked, then answered after a silence of five or ten minutes. Like a game of Grandmother's Footsteps, so the lopsided interaction would rush and halt for six or seven of these exchanges until broken off to be resumed the next day. 'As one goes north in the Scandinavian peninsula, particularly in Sweden,' wrote Reisman, 'what is called "the difficulty in expressing one's feelings" and the need for sincerity and honesty increase, while the amount of speech per hour decreases. Our neighbours felt they ought to visit, but perhaps one part of their silence was simply that they didn't have anything to say.'

Though there is doubtful value in comparing northern Swedish reticence with contemporary improvised music, certain phrases in Reisman's explanation coincide with the stated beliefs of musicians involved in this way of playing. In the magazine *Improvised Music in Japan*, first published in 2002, Japanese guitarist Taku Sugimoto and Viennese trombonist Radu Malfatti engage in dialogue on the issues that motivate them to play so sparsely, at such low volume. 'What I want to do,' says Malfatti, 'is attempt to create realms in which the senses are bound up together – are alert and attentive, resisting the desolation which our cultural environment seems to push upon us.'

This makes it clear that music, or improvisation, or any other categorisation of making sound within the context of art or entertainment, is not the central point. Instead, Sugimoto and Malfatti are discussing a course of action, a way of being fully alive in the moment, during the creation of sound. For Sugimoto, the problem lies with music's slippery capitulation to restless desire. Most music is designed as material for easy consumption but even the most impenetrable musics can be used and used up as a novelty. Sugimoto's dilemma hangs upon the vulnerability of musicians, their susceptibility to this enduring pressure, the way clear ideals can lapse into a decadent, stagnant circus act in which the performers enjoy the predictable grind as much as the audience.

On stage during an Italian concert in 1993, Malfatti realised that he had been improvising in the same way for too long. Angry with himself, he wrote a composition for solo trombone when he returned home – *Die Temperatur der Bedeutung* (*The Temperature of the Meaning*) – which was aimed at eradicating the old habits. To purge in this way seems radical when the resulting sounds are so sparse, so private, so intimately concentrated on the way a lip touches metal or a short breath enters a tube. From the opposite point of view, there is something uncomfortably 21st-century lifestyle in the implications of detox diets, changing your life in 10 easy steps, burning off the fat, not to mention the dangers of an aloof, risibly precious, chronically introverted withdrawal from society's noisy vulgarity. No path is safe for long from its own predictable grind.

I had read an interview with the Swiss percussionist Günter Müller in which he talked disparagingly of performance as a dubious excuse for spectacle and repetitious tricks. In recent years, his own approach to playing has changed completely, notably in giving up the drum kit for less showy tools. From preparing acoustic drums with various materials 25 years ago, he began to use microphones and electronic effects in the 1980s, then reached the present stage of processing sounds on the computer, playing these as loops on a minidisc and iPod, as well as using a cymbal, a Japanese frame drum and two small sheets of metal. I asked him to elaborate on this transformation.

As well as running his own label, For4Ears, Müller has recorded and performed with many musicians – Sugimoto, Otomo Yoshihide, Sachiko M, Christian Marclay and the Swiss duo Voice Crack, whose performances are like magic shows of what they call cracked everyday electronics, strange displays in which violent and remarkable sounds are pulled from an incredible array of lo-tech electronic devices. 'Until now I refuse to play a laptop as a live instrument,' Müller says, 'because of the physical aspect of my playing. I often play with a pair of headphones, using them as microphones in my hands, so controlling the laptop at the same time might be tricky. I prefer to prepare my material on computer at home quietly without rush. The other thing about physicality is that there is often a "danger" to play an acoustic instrument, perhaps especially drums, showing your virtuosity and using lots of well trained automatisms. In my opinion this has nothing to do with creating music, or at least it's boring! It is not interesting to spread out all your vocabulary and tell what a smart guy you are, but to try to contribute best in the specific situation with the help of your language.

'When I compare the playing situation with my current instrument to the one with the instrument I used to play, let's say 10 years ago, I feel one main difference: playing more with the material on minidisc and iPod and less with a drum set, it's now much easier for me to stand a bit outside to hear what's going on. Maybe it's a little similar to a mixing/editing situation. That means being focused on what's going on and being as much involved as possible. I'm choosing my material, my moves, more carefully, and this is important. It's still the same intention to improvise. It's not more conscious or intellectual. The only thing that has changed is the way of listening.'

a secret noise

But then there are expectations. 'I feel bad if there is an audience going to a concert expecting some virtuoso spectacle from a musician,' says Müller, 'because they know he is doing this stuff for years and years all the time. It's the most uninteresting thing you can do. It has nothing to do with improvisation, even though the concert might be announced like that.'

Then there is the audience. Just as you're about to go on stage to perform your improvisation for damp leaves, aerated confetti and contrabass bed socks at The Tunnel, Milan, you realise that the entire audience has rediscovered the lost art of conversation. What to do? The options are limited. You can stalk out to the microphone, deliver a lecture on the sanctity of your art and demand total hush. This will result in poor reviews and a severely alienated bunch of potential fans. You can sing a bunch of songs they all love, though the latest, greatest hit played on damp leaves may lack the necessary lift that the occasion demands. Alternatively, wrench the PA knobs round to 11, why not, and blast them with an hour of unbroken, consciousness shredding noise. Consequence? Their chatter will at least be crushed, though they may adjourn to the nearest bar to resume verbal intercourse, or they will talk loudly enough for you to be crushed. Now that many people regard musicians as a kind of sentient MTV, a background interference to be treated with the same utilitarian lack of love as their television sets, this is the most likely outcome.

Alternatively, daringly, play really, really, really quietly, in the hope that your whispers will spread stealthily through the room like fairy dust. Sometimes this works, though when it doesn't, you're in big trouble.

Extreme noise terror is a purifying balm, a rent in the fabric of the universe, a transgression against the forces of conservatism, corporeal denial and suppressed psychic energies. This is the received wisdom. But the truth is, playing brutally loud music is quite easy. Exhausting, perhaps, and disastrous for the ears in later life, but not in the same league of difficulty as playing really, really, really quietly. Playing on the threshold of silence can turn your body into a war zone of cramps and tremors, provoke clumsiness and mental panic, push your concentration levels beyond all previous limits, expose every flaw of structure and execution and finally turn a docile audience into a howling mob.

Listening to Taku Sugimoto's *Italia* CD, solo guitar improvisations recorded live in Bologna and Milan in November and December of 2000, I wonder how he does it. Having played solo concerts at these venues myself, and experienced the will to chatter that they engender, I assumed these pieces were recorded direct from the mixing desk with none of the ambient room sound mixed in. Either that, or there was no audience present at either gig. Then, listening on headphones with the volume way up, I can hear all sorts of little noises – chair creaks, amplifier hum, clothes rustling, somebody shifting in their seat, the odd explosion of something dropped. At one point, a door buzzer is pressed, followed by the sound of somebody standing up to deal with the intrusion, trying to be as discreet as possible.

What I'm really wondering is how he sustains this kind of poise over lengthy periods of time, how he holds an audience in a state of suspended expectation, drawing them into his microworld of partial gestures and exploratory calm without unleashing a battery of coughing and walkouts. Think of any classical music concert, an evening's entertainment in a diphtheria ward. There is a surface tension to Taku's playing, like liquid quivering above the rim of a cup. Break the surface, just with a breath, and everything spills. The miracle is, the break doesn't come, yet his playing never feels tight, fearful, flustered or aimless. This is far more difficult than it sounds.

The melodic clarity and movement of his early albums – *Opposite* and *Myshkin Musicu* – has become implicit, now only sensed through broken chains of blunted notes, softly hammered trills, faint slides, brief swarms of feedback hum, subtle distortion, minute scratches and queasy bent pitches. In 1995 there was a hint of Jim Hall playing Bill Evans in the ballad style of Lester Young, but as time has passed most evidence of guitar has gone. Sugimoto's playing has its moments of upheaval, but the range in which he works is so precisely mapped, so circumscribed, that it's possible to read him as a kind of cleric of the electric guitar. Loud, quiet, active, inactive, whatever he does is somehow secret and mysterious. A secret noise.

microscopic   aerophonic

Listen to this kind of work, or the compositions of Francisco Lopez and Bernhard Günter, at low volume, or even very high volume, and there may seem to be nothing on the CD. The microscope is on high magnification. In Tokyo, in 2000, Shunichiro Okada gave me a CD-R of his recent music. Throughout the recording there were just a few clicks, otherwise silence. My main reaction was amusement, though technical aspects of this search for silence made me realise that a new era had been entered.

Unlike the analogue formats of magnetic tape and vinyl discs, digital recording, storage and transmission are relatively silent in their operations. In 1975 I recorded a piece – *The Divination of the Bowhead Whale* – for Brian Eno's Obscure label. All the musicians were asked to pause for two long intervals during this semi-improvised composition. The beginning of these pauses was signalled by percussionist Frank Perry striking one of his Japanese resting bells. The interval would then last until the sustain from the bell had died away completely. These bells sustain for a surprisingly long time. Over two minutes of hard listening elapsed before the first musician came back in, though on the vinyl pressings the 'silences' were neutered by tape hiss, the crackle of poor vinyl pressings and a rumble from the unsophisticated turntable I owned in those penurious times. Remastering the album for a CD reissue raised the possibility of eradicating unwanted noise with digital tools that can distinguish noise from signal, though completely eradicating the sound of tape hiss leaves a strangely empty feeling to an analogue recording. The surface noise has gone but a subjectively satisfying remnant of hiss remains.

These problems no longer exist, even if others have replaced them. I asked cellist Mark Wastell, prominent in this new stream as well as being the proprietor of Sound 323, a small but meticulously stocked record shop in north London, if he felt that technology had played any significant part in this way of listening and playing. 'Why has this new procedure come about?' he says. 'When discussing it in purely musical terms, I do think that it is music informed by the digital era. The musicians have digital ears. By that I mean the contemporary players are listening to forms of music that did not exist 10 or so years ago: pre- and post-electronica, digital sound art, the post-techno scene, digital *musique concrète*, live laptop sound processing. AMM have always been a digital group, it's just taken the rest of the world 30 years to catch up, their influence must be acknowledged. Personally, I take influence from "still" art – the paintings of Robert Ryman and Agnes Martin – or from Japanese Butoh dance, where the smallest gestures speak volumes, and the solidity of sculpture and architecture. The nature of the way this music is performed can result in very still or static musicians. There is very little to actually watch. It's all about sound.'

Agnes Martin wrote these lines in 1973: 'I can see humility, delicate and white, it is satisfying, just by itself.' As ever, a new music appears and the rush to name it chokes the musicians in a cloud of dust. Wastell once favoured Reductionism as a way to describe it, though now rejects that. He also rejects terms such as sparse, barely audible, quiet and fragile, all of which suggest a weakness belied by the powerful impact the music can have on those who hear it. Silence is problematic, as usual, since it conveys a withdrawal from action, rather than the explorations of white practised by Ryman and Martin. Improvisation is little help, either. An openness to robust exchange is not part of this music, nor is the historical memory of automatism, expressionism and personal freedom out of which improvisation grew. 'A musician is defenceless in this genre,' says Wastell. 'He or she has nowhere to hide. His/her material is delivered with such care and diligence that it cannot be destroyed in ill-conceived collaborations. As Morton Feldman said, "Now that things are so simple, there's so much to do."'

If one predominant characteristic of this simplicity is the precise placement of small sounds in empty space, the other is high electronic tones that writhe in the air like miniature hummingbirds. Toshimaru Nakamura and Sachiko M are the original specialists in this field, Nakamura playing no-input mixing desk and Sachiko manipulating the sine tone pre-installed in a digital sampler. Albums such as Sachiko M's *Sine Wave Solo*, Toshimaru Nakamura's *Zero Gravity* and their duo album together, *do*, are like broadcasts from a lonely planet. Their squidging of soft buttons and fine tweaking of knobs and faders produces a whiskered, puttering murmur of spirit voices, bat chatter, submarine proximity detection, hypobranchial rasping and microchiropteran ultrasound that seems somehow inevitable and utterly right in its harmoniousness.

Bioacoustic research can explain this more comfortably than musicology. If I quote from one of the books on my shelves, *Sounds of Western North Atlantic Fishes* by Marie Poland Fish (I'm not making this up) and William H. Mowbray, that will suffice both as displaced description and approbation. 'Well-acclimatised captives in glass aquaria,' Fish and Mowbray observe in a brief discussion of pipefish and seahorses, 'loud clicks similar to snapping of finger against thumb associated with feeding and introduction into new surroundings (i.e., possible orientation) ... During preliminaries to copulation, occasional high level snaps often produced alternately by two fishes and, during actual embrace, loud and almost continuous high-frequency clicking.'

Despite the unfamiliarity of these upper frequency fine lines of sound, there have been precedents in Japanese music, though never in the context of improvisation. Perhaps it begins with *gagaku*, the elegant court music that fused influences from Korea, India and China during the seventh and eighth centuries and has survived with little apparent change until the present. So measured in the progress of its percussive markers that it draws the image of a footstep raised to move forward yet caught in a universal power cut, *gagaku*'s timbral constitution is a gaseous astringency of reeds, flutes and free reeds. Particularly striking is the *sho*, a set of bamboo reed pipes that was said to be an imitation of the cry of the phoenix. Another plateau is discovered. 'In the West chords tend to colour a melody and drive it on by setting it in situations of tension which require release, in music terms, by setting up chord progressions,' wrote William P. Malm in *Japanese Music and Musical Instruments*. 'The chords of the sho, however, do not serve this function. Rather they "freeze" the melody. They are like a vein of amber in which a butterfly has been preserved. We see the beauty of the creature within but at the same time are aware of a transparent solid between us and the object, a solid of such a texture that it shows that object off in a very special way.'

Ryoji Ikeda's high electronic tones and pulses are a more recent example, but in the 1950s composers at the NHK studio in Tokyo investigated similar phenomena. According to Joel Chadabe's book, *Electronic Sound*, electronic experiments began at NHK in 1953, pioneered by Toshirou Mayazumi, Minao Shibata and Makoto Maroi. The youngest of the three, Maroi, had visited Cologne in 1955 and imported the German influence into the set-up of Denshi Ongaku at NHK. Then in 1966, Karlheinz Stockhausen spent a little over a month in the NHK studio, creating *Telemusik* with the assistance of a group of technicians that included Hiroshi Shiotani, the recording engineer.

Mayazumi and Moroi had created interesting works that predated *Telemusik*, however, and they exude a confidence of their own. Toshirou Mayazumi's rigorously titled *Music for sine wave by proportion of prime number*, *Music for modulated wave by proportion of prime number* and *Invention for square wave and saw-tooth wave*, dating from 1954, are particularly impressive. Famous in Japan in the 90s as a movie soundtrack composer and daily television presenter of classical music, Mayazumi's early work has a visceral simplicity that balances formal restraint with a faintly unsettling (and almost certainly unintended) hint of the aliens-drank-my-alcohol role that electronic music was assuming in cinema in the 1950s.

One probable reason why such work seems so compelling and relevant now is the directness, the clarity, the sense of pure intent. Surrounded by banks of keyboards and sound modules, sound processing equipment from all eras, sample libraries, plug-in effects and a clutch of software programs representing the entire trajectory of electronic music, the contemporary composer may be tempted to envy the dearth of resources and consequent narrowing of choices that prevailed in the early days. These pieces were simple because they took a long time to make, the tools were primitive and the territory they explored was utterly undiscovered.

A connection to *gagaku* was explored on Otomo Yoshihide's *Cathode* album, recorded in 1999. Inspired by Toru Takemitsu's film composing and the historical novels of Ikenami Shotaro, the three compositions on *Cathode* synthesise the tendencies that were emerging in Japan at that time. Born in Yokohama in 1959, Otomo is one those musicians who organises, inspires and curates, developing opportunities for younger or lesser known players to perform or record and providing a focal point for a whole scene. His own work as a turntablist, sampler and guitarist has moved through dramatic changes, from working in hectic referential contexts such as Ground Zero, or the *Monogatari: Amino Argot* album he recorded with Carl Stone in 1994, to the rough and ready warmth of his New Jazz Quintet.

The modulating difference tones produced by the combination of Sachiko M's sine tones and Ko Ishikawa's *sho* on *Cathode* are specifically linked to *gagaku* by Otomo in his composition notes. As he points out, these tones will vary according to the position of the listener in the room. This was an effect investigated by La Monte Young from the 1960s onwards in his mathematical sine-tone works, installations rather than performances that set up an aerial architecture in which the listener is an equal determinant in the shape of the work. In his notes for "Cathode #2", a composition for nine players, Otomo writes: 'I'd like the listener to interpret this music for themselves. Please listen at a lower volume without concentrating on the sounds coming from the speakers, perhaps even from another room. It's okay to listen carefully but it is better to listen as if the sounds are part of the environment. This music exists outside of the frame created by the sound itself and it is the listener, not the composer who will discover the music here.'

The sound sources used in this quiet, powerful piece are extremely diverse: sampled composition on hard disk recorder, sine waves and contact microphone, mixing board and effect, violin, cello and contrabass, computer, voice, analogue synthesiser. In other words, centred within the body, prosthetic extensions of the body, devices outside the body, corporeal, acoustic, amplified, electronic, analogue, digital. What is striking is the closeness of all these sounds, not just in their texture but in the way they impact on the skin and enter the ears, fill the space of the room and interpenetrate the ambiguity of signals and silence. Who could possibly tell who is doing what? Perhaps not even the players themselves. The same is true if I listen to *Tears*, Sachiko M's duet album with vocalist Ami Yoshida. Working under the name of Cosmos, this duo defies any easy judgements of what is natural, human or digital. Their music may have grown from the microscopic focus of digital technology on the granularity of sound, its clarity and silence, its structural leanings towards transformation, loops, inhuman durations and extreme frequencies, but humans are infinitely adaptable.

Listening to saxophonist John Butcher's CD, *Invisible Ear*, is even more disorientating. Just a soprano saxophone, the microphone very close to the instrument, the recorded sound intimately absorbed by the recording process and melting into the listener's being. As Sadie Plant has said: 'Bodies are continually engineered by the processes in which they are engaged.' A member of the last SME group, before John Stevens died, Butcher acknowledges the role of technology in his return to this journey into the centre of the instrument. 'Recently I've revisited using the microphone as part of the instrument,' he writes, 'a consequence, I'd imagine, of working more closely with computer/electronic musicians.' So matter of fact, yet the playing is unearthly, elevated, profoundly distant and deeply embedded.

'Sound is always present as a momentary force, a temporal form,' writes sound artist Brandon LaBelle, 'because it is always deflected and refracting against its surroundings – it is always interfered with by other stimuli, by bodies and space. In this way, sound is never isolated.' The invisible ear is not really a metal thing, a saxophone or the institution of music; just digital technology, electronic feedback, interior and exterior, fingers, breath and air, the resonator of this room, the objects within the room, this moment, hearing actions from another time and place.

9 Epilogue: a book at bedtime

As 2002 drew to a close, Christmas night was so unusually mild that my neighbour Neill and I sat out on the deck, drinking red wine, Neill smoking a cigarette, both of us gazing out into the darkness of the garden and gently musing on the demands of music and its difficult place within the rhythms and routines of domestic life. Sound needs its own silence. Silence is not something that can be turned on and off like water from a tap or light in a room, but this is also true for social life. Interactions with people are not commodities to be accepted or rejected without communal agreement and negotiation.

Earlier in the day, Neill had showed me a copy of *Let's Build a Railroad*, a children's book of American songs collected in 1954 by his grandmother, Ruth Crawford Seeger. He had found it and bid for it on an auction website during the course of an ongoing search for records and other documents produced by his father and mother. His uncle, Pete Seeger, had said that songs in a book are like birds in a photograph. Words can be explosions on the deck of a ship, I thought, remembering Rabelais. 'A poem dreams irresistibly of flying,' wrote Makoto Ooka, but then he also wrote, 'Even the rims of clinking glasses make far more transparent sounds; and even the dying tone of the day's last train is sweeter than the sound of my "poetry".'

A song in a book is one kind of memory trace among many, after all. Our conversation in the garden lasted for some time, considering it was mid-winter. Short explosive cracks, fireworks probably, hammered the silent sky to the south of us, then ricocheted back from the slopes of Alexandra Park to our north. We could have been two farmers sheltering in no man's land, caught between the artillery of two opposing armies. Later, after my mother was safely back home, after Justine, Neill and the boys, and Justine's mother, had gone back to their house, after Eileen and Juliette were asleep, I watched a performance by Dexter Gordon, broadcast on a cable channel I can usually depend on to be unwatchable. Pleasantly surprised and pleasantly drunk, I felt almost scared by the risks Gordon took with logic, the way a line threatened to become lost and foolish as the mathematics grew increasingly wild and abstruse, yet always at the last moment, saxophone resolved with piano chords to set me at ease with the world.

Much later, more than a month in fact, two of these stories developed endings, if not resolutions, of their own. I asked Neill if he could recall memories of sound from his childhood. His mother, Peggy Seeger, practising banjo downstairs when he was in bed at night, a comforting memory, he said, and his father, Ewan MacColl, obsessively battling internal disorder with the vacuum cleaner during periods of depression. Even now, Neill said, if he was sleeping late after a gig or a nocturnal recording session, the noise of a vacuum cleaner nozzle bumping against the bedroom door could tip him into a downward spiral. Also at the end of January, the local paper ran a front page item on things that go bang in the night. Fears over mysterious 'explosions', there had been, and these inexplicable bangs had woken a number of residents on a number of occasions. Definitely not fireworks, all the residents agreed. We know nothing of these bangs, said the police. Definitely fireworks, said the local council. Call our noise nuisance line. Hoichi, the blind musician in Masaki Kobayashi's *Kwaidan*, came into my mind. Hoichi plays *biwa* every night on the haunted shores of the Straits of Shimonoséki, chanting the story of the battle at Dan-no-ura to the phantom army of the Heiké clan, wiped out in the final conflict between the Heiké and the Gengi clans. In fact, he has been in the cemetery, serenading ghosts. At the end of the story, he regains his soul, losing only his ears.

One evening in spring I watched the first heavy bombardment of Baghdad. Every explosion is a jolt to the system. Everything to say yet nothing to say. Another warm night and I sit outside in the garden, dazed by the sight and sound of so much destruction. Two huge bangs detonate in the distance, one to the south, from the direction of the 'mysterious explosions', the other to the north-east, from the direction of Tottenham. Not an echo this time. Who could set off fireworks on a night like this, I ask myself, feeling a growing anger at so much stupidity, though maybe the Iraqi Kurds of north London are celebrating the first major air strike against the regime they detest? Later I learned that this was the moment to mark NowRooz, the Persian new year.

Three days later, at 5.55 in the afternoon, an orange yellow sun falls into the rising white cloud of tree blossom that hovers over our garden. I imagine a sound, like hot egg yolk dropping slowly into snow. That night, unable to sleep, I listened through my pillows to the penetrating, insistent song of the electricity substation that hums to itself at the end of our street. Atmospheric conditions, levels of ambient noise and my focus of attention may appear to change the volume of this sound from absent to gently reassuring to oppressive. My awareness changes; the sound is constant.

afterword

I would like to thank:

... Cathy Lane, Angus Carlyle, Peter Cusack, John Wynne and the students and staff at the London College of Printing, Department of Sound Design, and Janice Hart, research co-ordinator, and Katherine Heap, research administrator, at the London Institute, for their support and encouragement throughout my tenure as a Visiting Research Fellow at LCP.

... Minoru Hatanaka at ICC, Tokyo, whose invitation to Japan in 2000 first launched this train of thought, to Rob Young, Chris Bohn and Tony Herrington at *The Wire*, Andrew Hultkrans at Bookforum, and Larry Sider at The School of Sound, who commissioned pieces which found their way into the manuscript.

... the artists who contributed visual work so generously – Mariko Sugano, Akio Suzuki, Max Eastley, Rolf Julius and Trevor Sutton – and to Jennifer Pike and Anna Stevens who gave permission to include the visual work of the late Bob Cobbing and John Stevens respectively.

... Neill and all the interviewees for the conversations.
... Justine Picardie, Robin Rimbaud, Andrew Brenner, Magnus Haglund and Tom Recchion for their encouragement in moments (or months) of negative progress.
... Pete Ayrton for his faith and patience.
... Russell Mills for his creative imagination and understanding.
... Eileen and Juliette for enduring my nocturnal disappearances into the top of the house, a general deterioration in cuisine and my sporadic need for comfort and cajoling at critical moments.

bibliography

Ashton Dore, *The Delicate Thread: Teshigahara's Life In Art*, Kodansha International, Tokyo, New York, London, 1997.

Bachelard, Gaston, *The Poetics of Reverie*, Beacon Press, Boston, 1971.

Bateson, Gregory, *Steps to An Ecology of Mind*, Paladin Granada, London, 1973.

Beckett, Samuel, *Krapp's Last Tape*, Faber and Faber, London, 1959.

Bernstein, David W., and Hatch, Christopher, *Writings Through John Cage's Music, Poetry + Art*, The University of Chicago Press, Chicago and London, 2001.

Bauman, Richard, and Sherzer, Joel, *Explorations In the Ethnography of Speaking*, Cambridge University Press, London, 1974.

Böhme, Gernot, 'Acoustic Atmospheres', in *Soundscape: Journal of Acoustic Ecology*, Vol. 1, No. 1, Spring 2000.

Böhme, Gernot, 'The Atmosphere of a City', in *Issues In Contemporary Culture and Aesthetics* (Maastricht), No. 7, 1998.

Briscoe, Desmond, and Curtis-Bramwell, Roy, *The BBC Radiophonic Workshop: The First 25 Years*, British Broadcasting Corporation, London, 1983.

Brophy, Philip, *Cinesonic: Cinema and the Sound of Music*, Australian Film Television & Radio School, North Ryde, NSW, 2000.

Cage, John, and Retallack, Joan (ed.), *Musicage: John Cage in Conversation with Joan Retallack*, Wesleyan University Press, New England/Hanover and London, 1996.

Calvino, Italo, *Six Memos for the Next Millennium*, Jonathan Cape, London, 1992.

Cendrars, Blaise, *Dan Yack*, Editions Denoël, Paris, 1927.

Chion, Michel, *Audio-Vision: Sound on Screen*, Columbia University Press, New York, 1994.

Choi, Jae-eun, *Work* (catalogue), Fondazione Mudima, Milan, 1998.

Collins, Nicolas (ed.), 'Not Necessarily "English Music"', *Leonardo Music Journal*, The MIT Press, Vol. 11, Cambridge, MA, 2001.

Connor, Steven, *Dumbstruck: A Cultural History of Ventriloquism*, Oxford University Press, Oxford, New York, 2000.

Coontz, Robert, 'The Planet That Hums', *New Scientist*, UK, No. 2203, 11 September 1999.

Corbin, Alain, *Village Bells*, Papermac, Macmillan Press, London, 1999.

Cox, Christophe, *Seeing Sounds Hearing Images*, exhibition catalogue, The Museum of Contemporary Photography, Columbia College, Chicago, USA, 2001.

Curiger, Bice, Christian Marclay interview, Züritip, Zurich, 1997.

Day, Timothy, *A Century of Recorded Music*, Yale University Press, New Haven and London, 2000.

Dickens, Charles, *Bleak House*, Oxford University Press edition, Oxford & New York, 1998.

Dunn, David, *Why Do Whales and Children Sing?* Earth Ear, Santa Fe, NM, 1999.

Foer, Jonathan Safran (ed.), *A Convergence of Birds: Original Fiction and Poetry Inspired by the Work of Joseph Cornell*, D.A.P., New York, 2001.

Forrester, Michael A, 'Auditory Perception and Sound As Event: Theorising Sound Imagery In Psychology', *Sound Journal*, 28 April 2000, URL: http://www.ukc.ac.uk/sdfva/sound-journal/forrester001.html [Accessed 2 May 2002].

Friedman, B. H. (ed.), *Give My Regards to Eighth Street: Collected Writings of Morton Feldman*, Exact Change, Cambridge, MA, 2000.

Galbraith IV, Stuart, *The Emperor and the Wolf: The Lives and Films of Akira Kurosawa and Toshiro Mifune*, Faber and Faber, New York and London, 2001.

Hamilton-Paterson, James, *Playing With Water*, Granta Books, London, 1998.

Hatanaka, Minoru (ed.), *Sound Art – Sound As Media* (catalogue), NTT Intercommunication Centre (ICC), Tokyo, 2000.

Hearn, Lafcadio, *Writings From Japan*, Penguin Books, Middlesex, UK, 1984.

Hess, Felix, *Light As Air* (catalogue), Kehrer Verlag Heidelberg, 2001.

Hiller, Susan, interviewed by Mary Horlock, *Paletten*, No. 245–246, Göteborg, April/May 2001.

Imada, Tadahiko, 'The Japanese Sound Culture', *The Soundscape Newsletter*, No. 9, September 1994, World Forum for Acoustic Ecology, Univ. of Oregon, URL: http://interact.uoregon.edu/MediaLit/wfae/readings/jpsoundculture.html [Accessed 7 February 2003]

Johnson, Steven, *Emergence*, Allen Lane, The Penguin Press, London, 2001.

Joyce, James, *Ulysses*, Picador edition, London, 1998.

Julius, Rolf, *Black (Red)* (catalogue), University of Massachusetts, Amherst, 2000.

Kahn, Douglas, *Noise Water Meat: A History of Sound In the Arts*, The MIT Press, Cambridge, MA, 1999.

Kawabata, Yasunari, *The Sound of the Mountain*, Penguin, Middlesex, UK, 1974.

Keil, Charles, and Feld, Steven, *Music Grooves*, The University of Chicago Press, Chicago and London, 1994.

Krause, Bernie, *Wild Soundscapes*, Wilderness Press, Berkeley, CA, 2002.

Kubisch, Christina, *Klangraumlichtzeit*, Kehrer Verlag Heidelberg, 2000.

Kyoka, Izumi, *Japanese Gothic Tales*, University of Hawaii Press, Honolulu, 1996.

Leach, Bernard, *Hamada: Potter*, Kodansha International, Tokyo, New York, London, 1975.

Malm, William P., *Japanese Music and Musical Instruments*, Charles E. Tuttle, Rutland, Vermont and Tokyo, Japan, 1959.

Michaux, Henri, *Darkness Moves*, University of California Press, Berkeley, 1994.

Miyake, Issey, *Making Things* (catalogue), Scalo, Zurich, Berlin, New York, 1998.

Moroni, Artemis, Manzolli, Jônatas, Von Zuben, Fernando, and Gudwin, Ricardo, 'Vox Populi: An Interactive Evolutionary System for Algorithmic Music Composition', *Leonardo Music Journal*, The MIT Press, Vol. 10, Cambridge, MA, 2000.

Needham, Joseph, *Science and Civilisation In China*, Vol. II, Cambridge University Press, Cambridge, 1956.

Nicolai, Carsten, *Polyfoto, Verlag für moderne Kunst* (catalogue), Nürnberg, 1998.

Nosé, Michiko Rico, *The Modern Japanese Garden*, Mitchell Beazley, Octopus, London, 2002.

Nyman, Michael, *Experimental Music: Cage and Beyond*, Cambridge University Press, UK, 1999.

Ooka, Makoto, *Elegy and Benediction: Selected Poems 1947–89*, Jitsugetsu-kan, Tokyo, 1991.

Pinch, Trevor, and Troco, Frank, *Analog Days: The Invention and Impact of the Moog Synthesiser*, Harvard University Press, Cambridge, MA, 2002.

Plant, Sadie, *Zeros + Ones*, Fourth Estate, London, 1998.

Plutschow, Herbert, *Rediscovering Rikyu and the Beginnings of the Japanese Tea Ceremony*, Global Oriental, Folkestone, UK, 2003.

Poe, Edgar Allan, *Poe's Tales of Mystery and Imagination*, J. M. Dent, London, 1908.

Proust, Marcel, *The Way By Swann's*, Allen Lane edition, London, 2002.

Richie, Donald, *The Films of Akira Kurosawa*, University of California Press, Berkeley, Los Angeles, London, 1996.

Sakane, Itsuo, *On Hiroshi Ishii and the Tangible Media Group Exhibit*, catalogue from Tangible Bits, NTT Intercommunications Centre (ICC), Tokyo, 2000.

Schafer, R. Murray, *The New Soundscape*, Universal Edition, London, 1969.

Schafer, R. Murray, *The Tuning of the World*, Alfred A. Knopf, New York, 1977.

Sebald, W. G., *Austerlitz*, Penguin Books, London, 2001.

Shimoda, Nobuhisa, and Mori, Nobuko, *Sound In the Future*, TOA Corporation, Kobe, Japan, 1996.

Sinclair, Iain, *Lights Out for the Territory*, Granta Books, London, 1997.

Small, Christopher, *Musicking*, Wesleyan University Press, Hanover, NH, USA, 1998.

Suzuki, Akio, *'A': Sound Works Throwing and Following* (catalogue), Stadtgalerie Saarbrücken, Germany, 1997.

Suzuki, Yoshiyuki, *Improvised Music from Japan 2002–2003*, Launch Issue, Tokyo, 2002.

Takei, Jiro, and Keane, Marc P., *Sakuteiki: Visions of the Japanese Garden*, Tuttle Publishing, Boston, Rutland, Vermont, Tokyo, 2001.

Takemitsu, Toru, *Confronting Silence: Selected Writings*, Fallen Leaf Press, Berkeley, California, 1995.

Tàpies, Antoni, *European Collections*, Centro de Arte Moderna, Lisbon, 1992.

Thompson, Emily, *The Soundscape of Modernity*, The MIT Press, Cambridge, MA, 2002.

Tomkins, Calvin, *Ahead of the Game: Four Versions of the Avant-garde*, Penguin Books, London, 1968.

Tomkins, Calvin, *Duchamp: A Biography*, Henry Holt and Company, Inc., New York, 1996.

Toop, David, *Ocean of Sound*, Serpent's Tail, London, 1995.

Virilio, Paul, *The Lost Dimension*, Semiotext(e), Autonomedia, New York, USA, 1991.

Williams, Harriet, 'Sizzling Skies', *New Scientist*, UK, No. 2272, 6 January 2001.

Wilson, Elizabeth, *The Sphinx In the City*, Virago Press, London, 1991.

World Soundscape Project, *The Vancouver Soundscape*, Simon Fraser University, Vancouver, undated (c. 1975).

Wörner, Karl H., *Stockhausen: Life and Work*, Faber & Faber, London, 1973.

Wright, Tom, and Katsuhiko, Mizuno, *Zen Gardens*, Suiko Books, Kyoto, 1990.

Yoshimura, Akira, *One Man's Justice*, Canongate Books, Edinburgh, 2003.

discography

Where possible, I have tried to list and indicate CD releases relevant to this book. If the recording was released on vinyl or some other format, or if I don't have the details of a CD reissue, then I have indicated that with the letter V for vinyl and MC for cassette. If it's a bootleg, then it's labelled with a B. If it's available only within one country then it's labelled with the appropriate abbreviation, ie. Jp for Japan. Needless to say, some of these old recordings, limited editions and non-standard formats will be difficult or near-impossible to obtain.

Akiyama Nakamura Sugimoto Wastell, *Foldings*, Confront 12.

Bailey, Derek, *Ballads*, Tzadik TZ7607.

Bailey, Derek, *Pieces For Guitar*, Tzadik TZ7080.

Bailey, Derek, *Solo Guitar Volume 1*, Incus CD10.

Bailey, Derek & Stevens, John, *Playing*, Incus CD14.

Bohman, Adam, *Last Orders*, Mycophile SPOR 03.

Bryars, Gavin, *Jesus' Blood Never Failed Me Yet*, Virgin CDVE 938.

Butcher, John, *Invisible Ear*, Fringes 12.

Cardew, Cornelius/Scratch Orchestra, *The Great Learning*, Organ of Corti 21.

Charles, Christophe, *Deposition Yokohama*, CH94.

Chopin, Henri, *Le Corpsbis & co*, Nepless PS 961 1001.

Cosmos, *Tears*, Erstwhile 024.

Cusack, Peter, *Your Favourite London Sounds*, LMC RESFLS1CD.

Cusack, Peter & Collins, Nicolas, *A Host of Golden Daffodils*, Plate Lunch PL 07.

Disinformation, *R&D2*, Ash International Ash 9.2.

Durand, Werner, *The Art of Buzzing*, X-tract x-t 2004.

Durrant/Lehn/Malfatti, *Dach*, Erstwhile 014.

Fascinato, Jack & Elliott, Dean, *Zounds! What Sounds/Music from a Surplus Store*, Junkyard JY 9206-2, (B).

Feld, Steven, *Rainforest Soundwalks*, Earth Ear EE1062.

Feldman, Morton, *All Piano*, LondonHALL, LoHALL do13.

Feldman, Morton, *Feldman/Brown*, Mainstream MS/5007, (V).

Fennesz, Christian, *Endless Summer*, Mego 035.

Fennesz, Christian, *Fennesz Plays*, Moikai M5.

Fujieda, Mamoru, *Patterns of Plants*, Tzadik TZ7025.

Grossi, Pietro, *Battimenti*, Ants AG03.

Grossi, Pietro, *Musicautomata*, Die Schachtel DS1, (limited edition V).

Günter, Bernhard, *Crossing the River (Night Music)*, Trente Oiseaux TOC012.

Chico Hamilton Quartet, *Spectacular!*, Pacific Jazz Records PJ-39, (V).

Hanson, Sten, *Text-Sound Gems & Trinkets*, Firework Edition Records FER 1037.

Hess, Felix, *Frogs 4*, 6818.566, (V).

Ikeda, Ryoji, *Matrix*, Touch TO:44.

Kagel, Mauricio, *Atem*, EMI C 063-28808.

Jeck, Philip, *Stoke*, Touch TO:56.

John Benson Brooks Trio, *Avant Slant (one Plus I =II?)*, Decca DL 75018, (V).

Julius, *(halb) Schwarz*, X-tract/Edition RZ 4001.

Julius, *Soba Field*, Small Music R210-314.

Kayn, Roland, *Tektra*, Barooni BAR 016.

Kubisch, Christina, *Dreaming of a Major Third*, Edition RZ LC 8864.

Lucier, Alvin, *Vespers and Other Early Works*, New World Records 80604-2.

M, Sachiko, *Sine Wave Solo*, Amoebic AMO-SAT-01.

Machida, Yoshio, *Hypernatural #2*, Soft Music som 101.

Marclay, Christian, *Footsteps*, RecRec 26, (V).

Marclay, Christian, *Record Without a Cover*, Recycled Records (no number), (V).

Matthews, Kaffe, *cdAnn*, Annette Works, Awcd0001.

Matmos, *A Chance to Cut Is a Chance to Cure*, Matador ole 489-2.

Mimeo/John Tilbury, *The Hands of Caravaggio*, Erstwhile 021.

Mingus, Charles, *Jazzical Moods*, Period Records OJCCD 1857-2.

Nicolai, Carsten, *empty garden (inside.out)*, Noto A1.

Oswald, John, *Plexure*, Avant AVAN 016.

Oswald, John, *Plunderphonics 69 96*, Seeland 515 CD.

Oval, *94 diskont*, Mille Plateaux MP CD 13.

Oval/Charles, Christophe, *Dok*, Tokuma TKCB-71355.

Pan Sonic, *A*, Blast First BFFP149CD.

Parker, Evan, & Rowe, Keith, *Dark Rags*, Potlatch P200.

Parker, Evan & Stevens, John, *Corner To Corner*, Ogun OGCD 005.

Peebles, Sarah, *108 – Walking Through Tokyo at the Turn of the Century*, Post-Concrete, Post-004.

Prime, Michael, *L-fields*, Sonoris SON-08.

Rahn, Eckhart, *Pachinko In Your Head*, Blue Rahn Studio 19004-2.

Riley, Terry, *Music For the Gift*, Organ of Corti 1.

Riley, Terry, *You're No Good*, Organ of Corti 5.

Roden, Steve/in be tween noise, *splint (the soul of wood)*, Interiorsounds/New Plastic Music (no number).

Rowe, Keith, *Harsh*, Grob 209.

Rowe, Keith & Nakamura, Toshimaru, *Weather Sky*, Erstwhile 018.

Rüsenberg, Michael, *Cologne Bridges Symphony*, Artelier Music NW5102 2.

Ruttmann, Walter, *Weekend*, Metamkine MKCD010.

Semper, Jonty, *Kenotaphion*, Charrm KEN01.

Shimizu, Jio, *Insert 'Delay' 35*, (MC).

Shiotani, Hiroshi/NHK Studio, *Hiroshi Shiotani's Work*, OUOADM 9301.

Singing Dogs, *The Singing Dogs*, Mr Pickwick SPC-5130, (V).

Snow, Michael, *The Last LP CD*, Art Metropole #1001.

Spontaneous Music Ensemble/John Stevens & Trevor Watts, *Face To Face*, Emanem 4003.

Spontaneous Music Ensemble, *Karyobin*, Chronoscope CPE2001-2.

Spontaneous Music Ensemble, *Low Profile*, Emanem 4031.

Stangl, Burkhard, *Ereignislose Musik – Loose Music*, Random Acoustics RA015.

Stockhausen, Karlheinz, *Cycle for one percussionist (in two different versions)*, Heliodor Wergo 2549 016,(V).

Stockhausen, Karlheinz, *Mikrophonie I/Telemusik*, Stockhausen 9.

Sugimoto, Taku, *Myshkin Musicu*, Slub Music (no number).

Sugimoto, Taku, *Opposite*, Hat Hut Records HatNoir 802.

Suzuki, Akio, *Odds and Ends*, Hören MIMI-012/13.

Takemitsu, Toru, *Coral Island, Water Music, Vocalism Ai*, RCA VICS-1334, (V).

Toru Takemitsu, *Film Music by Toru Takemitsu*, vols 1, 4, 5, JVC VICG-5124, 5127, 5128 (Jp).

Takemitsu, Toru, *In An Autumn Garden*, Voyage, Eclipse, DGG POCG-3652 (Jp).

Thaemlitz, Terre, *Means From An End*, Mille Plateaux MP CD 44.

Ticklish, *Ticklish*, Grob 212.

Tsunoda, Toshiya, *Pieces of Air*, Lucky Kitchen 016.

Various Artists, *An Anthology of Noise & Electronic Music*, volume #1, Sub Rosa SR190.

Various Artists, *Early Modulations: Vintage Volts*, Caipirinha Music CAI 2027.2.

Various Artists, *Film Music of Akira Kurosawa*, Toshiba-EMI TYCY-5637-41 (Jp).

Various Artists, *FluxTellus*, Tellus #24, (MC).

Various Artists, OHM: *The Early Gurus of Electronic Music*, Ellipsis Arts CD3670.

Various Artists, *Silence*, Spiral Editions 36CD-NO20 (Jp).

Various Artists, *WrK compilation*, Wrk004.

Vitiello, Stephen, *Bright and Dusty Things*, New Albion Records, NA 115.

Von Hausswolff, C.-M, *Operations of Spirit Communication*, Die Stadt DS31, (V).

Watanabe, Yurihito/yxetm+, *Mille Comédies – Le Double Inaudible*, Airplane AP1015.

Watson, Chris, *Outside the Circle of Fire*, Touch TO:37.

Watson, Chris, *Stepping Into the Dark*, Touch TO:27.

Watson, Chris, *Weather Report*, Touch TO:47.

Yoshihide, Otomo, *Cathode*, Tzadik TZ7051.

Yoshihide, Otomo & Stone, Carl, *Monogatari: Amino Argot*, Trigram TR-P908.

Yuko Nexus6, *Journal De Tokyo*, Sonore SON-18.

Zorn, John, *Cobra: Tokyo Operations '94*, Avant AVAN 049.

Zorn, John, *Film Works II: Cynical Hysterie Hour*, Tzadik TZ7315.

Zorn, John, *Songs From the Hermetic Theatre*, Tzadik TZ 7066.

index

Fiction
Crime
Noir

Culture
Music
Erotica

dare to read at serpentstail.com

Visit serpentstail.com today to browse and buy our books, and to sign up for exclusive news and previews of our books, interviews with our authors and forthcoming events.

| NEWS | cut to the literary chase with all the latest news about our books and authors |

| EVENTS | advance information on forthcoming events, author readings, exhibitions and book festivals |

| EXTRACTS | read the best of the outlaw voices - first chapters, short stories, bite-sized extracts |

| EXCLUSIVES | pre-publication offers, signed copies, discounted books, competitions |

| BROWSE AND BUY | browse our full catalogue, fill up a basket and proceed to our **fully secure** checkout - our website is your oyster |

FREE POSTAGE & PACKING ON ALL ORDERS ... ANYWHERE!

---

sign up today - join our club

Printed in the USA
CPSIA information can be obtained
at www.ICGtesting.com
JSHW012021140824
68134JS00033B/2809

9 781852 427894